T0319803

Academic Entrepreneurship

THE JOHNS HOPKINS UNIVERSITY SERIES ON ENTREPRENEURSHIP

Series Editor: Phillip H. Phan, *Johns Hopkins University, USA*

From its inception more than 130 years ago, The Johns Hopkins University has led the world in scientific discovery and innovation. Starting with the Master of Science in Management Science in 1916, the university has focused its lens on bringing the most up-to-date concepts to business education. In 2007, the university established the Johns Hopkins Carey Business School to transform business education through a uniquely humanistic, integrated approach to research. This series continues the tradition of discovery and innovation by bringing the best research in technological entrepreneurship and management in the form of book length original contributions and edited volumes on topics of contemporary interest and theoretical significance.

Titles in the series include:

The Competitive Dynamics of Entrepreneurial Market Entry
Edited by Gideon Markman and Phillip H. Phan

Theory and Empirical Research in Social Entrepreneurship
Edited by Phillip H. Phan, Jill Kickul, Sophie Bacq and Mattias Nordqvist

Academic Entrepreneurship
Translating Discoveries to the Marketplace
Edited by Phillip H. Phan

Academic Entrepreneurship

Translating Discoveries to the Marketplace

Edited by

Phillip H. Phan

Alonzo and Virginia Decker Professor of Strategy and Entrepreneurship, Johns Hopkins University, USA

THE JOHNS HOPKINS UNIVERSITY SERIES ON ENTREPRENEURSHIP

Cheltenham, UK • Northampton, MA, USA

Published by
Edward Elgar Publishing Limited
The Lypiatts
15 Lansdown Road
Cheltenham
Glos GL50 2JA
UK

Edward Elgar Publishing, Inc.
William Pratt House
9 Dewey Court
Northampton
Massachusetts 01060
USA

A catalogue record for this book
is available from the British Library

Library of Congress Control Number: 2015952686

This book is available electronically in the **Elgar**online
Business subject collection
DOI 10.4337/9781785363443

ISBN 978 1 78536 343 6 (cased)
ISBN 978 1 78536 344 3 (eBook)

Typeset by Servis Filmsetting Ltd, Stockport, Cheshire
Printed and bound by CPI Group (UK) Ltd, Croydon, CR0 4YY

Contents

List of contributors   vii
Acknowledgements   xviii

Research in translating discoveries to the marketplace   1
Phillip H. Phan

1   Translating Smart Kitchen technologies from the lab to the
    home   7
    William Hefley, Dan Ding, Aimee Rosenbaum, Megan Kiniry,
    Jason Somma, Skyler Berry, Katelyn Hazelbach,
    Matthew Michaels, James DeFelice, Meghan Duffy, Meredith Kearns,
    Ryan Magath, Jingzi Yang, Rachel Cawley, Brian Chatot,
    Samuel Deely, Bryan Bradley, Allison Dobos, Callie Rosenfeld,
    Rebekah Strouse, Ihinosen Dibua, Haoran Hu, Zachary Venema
    and Carolyn Weber

PART I   DRIVERS OF ENTREPRENEURIAL ACTIVITY

2   Poor opportunities in the academic labor market as a cause of
    spin-offs   39
    Silvio Vismara and Michele Meoli

PART II   ORGANIZING FOR COMMERCIALIZATION IN
           THE BIOPHARMACEUTICAL INDUSTRY

3   When do biotechnology ventures pursue international R&D
    alliances?   65
    Hakan Ener and Ha Hoang

4   A technology credit scoring model for the biotechnology
    industry?   93
    So Young Sohn, Kyong Taek Lim and Bo Kyeong Lee

5   The dynamics of R&D inertia in the pharmaceutical chemicals
    industry   115
    Srikanth Paruchuri

6   How corporate governance affects innovation in the
    pharmaceutical industry   155
    Phillip H. Phan, Gideon Markman and David Balkin

PART III   INSTITUTIONAL CAUSES AND POLICY
           CONSEQUENCES OF TECHNOLOGY
           ENTREPRENEURSHIP

7   The institutional inertias that constrain technology-driven
    economic development   185
    G. Reza Djavanshir

8   The economic impact of public universities in the United
    Kingdom   206
    Maribel Guerrero, David Urbano and James A. Cunningham

9   A comparative study of ecosystem development in regenerative
    medicine   218
    Adam J. Bock and David Johnson

Conclusion: directions for future research   251
Phillip H. Phan

Index   255

Contributors

David Balkin is Professor of Management at the Leeds School of Business, University of Colorado at Boulder, USA. He received a PhD in Human Resource Management and Industrial Relations from the University of Minnesota. Prior to joining the University of Colorado, he served on the faculties of Louisiana State University and Northeastern University. He has published over 60 journal articles. His current research focuses on the management of knowledge and innovation and the management of reward systems. One of his publications (co-authored with Luis R. Gomez-Mejia) was selected as the best article published in the *Academy of Management Journal*. Balkin is co-author of several leading texts on management and human resources that include *Management: People, Performance and Change* (2012) and *Managing Human Resources* (7th edition, 2012). He has served as Chair of the Management Department at the University of Colorado and also on advisory boards of non-profit organizations. Balkin serves as the associate editor for *Human Resource Management Review* and has previously served on the editorial boards of the *Academy of Management Journal* and the *Journal of Management*. He has served as an expert witness on cases dealing with employment and pay discrimination. Balkin has extensive international experience as a scholar and teacher and has been a Visiting Professor at the University of Toulouse (France), Copenhagen Business School (Denmark), Helsinki University of Technology (Finland), University of Regensburg (Germany), ESADE Business School (Spain), National University of Singapore, Hong Kong University of Science and Technology, HEC Montreal (Canada) and the Indian School of Business (India).

Skyler Berry graduated with a degree in Marketing and Supply Chain Management from the College of Business Administration at the University of Pittsburgh, USA. While at Pitt Business, he completed the Certificate Program in Leadership and Ethics (CPLE) and served as a member of the Allocations Committee on the Student Government Board.

Adam J. Bock is Senior Lecturer in Entrepreneurship at the University of Edinburgh Business School, UK. He studies entrepreneurial activity in uncertain contexts to explain why entrepreneurs commercialize new technologies and how they develop innovative business models. He has explored the motivations of academic scientists who become inventing entrepreneurs and the unique narrative capabilities of founder-entrepreneurs in technology-intensive industries. Bock is the co-author (with Gerry George) of *Inventing Entrepreneurs* (2008) and *Models of Opportunity* (2012), and has published articles in *Entrepreneurship Theory and Practice* and *Journal of Management Studies*. He is a fellow of the UK Higher Education Academy and a Member of the Royal Society of Edinburgh Young Academy. He co-authored *Entrepreneurship in the Research Context*, an online course for research scientists produced by Epigeum Ltd. Bock is the Co-founder of three university spin-out companies and has managed multiple angel networks. He mentors technology and social entrepreneurs around the world, and was the lead Advisory Board member for Power of Youth (Scotland). Bock has been a Visiting Scholar at the University of Wisconsin-Madison, Adjunct Professor of Entrepreneurship at Skolkovo Institute of Science and Technology (Moscow) and a visiting fellow at Imperial College London.

Bryan Bradley graduated with a Bachelor of Science in Business Administration degree in Marketing and a minor in Economics from the College of Business Administration at the University of Pittsburgh, USA. While at Pitt Business, he completed the Certificate Program in Leadership and Ethics (CPLE).

Rachel Cawley graduated from the College of Business Administration at the University of Pittsburgh, USA with a Bachelor of Science in Business Administration. While attending Pitt Business, she concentrated on marketing studies while also completing the Certificate Program in Leadership and Ethics (CPLE). The CPLE allowed Cawley to serve different consulting roles, including as a commercialization consultant where she explored different ways to bring a product to market. In addition to her work through the CPLE, she studied and worked abroad to complete her Certificate Program for International Business (CPIB). She spent a semester in Spain, taking classes and working with locals at the Salamanca Chamber of Commerce Gastronomic Innovation Center. Cawley is also the proud recipient of a 2014 David Berg Center Endowment grant.

Brian Chatot graduated with an Accounting degree from the College of Business Administration at the University of Pittsburgh, USA. While attending Pitt Business he completed the Certificate Program in Leadership and Ethics (CPLE). After graduating he is attending Katz Graduate School at the University of Pittsburgh to earn his Masters in Accounting. He is also pursuing his Certified Public Accountant (CPA) title.

James A. Cunningham graduated from J.E. Cairnes School of Business & Economics and the Whitaker Institute, National University of Ireland, Ireland. He is Professor of Strategic Management at Newcastle Business School at Northumbria University, UK. His research intersects the fields of strategic management, innovation and entrepreneurship and focuses on strategy issues with respect to principal investigators as scientific entrepreneurs and market shapers, university technology transfer commercialization, academic and technology entrepreneurship and entrepreneurial universities. His papers have been published in leading international journals. Cunningham has published seven books on the themes of strategy, entrepreneurship, technology transfer and technology entrepreneurship. His co-authored case studies have won international case writing competitions. He has completed several commissioned research reports, acted as mentor for start-up businesses and been a principal investigator on a range of national and international publicly funded projects including the Creative Edge funded by the Northern Peripheries Programme. He is currently a member of the editorial board of the *Journal of Technology Transfer* and member of the Academic Board for the University Industry Innovation Network. He led the establishment of TOPIK (Translation of Principal Investigator Knowledge), an online resource and community for scientists as principal investigators (www.topik.ie).

Samuel Deely graduated with a Bachelor's degree from the College of Business Administration at the University of Pittsburgh, USA. While at Pitt Business, he completed two majors in Marketing and Supply Chain Management, a Certificate in Leadership and Ethics and spent a semester in London. He begins his professional career in the Merchandising Trainee Program at Dick's Sporting Goods.

James DeFelice graduated with a Bachelor of Science degree in Finance from the College of Business Administration at the University of Pittsburgh, USA. While at Pitt Business, he completed the Certificate Program in Leadership and Ethics (CPLE) and a minor in Economics, as well as spending a semester studying abroad. After graduation, he will work in New York with AXA Advisors.

Ihinosen Dibua was an undergraduate student in the College of Business Administration at the University of Pittsburgh, USA. While at Pitt Business, he was pursuing the Certificate Program in Leadership and Ethics (CPLE).

Dan Ding received a PhD in Mechanical and Automation Engineering from the Chinese University of Hong Kong, China. She is Associate Professor at the University of Pittsburgh, USA in the Department of

Rehabilitation Science and Technology with a secondary appointment in Pitt's Department of Bioengineering. She is a Research Scientist at the Human Engineering Research Laboratories in the VA Pittsburgh Healthcare System. She is also a Testbed System Leader of the Home and Community Health and Wellness Testbed, and the Education Co-director, both within the National Science Foundation's Engineering Research Center (ERC) on Quality of Life Technology (QoLT), Pittsburgh. Ding's research interests include wearable technology for rehabilitation applications, assistive robotics and systems, and instrumented environments and ambient assistive living. Ding has published more than 120 papers in refereed professional journals and abstracts/conference proceedings as well as six book chapters. She is associate editor of *Research for the Assistive Technology Journal*. Ding is the recipient of several awards and honors including a 2005 research fellowship award from the Paralyzed Veterans of America and a 2004 Switzer fellowship award from the Department of Education and the National Institute of Disability Research and Rehabilitation.

G. Reza Djavanshir is Associate Professor at the Johns Hopkins Carey Business School in Baltimore, USA. He is a Doctor of Science in Systems Engineering and Engineering Management with expertise in the areas of global sourcing and supply chains, technology transfer and strategic planning, technology institutionalization, auto-poetic meta-systems design and systems integration strategies. He serves on the editorial review boards of *IEEE Technology & Society*, *IEEE IT Professional* and the *Scientific Journal of Administrative Development*. He has published in such journals as *IEEE Computer Society*, *IT Pro.*, *IEEE Transaction on Engineering Management* and the *Journal of Telematics and Informatics*. Djavanshir teaches in the areas of strategy architecture, systems designs and integration, global-sourcing strategy and telecommunication networks and systems.

Allison Dobos graduated with a Bachelor of Science in Business Administration degree with majors in Marketing and Finance from the College of Business Administration at the University of Pittsburgh, USA. While at Pitt Business, she completed the Certificate Program in Leadership and Ethics (CPLE) and was an active member of the business organization Phi Beta Lambda.

Meghan Duffy graduated with a dual Finance and Supply Chain Management degree from the College of Business Administration at the University of Pittsburgh, USA. While at Pitt Business, she completed the Certificate Program in Leadership and Ethics (CPLE), was a member of the Socially Responsible Investing Club, a member of the professional business fraternity Alpha Kappa Psi and studied in Copenhagen Denmark for a semester. After graduating she will work for Eaton Corporation in the Finance Leadership Development Program as a financial analyst.

Hakan Ener is Assistant Professor of Entrepreneurship at IESE Business School, University of Barcelona, Spain. He earned a PhD at INSEAD Business School in France and Singapore. His research interests focus on the ability of entrepreneurial firms to grow in new markets, especially through the lens of organizational learning theories. His work has won the worldwide Kenneth E. Clark Award from the Center for Creative Leadership.

Maribel Guerrero graduated from the Deusto Business School, Donostia-San Sebastian, Spain. Her PhD is from the Autonomous University of Barcelona (Spain) for a dissertation on 'The creation and development of entrepreneurial universities: an institutional approach.' She is a researcher at Deusto Business School and research fellow at Orkestra-Basque Institute of Competitiveness. Guerrero has taught postgraduate entrepreneurship courses in Spain and Mexico, and also taken part in research projects regarding entrepreneurship in Catalonia, the Basque Country and Northeast Mexico. She has published several books, book chapters and articles in academic journals on intrapreneurial activities within public institutions (entrepreneurial universities and academic entrepreneurship) and private organizations (corporate entrepreneurship). She is a reviewer for international journals and guest editor of some special issues. She is a member of the Spanish team involved in the *Global Entrepreneurship Monitor (GEM)* in Spain.

Katelyn Hazelbach graduated with a Marketing degree from the College of Business Administration at the University of Pittsburgh, USA. While at Pitt Business, she completed the Certificate Program in Leadership and Ethics and an additional certificate in Corporate and Community Relations. Upon graduation, she is attending the University of South Florida to complete an MBA and an MS in Sport and Entertainment Management.

William Hefley received a PhD in Organization Science and Information Technology from Carnegie Mellon University, USA. He also earned a MS in Engineering and Public Policy from Carnegie Mellon and a MSSM from the University of Southern California. He is Clinical Professor at the Naveen Jindal School of Management at the University of Texas at Dallas. From 2009 to 2015, Hefley was at the Joseph M. Katz Graduate School of Business and College of Business Administration at the

University of Pittsburgh. Prior to joining Pitt Business, he was Associate Director of a research center in the School of Computer Science at Carnegie Mellon University, Associate Teaching Professor in the Institute of Software Research, Assistant Teaching Professor in the Department of Social and Decision Sciences and Senior Member of the Technical Staff at the Software Engineering Institute, where he focused on transitioning advanced technologies into use across industry, government and academia. He has industry experience as an Executive Consultant with IBM, a Principal Consultant/VP with Q-Labs and as a Human Factors Engineering Specialist with the Lockheed Corporation.

Ha Hoang is Professor at ESSEC Business School, France. She received a PhD from the University of California-Berkeley, USA. Her research is focused on the dynamics of R&D alliance activity in the biotechnology industry, network-based research in entrepreneurship and entrepreneurial identity. Her work has been published in leading journals including *Administrative Science Quarterly*, *Academy of Management Journal*, *Strategic Management Journal* and *Journal of Business Venturing*.

Haoran Hu graduated with a Bachelor's degree from the College of Business Administration at the University of Pittsburgh, USA. While at Pitt Business, he completed the Certificate Program in Leadership and Ethics (CPLE). After graduation, he will pursue his career in the banking industry.

David Johnson is a Doctoral Candidate at the University of Edinburgh Business School, UK. His research focuses on regenerative medicine venturing, where he explores entrepreneurial coping strategies, sensemaking and entrepreneurial ecosystem development under uncertainty. Johnson's academic studies began in science and included research at the Roslin Institute into immunogenetics and disease resistance. Prior to his doctoral studies, he spent several years working for global pharmaceutical companies and during this time he obtained an MBA. He is especially interested in university technology transfer, in particular, university spin-out ventures. This interest has resulted in him reaching the semi-final of the world's largest biotechnology business plan accelerator program with an innovative life science diagnostic tool. During his doctoral research, Johnson has been a Visiting Scholar at the Wisconsin School of Business at the University of Wisconsin-Madison, USA.

Meredith Kearns graduated with a Bachelor's degree in Business Administration from the College of Business Administration at the University of Pittsburgh, USA. While at Pitt Business, she studied General Management focusing on Marketing and Human Resources as well as completing a Certificate in Leadership and Ethics (CPLE). Kearns was involved in the Pitt Fashion Business Association (FBA). She was an active member as a freshman and in sophomore year, took over the alumni relations chair in her junior year before serving as president in her senior year.

Megan Kiniry graduated with a Bachelor of Science in Business Administration from the College of Business Administration at the University of Pittsburgh, USA. She completed the Certificate Program in Leadership and Ethics (CPLE) and is Digital Adviser for retail clients at eBay Inc.

Bo Kyeong Lee is a PhD candidate at the Department of Information and Industrial Engineering, Yonsei University, South Korea. Her research areas are the technology-based credit scoring model, microcredit and evidence-based policy evaluation.

Kyong Taek Lim obtained a Master's degree from the Department of Information and Industrial Engineering, Yonsei University, South Korea. He works for the Korea Credit Bureau.

Ryan Magath graduated with a Bachelor of Science in Accounting from the College of Business Administration at the University of Pittsburgh, USA. While at Pitt Business, he completed the Certificate Program in Leadership and Ethics (CPLE). Magath is currently working for Deloitte as an Audit Intern before returning to Pitt to complete his Masters in Accounting.

Gideon Markman is Professor of Strategy, Entrepreneurship and Sustainable Enterprise at Colorado State University (CSU), USA. He studies competitive strategy, entrepreneurship and innovation. His research has been published in many leading journals. Markman earned the prestigious Best Teacher Award in 2010; he teaches the Capstone Strategy classes at CSU, and has taught in diverse institutions and contexts in the USA and other countries. He is an editorial board member with the *Journal of Management, Journal of Management Studies* and *Strategic Entrepreneurship Journal*. Markman founded and funded the Sustainability, Ethics, and Entrepreneurship (SEE) Conference – a unifying event that is supported by several universities and the Kauffman Foundation. In addition, Markman founded the Front Range Management Research Seminar, a research event often held in Colorado. He is an expert in business model innovation and has consulted large enterprises such as Deutsche Telekom, Bosch Siemens, ChoicePoint, Mary Kay Cosmetics and Worldspan, as well as private and family firms, start-ups and non-profit organizations (Altarum Institute).

Michele Meoli is Assistant Professor of Corporate Finance at the Department of Engineering, University of Bergamo, Italy. He is a member of the CISAlpino Institute for Comparative Studies in Europe (CCSE), University of Bergamo and University of Augsburg. He was Marie Curie Research Fellow at the Centre for Econometrics Analysis, Cass Business School (City University London). His research interests include corporate governance, initial public offerings valuation, academic entrepreneurship and governance in higher education systems.

Matthew Michaels graduated with a Bachelor of Science in Business Administration from the College of Business Administration at the University of Pittsburgh, USA. While at Pitt Business, he majored in Finance, with a minor in Economics and pursued a Certificate in Leadership and Ethics. Post graduation, Michaels will work with Dick's Sporting Goods in their Merchandising Trainee Program.

Srikanth Paruchuri is Associate Professor in the Smeal College of Business, Pennsylvania State University, USA. His PhD is from Columbia University, Master's in International Business is from the Indian Institute of Foreign Trade, New Delhi and Bachelor's in Technology specializing in computer science is from the Regional Engineering College, Warangal, India. His work focuses on the evolution of organizational capabilities (specifically R&D capabilities), technologies and industries. He investigates these aspects by employing diverse theoretical lenses including social networks (of individual scientists and firms), social movements and environmental jolts. His work has appeared in journals such as the *Academy of Management Journal, Organization Science, Management Science, American Sociological Review, Economic Geography Journal* and *Journal of Management Studies*. His teaching interests are in the areas of strategy and innovation management. He serves on the editorial boards of *Academy of Management Journal* and *Organization Science*.

Phillip H. Phan received a PhD from the University of Washington, USA. He is Professor at the Johns Hopkins University Carey Business School and Core Faculty at the Johns Hopkins Medicine Armstrong Institute for Patient Safety and Quality. He is Academic Program Director of the Carey Business School's Executive MBA and MSc in Health Care Management and Strategy. He is Visiting Professor of Medicine at the National University of Singapore Yong Loo Lin School of Medicine and serves on the grants committee of the Center for Health Services and Policy Research at the National University of Singapore Saw Swee Hock School of Public Health. Previously, he held the Pauline and Warren H. Bruggeman '46 Distinguished Professorship at Rensselaer Polytechnic

Institute, and the Bosch Foundation Public Policy Fellow at the American Academy in Berlin. Phan's research focuses on the governance of innovation in technology, healthcare services and biomedical science. His current work focuses on technology-mediated innovation in transitions of inpatient care and patient discharge planning conducted at the Johns Hopkins Hospital and the Singapore National University Healthcare System. He has published more than 90 peer-reviewed research articles in leading journals. He is co-editor of the *Academy of Management Perspectives*, senior editor of the *Journal of Business Venturing* and associate editor of the *Journal of Technology Transfer*. He has presented his healthcare services research at the Academy of Management, the Society for General Internal Medicine, the American College of Neuropsychopharmacology, Alliance for Academic Internal Medicine.

Aimee Rosenbaum graduated with a Bachelor of Science in Business Administration from the College of Business Administration at the University of Pittsburgh, USA. While at Pitt Business, she completed a major in Accounting as well as the Certificate Program in Leadership and Ethics (CPLE).

Callie Rosenfeld graduated with a Global Management major from the College of Business Administration at the University of Pittsburgh, USA. She works for PNC Financial Services Inc. as part of their Human Resources Development Program.

So Young Sohn received a PhD in Industrial Engineering from the University of Pittsburgh, USA and MS degrees in Management Science from Imperial College London and Industrial Engineering from KAIST, South Korea. She is Professor of Information and Industrial Engineering at Yonsei University, Korea. Sohn is an expert in the area of technology financing, specializing in the development of technology credit scoring models. Her pioneering framework for a technology rating system has been implemented by the Korean government agency that is responsible for managing the technology credit guarantee fund. In 2007 she was awarded Outstanding Female Scientist of the Year (Engineering area) in Korea. She has published articles in many leading journals and is also an inventor with several patents in related areas. She served as editor-in-chief of *IE Interfaces* and the *Journal of Engineering Education Research*. She is a fellow of the Korean Academy of Science & Technology and Vice President of the Korean Institute of Industrial Engineering.

Jason Somma is an Intellectual Property and Licensing Associate with the Office of Technology Management in the Innovation Institute at the University of Pittsburgh, USA. Within the Innovation Institute, he is involved with drafting and negotiating various transactional agreements including confidentiality, inter-institutional and license agreements relating to technologies developed from university research; evaluating emerging technologies for their commercial potential and patentability; and management of outside counsel in preparing and prosecuting patent applications, with a focus on medical imaging, electrical engineering and software-related technologies. He holds a JD from the University of Pittsburgh School of Law, and was awarded a BS in Engineering Physics and a BA in Music (Jazz Studies), both from the University of Pittsburgh. Somma has held externships with the Chief Justice of the Supreme Court of Pennsylvania and the US Court of Appeals for the Third Circuit, and is a Registered Patent Attorney with the US Patent and Trademark Office.

Rebekah Strouse graduated with a Finance and Human Resources degree from the College of Business Administration at the University of Pittsburgh, USA. While at Pitt Business, she completed the Certificate Program in Leadership and Ethics (CPLE). After graduation, she works as a Human Resource Generalist with a focus on compensation.

David Urbano is Professor of Entrepreneurship at the Department of Business, Universitat Autonoma de Barcelona, Spain. He obtained a PhD from the European Doctoral Programme in Entrepreneurship and Small Business Management at UAB-Växjö University, Sweden. Urbano's research focuses on the conditioning factors for entrepreneurship in different contexts. His work adopts an institutional perspective and combines quantitative and qualitative methodologies. He has published several books as well as articles in international journals. He is a research fellow in the *Global Entrepreneurship Monitor (GEM)* and in the Panel Study for Entrepreneurial Dynamics (PSED). He has been editor of various special issues of refereed international journals and is a member of the editorial board of several academic journals. Urbano has been a visiting scholar at international and Spanish universities. He is a consultant in entrepreneurship in several projects for the Catalan and Spanish governments, the European Union, Organisation for Economic Co-operation and Development and the private sector, teaching several courses and seminars and advising in this area (innovation, new firm creation, corporate entrepreneurship, family firms, small and medium-sized enterprise management).

Zachary Venema has an Accounting degree from the College of Business Administration and a minor in Political Science from the University of Pittsburgh, USA. While at Pitt Business, he completed the Certificate Program in Leadership and Ethics (CPLE). After graduating, he works for Ernst & Young in their Washington, DC area office in the Assurance practice.

Silvio Vismara is Associate Professor of Corporate Finance at the University of Bergamo, Italy. His research is in the areas of entrepreneurial finance, mainly on initial public offerings, academic entrepreneurship and crowdfunding. Vismara is associate editor of *Small Business Economics*, member of the Editorial Review Board of *Entrepreneurship Theory and Practice* and author of articles in journals such as *Entrepreneurship Theory and Practice, Small Business Economics, Financial Management, Journal of Corporate Finance, Journal of Banking and Finance, European Financial Management* and *Journal of Technology Transfer*. He is Co-founder and Co-director of the CISAlpino Institute for Comparative Studies in Europe (CCSE). He is scientific consultant for the Italian Stock Exchange and founder of Universoft, a spin-off company from the University of Bergamo.

Carolyn Weber is a Technology Marketing Associate at the Office of Technology Management, University of Pittsburgh, USA. She has been with the office since 2000, first accepting the Katz Tech Fellowship position, sponsored by the Heinz Foundation, after graduating from the Joseph M. Katz Graduate School of Business at the University of Pittsburgh. Prior to joining the University of Pittsburgh, Weber worked in the retail pharmacy area as a Pharmacist/Manager for Thrift Drug Store for 18 years. She received a BS in Pharmacy from the University of Pittsburgh in 1980 and MBA from the Katz Graduate School of Business in 2000.

Jingzi Yang is a graduate student from the College of Business Administration at the University of Pittsburgh, USA. While at Pitt Business, she completed a double major in Accounting and Finance with an Economics minor, as well as the Certificate Program in Leadership and Ethics (CPLE). After graduation, she will pursue her Certified Public Accountant (CPA) title.

Acknowledgements

Chapter 1

The authors thank two anonymous reviewers for their important and very helpful suggestions for improvement. We also thank the participants of the Paper Development Workshop at the Technology Transfer Society 2014 Annual Conference. In addition, we thank Katherine Seelman, School of Health & Rehabilitation Sciences, University of Pittsburgh, for her valuable review. Generous support for the Certification Program in Leadership and Ethics (CPLE), and for this research, is provided by the David Berg Center for Ethics and Leadership at the Joseph M. Katz Graduate School of Business and College of Business Administration at the University of Pittsburgh through the David Berg Foundation of New York. The Smart Kitchen work is supported by the National Science Foundation, Quality of Life Technology Engineering Research Center (grant no. EEC 0540865) and with resources and use of facilities at the Human Engineering Research Laboratories (HERL), VA Pittsburgh Healthcare System. This material does not represent the views of the Department of Veterans Affairs or the United States government. The authors declare that they have no conflict of interest. No commercial party having a direct financial interest in the results of the research supporting this chapter has or will confer a benefit on the authors or on any organization with which the authors are associated.

Chapter 3

The authors thank Gautam Ahuja, Jenny Kuan, Joanne Oxley, Subramanian Rangan, Robert Seamans, Rosemarie Ziedonis, as well as conference and seminar participants at the 2015 Technology Transfer Society Annual Conference, Baltimore, Maryland, USA for their valuable comments. Ananth Raman provided helpful research assistance.

Chapter 4

This work was supported by the National Research Foundation of Korea (NRF) grant funded by the Korea government (MSIP)

(2013R1A2A1A09004699). Yonghan Ju participated in this research as a graduate research assistant. We are indebted to Professor William Hefley for many insightful comments that improved this manuscript.

Chapter 5

I thank Don Hambrick, Hayagreeva Rao, Heather Haveman, Henry Tosi and Wei Shen for providing helpful comments on earlier versions of the manuscript.

Chapter 7

The author would like to thank Nick Brock for his editorial contributions to this chapter.

Chapter 8

A previous version of this chapter was presented at the 2014 Technology Transfer Society Conference held on 24 October in Baltimore, MD, USA. The authors wish to acknowledge the anonymous reviewers for their comments and feedback that have helped shape this chapter. David Urbano acknowledges the financial support from the projects ECO2013-44027-P (Spanish Ministry of Economy & Competitiveness) and 2014/SGR/1626 (Economy & Knowledge Department, Catalan government).

Chapter 9

Funding for this research was provided by the Economic and Social Research Council (grant no. ES/J500136/1) and the University of Edinburgh Business School. We are also grateful for institutional support from the Holtz Center for Science and Technology Studies at the University of Wisconsin-Madison and the Wisconsin School of Business at the University of Wisconsin-Madison.

Research in translating discoveries to the marketplace

Phillip H. Phan

Technology commercialization has drawn widespread attention from academia and policymaking, leading to an increasing volume of published papers. However, not all topics in this field have received equal attention; for example, the translation phase of the commercialization process is not well understood. Translation is where the scientific concept or paradigm has to be converted into a working application before it can be considered a funding opportunity for commercialization. This stage of the process, between bench discovery and proof of concept, represents the most financially and organizational challenging phase of the commercialization cycle. Funding is limited because translation is considered not novel enough for discovery-based funding. But because the idea is still in its early stages the distance to a working prototype may be too great for commercial or venture funding. Further, what is ultimately acceptable to the marketplace is generally unknown in this process. In life science, the translation process begins with target validation; in software, it is the alpha version; in materials science, the physical proof of the theoretical construct; and so on. This development cycle is typified by trial and error learning; in which innovators can look for clues in analogous solutions to guess at the appropriate form factor, design or composition. This 'best guess' is tested iteratively by exposing the ideas to external stakeholders (consumers, regulators, suppliers and so on) before formal product development can commence. By no means is Steve Blank's Business Canvas methodology in the National Institutes of Health/National Science Foundation (NIH/NSF) funded iCorp[1] program the only approach, but it represents a good example of such a process.

The purpose of this volume is to illustrate how the lesser known aspects of technology commercialization at the regional, institutional and organizational levels of analyses, with attention to translation, can be approached. The book opens with a case study of a technology translation project. Part I discusses how the lack of academic job opportunities can lead to more technology spin-offs. Part II turns our attention to the organizational aspects of technology commercialization, with special reference to the life science industry. In Part III, we look at the institutional causes and economic consequences of technology commercialization.

We begin with the case study by Hefley et al. in Chapter 1 that reports on the translation of the Human Engineering Research Laboratories' (HERL) Smart Kitchen technologies to commercial use by a student team from the Certificate Program in Leadership and Ethics (CPLE) course at the University of Pittsburgh. The components of the Smart Kitchen were subjected to a formal Technology Roadmapping to identify possible commercialization pathways. The team began by delineating the focal populations (Wounded Warrior/Traumatic Brain Injury, Physically Disabled, Aging and Mass Market) of interest. They then developed technology roadmaps, addressing short- and long-term commercialization pathways, for each population. By examining multiple target populations, the team demonstrated the important insight that commercialization pathways are not a singular route but are many that may depend on a number of factors such as target population and supporting institutions (for example, the Wounded Warrior and Physically Disabled are supported by Federal freedom of physical access regulation and facilitation programs) in the target space. Another lesson was that research projects moving toward commercialization may need to augment their staff and resources to address technology commercialization needs, a common theme in the research on translation science.

Chapter 2 by Vismara and Meoli addresses the question of where academic start-ups come from. A rapidly emerging phenomenon is the start-up as an employment alternative for PhD trained scientists. The fact that technology start-ups, given their risks, represent a form of alternative employment is itself an interesting notion. First, because existing studies on individual motivations to establish academic spin-offs are typified by entrepreneurial grand visions and passion for the technology or need to solve a problem. Interestingly, firms created because of an entrepreneurial vision or passion do not, the data in this chapter suggest, outperform start-ups created as employment substitutes. In the longitudinal study of 559 spin-offs from 85 Italian universities in the period 1999 to 2013, and controlling for university- and context-level factors, the authors found that a paucity of academic jobs at the regional level is correlated with a higher propensity to create new technology enterprises. Accordingly, they argue that academics sometimes become entrepreneurs as a second-best solution, because of shortcomings in the market for knowledge. This effect is negatively moderated by the faculty members' teaching load in technology-based spin-offs, and by administrative support in non-technology spin-offs. The authors conclude that the lack of administrative support might create an incentive to spin-off non-technology-based firms, replacing the role of the administrative staff.

In Part II, Chapter 3 by Ener and Hoang looks at why technology ventures go international. Typically, technology ventures often develop products domestically and license them out to large companies for worldwide commercialization. This is because local demand markets allow these ventures to refine their products and provide a hedge against the political and currency risks encountered in international markets. However, the authors show that international research and development (R&D) alliances can provide an alternative and potentially more rewarding path to growing foreign markets. They conjecture that such a path is especially attractive for firms underperforming in terms of product development relative to their aspirations. Their analyses of US-based biotechnology ventures show that low performance leads ventures to collaborate internationally while high-performing ventures refrain from international R&D alliances. This is a somewhat counter-intuitive finding, since international alliances add a level of complexity that a domestic focus does not have. However, if the firm's domestic R&D efforts are not paying off, perhaps because demand markets are matured or regulatory processes are too costly to overcome, a 'go international' strategy may represent a lower risk proposition. The authors conjecture that this novel commercialization channel turns out to be a response to the failure in developing novel products, which is a departure from the traditional way to think about international strategy in general, and innovation management in particular.

In Chapter 4 Sohn and colleagues propose a technology credit scoring model for the biotechnology and pharmaceutical industries. Technology scoring models are popular in the management of technology commercialization. They allow managers to determine the stage of maturity of a technology in order to make the appropriate investment decisions for further development. Sohn et al.'s proposition of a technology credit scoring model is unlike traditional technology scoring models in that it accounts for the technology *and* firm-level attributes to determine readiness for commercialization. This approach recognizes the importance of firm capabilities for successful commercialization, in addition to the maturity of the base technology. The results of their logistic regression analysis show that both technology and marketability factors play the most important roles in industrial biotechnology, while management factors and firm-specific characteristics are more influential in pharmaceutical companies.

Chapter 5 by Paruchuri investigates how changes in the nature of R&D in the pharmaceutical chemicals industry is impacted by and affects changes in the technological and economic landscape in which such activities are conducted. He uses the Dow Chemical company as the case study to explore the core assumption that organizations cannot change faster than their environments. Apart from the performance implications of change, which are well characterized in the literature, he explores how organizational inertia affects the content and process of change in the organization's R&D capability. Following this chapter, Phan et al. explore the impact of ownership and control on research intensity, patenting and new product introductions over a five-year period for 86 publicly listed pharmaceutical firms. In combination with the chapters by Sohn et al. and Paruchuri, readers should be reminded of the importance of governance, strategic and organizational capabilities to the life science firm's R&D activities.

In Chapter 6 Phan et al. find that the presence of block private and insti-tutional shareholders – controlling for firm size and prior performance – is positively associated with innovation activity and its outcomes. Indeed, the fact that chief executive officer (CEO) duality, in which the CEO also serves as chair of the board, is positively related to R&D expenditures, and that insider-dominated boards are positively related to new product introductions suggests a more sophisticated discussion of the interplay between board independence and managerial discretion is in order. In the literature, there is a sense that management-dominated boards can lead to value destruction because when decision control and management are combined, managers can make investment decisions at the expense of shareholders. However, when long-term irreversible investments of capital are required to drive innovation, the ability for managers to keep investing may spell the difference between success and failure. Therefore, sustained support by the board of directors to resist the short-term ten-dencies of public shareholders is critical. Combining decision control and management *can* yield positive effects in specific circumstances and the management-dominated board may support more risk-taking and innova-tion. Therefore, 'best practice' recommendations for 'independent' (that is, outsider-dominated) boards should be reconsidered for firms engaged in high risk innovation activities with uncertain outcomes.

In Part III, in Chapter 7 Djavanshir introduces the volume's discussions on the institutional precursors to technology-driven economic develop-ment, and the policy implications for government programs and public universities designed to foster regional development. Unlike other chapters on the institutional enablers of technology-driven economic develop-ment, Djavanshir conjectures that in certain developing and transitioning countries (DTCs), strategies to promote innovation, technology transfer and economic development are unsuccessful because of institutional impediments. In these countries, although governments and businesses in the private sector spend billions of dollars on technology transfer and innovation, their economic development efforts do not achieve their desired strategic goals. To understand why, he draws upon the rich institutional literature to identify the causal factors behind the problems these countries face. Djavanshir discusses how the systemic constraints in a country's regulative, normative and cultural-cognitive institutions act as inertial dampers to their technology transfer, development and entrepreneurial strategies, which ultimately prevent technology-driven economic development processes from achieving the desired strategic goals.

Following the discussion on institutional impediments, in Chapter 8 Guerrero and colleagues study the less understood natural role of universities in economic development. Given the complexity of university functions, previous studies have shown mixed evidence on the economic impact of university teaching, research or entrepreneurial activities by adopting different theoretical approaches and methodologies. According to the microeconomic foundation of endogenous economic theory, the authors in this exploratory study attempt to contribute to a better understanding of the regional economic impact of entrepreneurial universities' activities (teaching, research and entrepreneurship). Their proposed model was tested with a two-stage least square regression weighted by regions using the data of 147 UK public universities located in 74 of the 139 NUTS-3 regions of the country (European nomenclature of territorial units). They found the measure of teaching is strongly correlated with economic development, while the correlation between research and entrepreneurship measures is much weaker. This is in contrast to the work on technology transfer in universities that attempt to show a strong correlation between technology entrepreneurship and wealth creation through employment, the introduction of new goods and services and the corresponding increases in trade. Their study demonstrates that human capital development is a more direct and sustainable route to economic welfare, since university human capital is more general (more fungible and responsive to changes in the economic competitive landscape for labor) than entrepreneurial capital, which is more specific to the form of activity against which such capital is deployed.

Chapter 9 by Bock and Johnson studies two university-centric regenerative medicine ecosystems to explore the characteristics of venturing activity and ecosystem development under irreducible uncertainty. In the field of regenerative medicine, new ventures face unformed markets and inconsistent industry practices. The situational analysis reveals multi-level effects. At the micro-level, entrepreneurial coping strategies are significantly affected by cultural artifacts generated by the ecosystem university. At the macro-level, entrepreneurial ecosystems may develop along different paths, generating idiosyncratic contexts for venturing activity. The authors present a model of entrepreneurial ecosystem development with implications for theories of entrepreneurial behavior as well as policy practice in developing technology sectors.

Taken as a whole, this volume tries to energize the research in technology commercialization and entrepreneurship by looking at the less well-researched parts of the development cycle. It looks at the problems attending translation (identification of the fit between firm-level R&D capabilities and stage of technology maturity, sustaining high risk investments and situations where collaborations pay off); the institutional impediments of technology-driven economic development; the development of general versus specific human capital and the implications for risk-taking and wealth creation; and the role of universities in economic and industry development. Each of these chapters are not meant to be taken as exhaustive examples of the represented research but rather guideposts to potentially interesting and productive paths for future research.

NOTE

1. http://steveblank.com/2012/03/26/the-national-science-foundation-innovation-corps-what-america-does-best/ (accessed 2 August 2015).

1. Translating Smart Kitchen technologies from the lab to the home

William Hefley, Dan Ding, Aimee Rosenbaum, Megan Kiniry, Jason Somma, Skyler Berry, Katelyn Hazelbach, Matthew Michaels, James DeFelice, Meghan Duffy, Meredith Kearns, Ryan Magath, Jingzi Yang, Rachel Cawley, Brian Chatot, Samuel Deely, Bryan Bradley, Allison Dobos, Callie Rosenfeld, Rebekah Strouse, Ihinosen Dibua, Haoran Hu, Zachary Venema and Carolyn Weber

INTRODUCTION

With changes in federal law regarding ownership of university-developed innovations, university-industry technology transfer is seen as a means to accelerate the commercialization of newly developed university technologies and promote economic development and entrepreneurial activity (Siegel et al., 2004). Many university-developed advanced technology innovations, including those focused on improving the quality of life for their users, move from research and development, usability studies and clinical research into various stages of commercialization (Seelman, 2013). However, this transition often requires surmounting many challenges and barriers to successful commercialization and widespread adoption (Anokhin et al., 2011; Ball and Preston, 2014; Borisoff, 2010; Martin, 2007; Miller and Acs, 2013; Nath et al., 2013; Sheth and Ram, 1987; Seelman, 2013).

Successful technology transfer can have measurable benefits for the universities and their innovators. McDevitt et al. (2014) reported $2.6 billion total income received by reporting universities. In addition to these revenue generation results, other benefits from technology transfer noted in this study include increased opportunities for funding as a result of technology transfer programs, promotion of a culture of entrepreneurship and innovation, increased student success, public benefits through both universities meeting their public missions and improved quality of life, and economic development. Economic development results reported were $36.8 billion of net product sales generated, with start-up companies related to innovations from 70 academic institutions providing work for almost 16 000 full-time employees. They also report increases in licensing, start-ups and cumulative active licenses, with over 40 000 cumulative active licenses, 5145 issued US patents, 6372 new licenses and options executed and 705 new start-up companies formed.

Regarding student success, Martin et al. (2013), in their recent quantitative review of the entrepreneurship education literature, found significant relationships between entrepreneurship education, training and entrepreneurship-related human capital assets, and entrepreneurship outcomes, with academic-oriented education having a stronger relationship than training. Thus, entrepreneurship education has been shown to enhance relevant knowledge and skills, as well as result in positive outcomes. Focusing more specifically on innovation and commercialization of university-developed technologies, several approaches have been applied. Incubators and proof of concept centers have been developed to move technology out of the university (Gulbranson and Audretsch, 2008; O'Neal, 2005; Phan et al., 2005). One such example in the biomedical space is Washington University's IDEA (Innovation, Design, and Engineering in Action) Lab, which is a biomedical design and entrepreneurship incubator (Som et al., 2014). Fostering start-ups are another pathway for commercialization of university technologies (Swamidass, 2013).

Universities have explored education-based initiatives. Numerous schools have implemented Bench to Bedside initiatives to bring technology into use, often involving students in these projects. Johns Hopkins has implemented a two-semester graduate course sequence known as 'Discovery to Market' that provides both instruction in technology transfer and commercialization and a hands-on project (Phan, 2014).

The purpose of this chapter is to report the results of a service-learning project designed to explore potential technology transfer pathways for a suite of assistive technologies – the Smart Kitchen (Ding et al., 2014; Mahajan et al., 2013; Telson et al., 2013; Wang et al., 2013; Yiin, 2014). The Smart Kitchen is being developed by the Human Engineering Research Laboratories (HERL). Our approach was guided by existing models of technology transfer (Anokhin et al., 2011; Siegel et al., 2004), as well as by processes of quality of life technologies (QoLT) development (Schulz et al., 2012). We ask the question: What are the potential pathways to successful commercialization of the Smart Kitchen innovations? In order to address this question, we explore the related questions of (a) are the potential pathways identical for all three components of the Smart Kitchen?; (b) are the potential pathways identical for all target user populations?; and (c) what resources and capabilities are necessary to innovate and commercialize the Smart Kitchen?

QoLT are designed to impact the quality of life of individuals who use them (Schulz et al., 2012). Most people want to live in the settings that they are accustomed to for as long as they can (Seelman et al., 2007). In recent years, research has focused on technologies that can assist in achieving this goal of independence for individuals with, or at risk of, impaired functioning due to trauma, chronic disorders or aging (Schulz, 2013; Schulz et al., 2012). These QoLT are intelligent systems and devices responding to the unique needs of older adults and persons with disabilities (Seelman et al., 2007). In a study using a nationally representative sample of US baby boomers (aged 45–64) and older adults (aged 65 and up), most of these individuals were willing to pay for help with kitchen or personal care activities (Schulz et al., 2014). However, this study noted that, based upon the amounts individuals were willing to pay and the third-party payer models in place (Medicare and insurance), these technologies would have to be cost-effective to gain market and payer acceptance. To accomplish this, these QoLT must successfully move from the laboratories into the marketplace and into the home, where they can provide assistance to those who need it and relief for caregivers, at costs that are within the willingness to pay of both users and payers.

Technology transition of assistive technologies for people with disabilities has been an area of active focus for some time. A decade ago, Lane (2003, p. 334) summarized existing technology transfer work within this field. He described technology transition as 'a value-added process that encompasses a continuum of related activities from laboratory innovation through market consumption.' Along this continuum there also exist a number of policy and regulatory tensions – tensions caused by technologies radically different from those envisioned when regulations were established, as well as tensions relating to financial considerations and healthcare cost and reimbursement guidelines (National Council on Disability, 2000; Seelman, 2013).

As Bauer (2003, p. 285) described the situation,

> Technology transfer has generally had little impact on the assistive technology industries serving small highly fragmented 'disability markets.' Persons with disabilities often require specialized, relatively sophisticated technology.

Third-party payer reimbursement rates and the low levels of disposable income among disability populations often cap product pricing. Transferring technology to these industry segments therefore poses special challenges.

This challenge is one that clearly highlights these tensions. Bauer (2003) points out the concern regarding third-party payer reimbursement rates, while more recently Schulz et al. (2014) point out user willingness to pay some amounts for these technologies, but the overcaution that these technologies must be cost-effective because of these third-party payer pressures. Wagner and Bremer (2001, p. S49) also note an additional challenge to the commercialization and use of certain technologies. QoLT or assistive technologies that are not medically necessary are often not covered by Medicare, Medicaid or insurance programs, thus potentially hindering the introduction and uptake of these new technologies.

Nonetheless, multiple laboratories are addressing the needs of these 'disability markets' by addressing QoLT. However, it has been claimed that invention is not the great challenge in reaching these populations, but rather that the 'bottleneck comes in the transfer of the technology into the commercial sector' (Wagner and Bremer, 2001). As Leahy (2003, p. 305) pointed out, 'many useful products are already invented, but they are not available to consumers, because the inventors lack resources to move the invention to the marketplace.'

Numerous previous studies have examined technology transfer of assistive technologies (for example, Bauer, 2003; Borisoff, 2010; Lane, 2003; Leahy, 2003; Schulz and Beach, 2013; Seelman, 2013; Stone, 2003; Wagner and Bremer, 2001). Other studies have examined assistive technology development efforts as service learning (Goldberg and Pearlman, 2013; Livingston, 2010).

One of the challenges highlighted by Wagner and Bremer (2001) is a need to understand which technology transfer practices will work in differing situations, with different types of technologies or for different markets. Commercialization pathways could include intellectual property protection through patents, retaining ownership of an innovation and bringing the innovation to market, sharing the innovation through licensing it or developing (or co-developing) it with partners or by selling the innovation (Datta et al., 2012; Webster and Jensen, 2011).

A technique that can be applied to address these differences in situations, technologies and target populations, capturing possible technology transfer pathways to commercialization and use is Technology Roadmapping (TRM). TRM is a strategic decision process framework that supports enterprise innovation activities, has attracted the interest of an increasing number of academics and practitioners and has been applied in many different industrial sectors and organizations (Carvalho et al., 2013; Lee and Park, 2005; Lee et al., 2011; Moehrle et al., 2013; Phaal et al., 2004; Phaal et al., 2010; Vatananan and Gerdsri, 2012). The technique originated at Motorola (Richey and Grinnell, 2004; Willyard and McCless, 1987). It is flexible and customizable to fit the strategic context in which it is being applied (Lee and Park, 2005; Phaal et al., 2004; Vatananan and Gerdsri, 2012).

Roadmaps are often used to link technologies to strategic goals and future market opportunities (Fenwick et al., 2009; Probert et al., 2003). In this way, TRM can serve to help principal investigators plan their activities as boundary spanners (Mangematin et al., 2014), helping to design pathways to market opportunities. For example, Chang (2010) identifies a series of internal capabilities and environmental drivers that can explain e-business adoption through the proposed roadmap.

Zurcher and Kostoff (1997) applied TRM to the development of fuel-efficient non-polluting cars. Recent applications include sustainable information technology (Harmon et al., 2012), services, devices and technologies for Smart Cities development (Lee et al., 2011), e-business adoption (Chang, 2010) and Internet security technology (Fenwick et al., 2009).

A technology roadmap is often represented using a multi-layer graphical representation of a plan that connects technology and products with market opportunities (Carvalho et al., 2013; Probert et al., 2003). Figure 1.1 depicts the technology roadmap format depicting a multi-layer, time-based chart that links resources and competencies, the technology

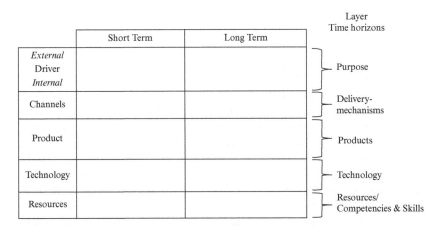

Source: Adapted from Carvalho et al. (2013), Wells et al. (2004) and Probert et al. (2003).

Figure 1.1   Technology roadmap format

and its development and market drivers. It introduces the concept of market channels to explore means of linking the technology under development with the targeted populations.

THE SERVICE-LEARNING PROJECT

The service-learning project (Decker, 2000; Tsang, 2000) was a key component of the Fall 2013 Leadership in the Social Environment (LSE) course. This course is an integral part of the Certificate Program in Leadership and Ethics (CPLE) in the College of Business Administration at the University of Pittsburgh.

Project Participants

The service-learning project was a collaborative effort between the CPLE Class of 2015, faculty and students from HERL and technology transfer experts from Pitt's Innovation Institute, the university's technology transfer office.

While team-based design courses focused on products for people with disabilities have become relatively common, often supported by training grants such as the National Science Foundation's Research to Aid Persons with Disabilities course grants (Goldberg and Pearlman, 2013), this course was significantly different, as it involved business students and focused on commercialization, rather than development, of assistive technologies.

CPLE Undergraduate Team

The CPLE team consisted of the 20 undergraduate students of the CPLE Class of 2015. Our CPLE initiative is the only program across the country that offers undergraduate business students an integrated and sustained program of study into the relationship between leadership and ethics. It contributes to a student's preparation for a career in business by providing hands-on experience into the complex nature of ethical leadership in today's business environment. The CPLE is designed to strengthen the Bachelor of Science in Business Administration (BSBA) program. Thus, students pursuing the CPLE must also be enrolled within the College of Business Administration.

This program is a unique opportunity for undergraduate business students who wish to explore the relationship between leadership and ethics. It contributes to the student's preparation for a career in business by helping to foster contacts with organizations committed to leadership and ethics. The CPLE curriculum is based on the belief that students ought to experience a sustained and integrated exposure to ethics and leadership in organizations. It is also based on the assumption that an emphasis on leadership, without proper consideration of ethics, will not generate leaders who approach their roles with a sense of responsibility and accountability; while an emphasis on ethics, without proper consideration of leadership, will not produce leaders with the necessary tools to develop and implement their vision and understanding of ethics. Thus, leadership and ethics must be considered together. Courses within the CPLE curriculum focus on the development of five key competencies areas: ethical awareness and decision-making; relational leadership; high impact communication; team project management; and civic/social engagement.

Human Engineering Research Laboratories (HERL)

HERL is a collaboration between the University of Pittsburgh, the VA Pittsburgh Healthcare System and UPMC Health System. HERL is dedicated to wheelchair and mobility research, specifically by improving the mobility and function of people with disabilities through advanced engineering in clinical research and medical rehabilitation. HERL also studies athletics in rehabilitation, assistive living spaces, the efficiency of wheelchair transfers, clinician training and force and vibration on wheelchair users. HERL is affiliated with the QoLT Center, a National Science Foundation Engineering Research Center for Quality of Life Technologies. The QoLT Center is a unique partnership between Carnegie Mellon and the University of Pittsburgh that brings together a cross-disciplinary team of technologists, clinicians, industry partners, end users and other stakeholders to create revolutionary technologies that will improve and sustain the quality of life for all people. The QoLT Education and Outreach mission is to create a growing community of engineers, scientists, practitioners and consumers who are intellectually prepared and motivated to create and apply technology to benefit people with disabilities and older adults.

Innovation Institute

The mission of the Innovation Institute is to facilitate the translation of research into innovations and start-ups that have impact. It has emphases on commercialization, entrepreneurship and economic development. Licenses and options, patents and support for start-ups are key activities, as well as a variety of training programs and innovation events.

Project Purpose

This project involved an analysis of technology commercialization options for a set of technologies that HERL is continuing to develop. As the class undertook the project to assist HERL, their primary focus was on analysing technology commercialization options for the Smart Kitchen. This focus was not just on developing a simple marketing plan for the Smart Kitchen technologies, but explored multiple pathways to commercialization, tailored to different populations; developed proposed approaches to pathways to commercialization and licensing of these emerging technologies; and addressed the issues and needs of business and policy ecosystems affecting these multiple populations.

The service-learning project embedded within this course engaged students through professional activism (Decker, 2000), linking students with community needs. In this case, the linkage was multi-level, as one level was linking students with their client at HERL, but also linking them with stakeholders, in this case, a large potential user population and their needs. It has been argued that participation in service-learning projects that benefit a larger community can substantially enhance student learning, support life skill development, increase a sense of civic responsibility and provide a foundation for future professional practice aware of professional, social and civic responsibilities (Tsang, 2000).

The CPLE competency of civic/social engagement is evidenced in a number of substantial, measureable impacts of the CPLE curriculum. These include a positive impact on the local community, primarily through the efforts of students who have worked with local business owners and leaders, have provided opportunities and opinions for local businesses and helped to improve local business and non-profits at no financial cost to the organization. In this project, our community focus was on HERL and potential commercialization partners.

Possible recipients of the social impacts of this course could go far beyond local businesses. Beneficiaries of the outputs from this course could include the target populations of potential users of the Smart Kitchen. Second, the university and its technology transfer units could benefit, as the university has approximately $700 million in funded research (University of Pittsburgh, 2014), and the results of this project may help other projects plan for commercializing their research. Results could also potentially be useful to funding agencies, especially with increasing emphases on industry-university collaborations and commercialization of research. Lastly, this research could have an indirect impact on taxpayers, seeing federally funded research put to work in addressing target populations and potentially lowering caregiving costs in these populations.

The project addresses a critical need as identified by our research partner. This project represents an important experiential exercise that will lead students to develop an understanding of the subtle connections between the role of the individual leader and an organization and its social environment. Students were introduced to concepts of technology transfer via lectures and interaction with experts from the Innovation Institute, licensing via lecture and technology roadmaps through lecture and a hands-on workshop.

On completion of the course and its service-learning project, students accomplished the following:

- Developed an understanding of macro-level concepts related to corporate social responsibility (CSR) and corporate social performance (CSP) as a leadership model for managing the relationship between organizations and society. Students applied CSR/CSP concepts in examining potential participants in the technology commercialization pathways, and explored the relationships between these potential participants and the target populations.
- Participated in a team case presentation to a client, in which student teams were charged with applying course concepts to a case problem relevant to their client, HERL. At the conclusion of the course, students made a presentation to their client, responded to questions and delivered a 129-page report to the client (Certificate Program in Leadership and Ethics Class of 2015, 2013).
- Developed an ability to apply the concepts of CSR by completing a community impact project that included recommendations concerning CSR within a contemporary business context. These recommendations were embedded in the body of the report prepared by students.
- Enhanced their project management skills by working in one or more small teams as part of a larger class project. Students were divided into teams, with each team focusing on a distinct potential user population of the Smart Kitchen and one team performing an overall coordination and planning role. This allowed for collaboration across teams and coordination of activities among teams to produce an integrated final report and presentation.

These activities provided a model for engaging business students in translational research commercialization, applying a cross-disciplinary approach, serving a role as translator, bridging business concepts for the HERL research team. Their efforts clearly met the CPLE raison d'être – students ought to experience meaningful and experience-based exposure to ethics and leadership in different organizational settings. The technology of the Smart Kitchen, its potential user populations and the possible commercialization pathways to bring this technology to the market in order to be useful to these populations provide a rich view into multiple organizational settings for project participants. The next section introduces the suite of Smart Kitchen technologies.

THE SMART KITCHEN

The 'Smart Kitchen' is a suite of technologies being created by HERL (Ding et al., 2014; Mahajan et al., 2013; Telson et al., 2013; Wang et al., 2013; Yiin, 2014). A key attribute of the Smart Kitchen is incorporating prompts to assist users with activities of daily living (ADL) (Wang et al., 2013). This is one example of technologies encompassed by the broader concept of a Smart Home – a home that utilizes sensing technology and networking infrastructure with intelligent software to enhance the quality of life of those living in the house (Augusto, 2012).

There are a number of issues driving the development of the Smart Kitchen. These include a growing population of older adults and people with disabling conditions, with 11 million needing personal assistance with everyday activities. Caregiver issues include a caregiver shortage and burden, a growing gap between caregiver supply and demand and caregiver demands outside the home – 25 percent of families care for someone outside the home and one third of nursing home admissions are due to caregiver burnout. Increasing costs are also drivers: both soaring homecare costs borne by families and third-party payers and increasing costs of institutional care, where a one-month delay in Alzheimer's disease and dementia nursing home admissions could save \$1.12 billion annually (US Census; Graham, 2014; Johnson et al., 2000; National Center on Caregiving, 2005; Smialek, 2013; Stone and Wiener, 2001; Zywiak, 2013). As these savings indicate, if the Smart Kitchen technologies prove to be effective in keeping residents safe in their home environments and away from nursing homes, that would save insurance costs for a comparatively lesser preliminary investment in technology infrastructure and support (Chan et al., 2008).

The three technologies comprising the Smart Kitchen are the Cueing Kitchen, KitchenBot and the Interactive Display. These technologies can be deployed as an integrated Smart Kitchen, or could potentially be deployed separately. Having these options allows the end user (or caregivers) to pick and choose which pieces will work best for them and ultimately make it a more effective product. When the 'Smart Kitchen' is referred to in this chapter, the entire suite of technologies described below is being referenced.

Cueing Kitchen

The Cueing Kitchen is a cognitive orthosis with advanced sensing and prompting tools designed to satisfy needs that individuals, such as people with traumatic brain injury (TBI), face in their activities around their kitchen, specifically focusing on meal preparation tasks (Mahajan et al., 2013). The Cueing Kitchen is comprised of sensors and lights, which are activated by a unique software program. When the software prompts for a certain item in the kitchen, the sensors and lights become activated in order to assist the user. The lights are attached to the handles and light up to show that something is located within the cabinet. The sensors are used in order to judge whether something is not closed or turned off properly. The sensors also help to control the switch for water, the oven and stove, along with the refrigerator door. In addition, the normally frosted glass cabinet doors can become transparent to provide additional locational cues to users.

KitchenBot

The KitchenBot design incorporates an overhead mounting system for a dynamic robotic manipulator to assist individuals with physical disabilities in tasks associated within a kitchen environment. The KitchenBot has three main components. First, a wall mounted track allows the KitchenBot to move along the cabinets. Second, a vertical column drives horizontally, guided along the track. Third, a commercially available six-degree of freedom robotic manipulator mounts to the vertical column (Telson et al., 2013). The KitchenBot uses this mechanical arm to lift items up and move them from point A to point B. This arm works with the Cueing Kitchen to open up cabinet doors, turn on and off the faucet and to pick up and to place down items. The arm can be controlled two different ways: with a joystick or through voice activation.

Interactive Display

The Interactive Display is a hologram that is reflected onto a surface. This display is able to detect certain objects to assist with the compiling of ingredients for recipes. The display works with the software that is used for the Cueing Kitchen, which makes it very easy to go from start to finish when making a recipe.

For purposes of examining potential technology transition of these technologies, each of the three technologies can be transitioned together or separately. Having these options allows the commercial developer or perhaps even the end user to pick and choose which pieces will work best for them and ultimately make it a more effective product.

METHODS

Analyses of Target Populations

This study examined the potential for moving these technologies into use by four populations, each of which are described in the following paragraphs. The three primary target populations explored were Wounded Warriors and individuals with TBI, individuals with physical disabilities and aging individuals (65+). As justified below, the analyses also considered a potential mass market user population.

Wounded Warrior/Traumatic Brain Injury

Wounded Warriors (WW) are veterans and service members who incurred a physical or mental injury, illness or wound, co-incident to their military service on or after September 11, 2001. Individuals with TBI are those who have a severe brain injury. The number of veterans returning from Operation Enduring Freedom (OEF), Operation Iraqi Freedom (OIF) and Operation New Dawn (OND) with TBIs was 253,330, while 1,715 veterans of the same campaigns experienced amputations (Bauer, 2013). Approximately 1.7 million people in the United States sustain a TBI each year from all sources (Faul et al., 2010). The current estimated number of TBIs in the United States is 3.2 million people, with 43.3 percent having residual disability one year after hospitalization with TBI.

TBIs are caused by a diverse range of events and are typically classified as mild or severe. Depending on the severity of an injury, an individual's cognitive behavior, speech, sensory and perceptual senses can all be affected. Various cognitive deficits such as problems with memory, attention, planning and executive functions affect individuals who have experienced TBI (Sohlberg and Mateer, 2001). These cognitive deficits can have an impact on an individual's completion of ADL independently.

While ADL are basic self-care tasks, instrumental activities of daily living (IADL) are those complex skills needed to successfully live independently. Cooking tasks have been identified among ADLs as essential skills for living independently (Graves et al., 2005; Horsfall and Maggs, 1986; Mechling, 2008). Individuals with TBI may encounter difficulties in independently completing certain IADL, such as meal preparation, due to problems with attention, cognition, memory and executive functions (Mahajan et al., 2013). They also report a number of kitchen activities, ranging from following recipes to appropriately turning appliances off, as a source of stress (Mahajan et al., 2013). Remembering the location of items and keeping track of recipe steps are the two most difficult activities for adults with TBI in performing kitchen tasks (Wang et al., 2013).

Physically disabled
People with physical disabilities have physical impairment that have substantial and long-term effects on their ability to carry out day-to-day activities. The physically disabled population considered in this study range from ages 18–65. Physically disabled individuals deal with impairments such as 'any physiological disorder or condition, cosmetic disfigurement, or anatomical loss affecting one or more of the following body systems: neurological, musculoskeletal, special sense organs, respiratory (including speech organs), cardiovascular, reproductive, digestive, genitourinary, hemic and lymphatic, skin, and endocrine' (Title 28 CFR 35, 1991). In 2012, adults with disabilities comprised 19,650,900 out of 194,611,800, or an estimated 10.1 percent, of working age Americans (ages 18–64) (Cornell, 2012).

The ability to adequately reach for objects impacts ADL (Holliday et al., 2005). Such functional limitations, which are required for interacting within a kitchen environment, can be caused by the natural progression of a medical condition, such as a physical disability, as well as by other causes such as aging or trauma. Individuals with limited or no upper limb ability have identified the kitchen as a desirable site for accommodating an assistive robotic device (Stanger et al., 1994). Kitchen tasks that have been identified by potential users as those where they require at least frequent assistance were moving hot objects from the stove, moving hot objects from the oven, putting in/taking out heavy objects, carrying heavy objects, stabilizing pots on the stove and opening/closing/reaching a cabinet above the countertop (Ding et al., 2014).

Aging
Kohlbacher and Herstatt (2008) have identified demographic shifts, in both aging and shrinking populations in many countries, as a major societal challenge. By 2050, the aged population (older than 65 years) in the United States is projected to be over 88 million Americans, more than double the aged population in 2010 (Vincent and Velkoff, 2010). While many consider the so-called 'silver market' to be those age 50 and over, this study limited its focus to an aging and elderly population that includes individuals aged 65 and above. These individuals are more vulnerable to be

affected by dementia, Alzheimer's and physical disabilities. Additionally, over the next 15 years the aging and elderly populations are anticipated to increase by 6 percent in the make-up of the American population. Of this aging population, in 2012, an estimated 35.8 percent (14,966,400 out of 41 823 600) of Americans aged 65 and over reported a disability (Cornell, 2012). The caregiver shortage and desires for continued independence in ADL also impact the aging population.

Kohlbacher and Hang (2011, p. 88) identified the aging population as being likely to adopt innovations that 'target non-consumption and help to support and enrich elder people's lives and work.' In a study of user preferences of baby boomers and older adults regarding technology versus human assistance and control over such technology in the performance of kitchen and personal care tasks, Beach et al. (2014) found that these populations may indeed be potentially receptive markets for the adoption of QoLT systems.

The Smart Kitchen is such an innovation. Other researchers have explored similar innovations for this population, for example, Pigot et al. (2008) examined recipe assistance for an aging population. These innovations may be useful to this population, as about one in ten adults aged 55 years and over have difficulty reaching (11 percent) or grasping (9.4 percent), with these rates tripling between the ages of 55–64 years and 85 years and over (Schoenborn and Heyman, 2009).

Mass market

In addition, the analyses also examined transition of the Smart Kitchen technologies to the mass market, as it was considered that broader adoption of these technologies may provide commercialization incentives that could have spill-over effects for the primary target populations, especially as Bauer (2003, p. 285) noted the difficulties in technology transfer to 'small, highly fragmented "disability markets."' Because the purchase price of many assistive technology products (for example, the Smart Kitchen suite) is strongly influenced by third-party reimbursement policy (for example, Medicare, Medicaid, private insurance) and the legislations that shape these policies, rather than by competitive market forces (Bauer, 2003; Seelman, 2013), the CPLE project team also studied a fourth potential population – the mass market.

ANALYSES

The students undertook an analysis of the commercialization prospects of HERL's Smart Kitchen and its components to identify possible technology roadmaps and pathways to bring the Smart Kitchen technologies to market. For each of the four target populations, barriers and market drivers were identified (Nath et al., 2013), a long-term technology roadmap was developed, an implementation plan was proposed, financial needs for these implementation plans were estimated and Strengths, Weaknesses, Opportunities and Threats (SWOT) analyses were conducted to address the strategic positioning of HERL to address the needs of the target population. Further, a proposed plan for HERL's next steps was developed for each population.

Prior to developing their roadmaps, students undertook a technology roadmap workshop, and were provided with access to background materials (for example, Garcia and Bray, 1997). Five technology roadmaps were developed, with four of the five roadmaps unique to each population that was analysed (Wounded Warrior/Traumatic Brain Injury, Physically Disabled, Aging and Mass Market). The fifth roadmap is a coordinated roadmap, which serves the purpose of combining and emphasizing common or similar points amongst all of the four populations.

Each technology roadmap organizes various categories of information that pertain to the commercialization of the HERL technologies. The technology roadmaps developed are discussed in greater detail below. The roadmaps show the various categories along with the corresponding important points. Key categories shown in the roadmaps are: Drivers (both External and Internal), Market Channels, Product Characteristics, Technology Demands and Resource Requirements, as shown in Figure 1.1.

Analyses of these roadmaps led to a set of recommendations for HERL's short- and long-term plans. The goal of the analyses and recommendations was to provide HERL with a coherent, comprehensive guideline and potential pathways for commercializing the Smart Kitchen. With these recommendations, HERL can further explore these pathways to bring their technology from the labs to product stage and then into the market to provide assistance to the targeted user populations.

DELIVERABLES

These analyses were documented in a set of deliverables, described below, and presented to the HERL client in a comprehensive report and presentation (Certificate Program in Leadership and Ethics Class of 2015, 2013).

Technology Roadmap

The technology roadmaps were the first category of deliverables presented within the client report (Certificate Program in Leadership and Ethics

Class of 2015, 2013). These roadmaps organize various categories of information that pertain to the potential commercialization of the HERL technologies. The first part of the deliverable is a chart that shows the various categories along with the corresponding important points. The second part of the deliverable contains further details and information regarding what was noted in the chart. This allows for more detail in order to elaborate on each point, while also providing the ability to have everything organized and presented within a single high-level roadmap chart.

There were five technology roadmaps developed. Four of the five roadmaps are unique for each population that was analysed (Wounded Warrior/Traumatic Brain Injury, Physically Disabled, Aging and Mass Market). The fifth roadmap is a coordinated roadmap. The roadmaps and commercialization pathways proposed are discussed in the next subsections.

Commercialization Recommendations

The second deliverable was a set of recommendations for various ways of commercializing the Smart Kitchen. Unlike the technology roadmap, there are only four sets of commercialization recommendations; each of these sets was unique to the specific target population and their needs. Included within this deliverable were several sections: a stakeholder analysis; implementation risks; collaborative opportunities/potential partnerships; methods for technology transfer; resources needed; and suggested staffing needs.

Technology Transfer Implications for the Commercialization Recommendations

A further analysis relating to the commercialization recommendations was presented. The first component of this analysis presented a risk assessment for identified risks associated with the specific commercialization recommendations. The second explained the resources needed to commercialize the products along with the anticipated costs associated with each commercialization channel. Finally, the analysis identified staffing needs recommended for commercializing these products.

The resources and staffing identified as being potentially useful in commercializing the Smart Kitchen are summarized in Table 1.1.

Strengths, Weaknesses, Opportunities and Threats (SWOT) Analysis

The SWOT analysis is a way to analyse HERL's position in the market with regard to their strengths, weaknesses, opportunities and threats. This is a

Table 1.1 Resources and staffing needs suggested for proposed commercialization pathways

Resources	Staffing needs
University technology transfer office	Product marketing specialists
Informational resources	Product education trainers
Smart Kitchen website	Spokesperson/lead user
Product briefs/sales sheets	Commercialization specialist

way for HERL to be aware of how competitive they and their products are in the market. It allows the opportunity for HERL to improve on their weaknesses, maintain their strengths, stay aware of their threats and take advantage of their opportunities. The SWOT analysis is a popular method used by a variety of companies and an efficient way to begin the initial analysis of where they stand within the market. SWOT analysis results allow HERL to examine their positioning and the potential pathways for their Smart Kitchen technologies in the context of each of their target populations.

Recommendations

These analyses also led to a set of recommendations for HERL's short- and long-term plans. Recommendations were provided for each target population. The key overall recommendations were to:

1. Work with the Innovation Institute to create plans for patenting and licensing the components of the Smart Kitchen.
2. Partner with insurance companies, not-for-profit groups and kitchen manufacturers to more effectively produce and market the Smart Kitchen and its separate components.
3. Create a sales kit and instruction manual to make the Smart Kitchen more marketable through broad awareness.

The next subsection provides greater detail on the roadmaps and potential commercialization pathways proposed.

Roadmaps for Pathways to Commercialization

Five technology roadmaps were prepared. Four of the five roadmaps are unique for each population that was analysed (Wounded Warrior/ Traumatic Brain Injury, Physically Disabled, Aging and Mass Market).

*Table 1.2   Proposed commercialization recommendations for each target
            population*

Target population	Commercialization recommendations
Wounded Warrior/Traumatic Brain Injury	Patent protection Product licensing agreement for domestic manufacturing and distribution Partnering with providers (assisted living/nursing homes) and third-party payers (insurance companies) Product licensing agreements for international markets
Physically Disabled Note: *Demand predicted as being focused on KitchenBot*	Patent protection License technology to an aligned outside company, such as a spin-off company Product licensing agreements for international markets
Aging	Patent protection Product licensing agreement Partnering with providers (assisted living/nursing homes) and in-home care agencies, as well as third-party payers (insurance companies) and special interest groups, such as the AARP
Mass Market Note: *Demand predicted as being focused on Cueing Kitchen and Interactive Display*	Patent protection Product licensing agreements Reach spill-over markets
All	Awareness and marketing campaign to reach target populations, their families and caregivers, providers and payers, as well as special interest groups. These materials can be distributed to potential users/customers and other relevant organizations to raise awareness of the technology and its impacts.

The fifth roadmap is a coordinated roadmap, described below. Examples of these roadmaps are found in the paragraphs below. Through the use of the roadmaps and supporting recommendations, the class project developed a number of proposed pathways to commercialization, as shown in Table 1.2.

Coordinated Roadmap

The coordinated roadmap, shown in Figure 1.2, combines similar, common concerns across the four populations examined.

	Short Term	Long Term
External Driver *Internal*	Need for assistance Assisted living costs Improved quality of life Debug device	Healthcare costs Family concerns Increasing Desire for populations independence Energy efficient In-home mobility Reduce costs
Channels	License arm Patent tactics Form partnerships	License abroad
Product	KitchenBot Track Cover Voice Control Cueing Kitchen Joystick Control Interactive Display Assistance KitchenBot Storage	Part Replacement Customized Bundles Additional Recipes Advanced Inventory
Technology	Voice Activation Software Increased Speed Increased Weight Capacity How-to-Videos	Technological Improvements Software Updates Mobile App Integration
Resources	Funding Sources HERL Kitchen Designers	Health Insurance Companies

Figure 1.2   Coordinated technology roadmap

Wounded Warrior/Traumatic Brain Injury roadmap

This team channeled its research to the Wounded Warrior (WW) and Traumatic Brain Injury (TBI) populations. Figure 1.3 depicts a detailed summary and analysis of the team's proposed commercialization efforts for this target population.

Physically Disabled roadmap

The Physically Disabled team's research revolved around its population's desire for more independence, such as the ability to cook dinner without the assistance of a family member or caregiver. This roadmap focused primarily on the KitchenBot. Figure 1.4 depicts the technology roadmap for the physically disabled target population.

Aging roadmap

The aging population can be reached through commercialization by licensing the Smart Kitchen technologies to a larger firm that has the resources and connections to reach this target population.

Additionally, the Smart Kitchen could be introduced in assisted living settings and nursing homes, potentially as lead users (Franke et al., 2006)

	Short Term	Long Term
External Driver *Internal*	Cost of Assisted Living WW: Ongoing Conflicts Role/Involvement of Caregivers	Improved Safety Precautions TBI: Increased Populations Desire for Independence
Channels	License Product Create Partnerships	Patent Protection License Abroad
Product	Smart Kitchen Sensory Design	Part Replacement Customized Bundles Additional Recipes WW: Technology in Mortgage Free Homes Sold in New Homes
Technology	Refine Current Products Speed-Up/Stronger Arm Increased Technology	Technological Improvements Software Updates Develop Apps
Resources	HERL Assisted Living Homes WW: Government Grants	Website Health Insurance Companies TBI: Relations with Brain Specialists

Figure 1.3   Wounded Warrior/Traumatic Brain Injury technology roadmap

	Short Term		Long Term	
External Driver *Internal*	Improves Quality of Life Joystick & Voice Control Debug Device Safety Regulation Liability	Cost to Install Price Sensitivity How-to- Videos Fulfill Mission Commercialize	Payers Price Promotions Energy Efficient In-Home Mobility Reduce Costs Sales Kit Revenue Sources	Service Outside of Home Contracts Perform Research
Channels	License arm Patent Form partnerships		Ongoing Renewal Fees Outsource Production License Abroad	
Product	KitchenBot Voice Control		Multiple Designs Testimonials Extend Track	Home Designers Water Resistant Arm Child-Friendly
Technology	How-to-Videos Increased Weight Capacity of Arm Increase Voice Capabilities		Software Updates Improve Technology	Detachable Arm Mobile App Aesthetics
Resources	Partners Funding Sources Knowledge of Regulations		Associated Fees Outsource Production	Contracts Mobile App

Figure 1.4   Physically Disabled technology roadmap

to provide direct feedback on implementation and use of the products and to further inform ongoing development of the Smart Kitchen to meet the needs of the user populations. Third-party payers, such as insurance companies, could also be engaged with to subsidize costs for individuals seeking the product, perhaps offsetting increased costs for assisted living or nursing home by delaying admission and keeping the aged in their own familiar settings. These payers may also serve as an additional communication channel to reach more consumers and make them aware of options utilizing the Smart Kitchen technologies.

Mass Market roadmap
In their analyses of the mass market population, channels such as restaurants and cooking schools were identified in the short term, and it was suggested to eventually move toward commercialization paths that could reach individual consumers with sufficient disposable income to afford a kitchen redesign in the longer term. These consumers are looking for increased efficiency in the kitchen, as well as instruction on how to cook new, unique recipes with the help of the Cueing Kitchen.

DISCUSSION

This project developed insights into commercialization for both the student participants and their researcher clients. They determined that Smart Kitchen may develop into a lucrative technology to commercialize, with significant royalty opportunities accruing to the university and inventors, as technology transfer pathways are developed to mature these technologies and move them into the commercial marketplace.

Addressing our research questions, we identified a number of potential pathways to successful commercialization of the Smart Kitchen innovations. Leahy (2003) had introduced three possible pathways for technology transition of assistive technologies: standard licensing, e-commerce and market cultivation, while Anokhin et al. (2011) suggested four possible modes of commercialization for misfit technologies: internal development, partnering, spin-offs and externalization. All of these mechanisms were incorporated into the technology roadmaps and recommendations developed, with the exception of e-commerce. The complexity of the Smart Kitchen technology, coupled with its need to be integrated into a kitchen by a competent contractor/installer, eliminated the e-commerce option from further consideration.

In examining the four technology roadmaps developed, we determined that the potential pathways are not identical for all three components of the Smart Kitchen. Two populations (Wounded Warrior/Traumatic Brain Injury and Aging) were very similar in the proposed pathways, while the Physically Disabled pathway was similar, but focused primarily on the KitchenBot technology of the Smart Kitchen and is a potential pathway to a spin-off company for the niche market of the KitchenBot. The Mass Market population had similar pathways, although significantly different partnering opportunities suggested for reaching a wider variety of spill-over markets within the mass market. These partnership opportunities included partnering with a restaurant chain or cooking schools – a spill-over market; kitchen designers – fitting the technology into a typical home; high-end consumers – remodeling their homes; and kitchen or appliance manufacturers – extending current product lines with the Smart Kitchen technology.

As discussed earlier, a number of resources and capabilities were recommended as necessary to innovate and commercialize the Smart Kitchen. These included the use of the university technology transfer office, development of informational resources, such as a Smart Kitchen website and product information for the education of potential users and funders, and enhancing the HERL research team with personnel to support technology transfer. These personnel could include product marketing specialists to raise awareness and understanding of Smart Kitchen, product education trainers who can provide user training and support Smart Kitchen training and awareness activities, and commercialization specialists to support licensing and partnership development. The role of spokesperson/lead user would be undertaken by someone who uses the Smart Kitchen, has domain expertise and can serve as an advocate or product evangelist (Steinhardt, 2010) for the Smart Kitchen. Either this role could be filled internally or externally, although Sindhav (2011) argues that consumers are more likely to become product evangelists when they help co-create the product, so an external spokesperson/lead user may be ideal.

Further research and commercial availability of these technologies would allow HERL to fulfill its mission to improve the quality of life through use of the Smart Kitchen, and would have a direct impact on the target populations, their families and caregivers. Potential partnerships could provide opportunities for relationships in a number of different channels to reach broader markets with these technologies. These partnerships could be with companies for joint development and commercialization, as well as with interest groups to build market credibility and awareness (for example, Wounded Warrior Foundation and AARP).

CONCLUSIONS

This service-learning project provided students with opportunities that relate to real-world experiences. It provided them with experience in identifying stakeholders, understanding stakeholders and their needs and working with multiple stakeholders. While doing this, they learned to consider both business and societal/stakeholder impacts and apply these considerations in their analyses.

They also gained significant experience working one on one with a client in a complex project, while learning and overcoming the challenges of managing complex projects. One such challenge was in addressing the client's needs and wants, while still accomplishing the task at hand. During this class project, they both collaborated with peer teams and gained experience in both direct and indirect leadership throughout the entire analysis and documentation process. They combined peer input, online research, sponsor input and other information together to create a final product, and presented this report and presentation to their client and interested parties. This service-learning project was a hands-on experiential learning opportunity that introduced students to concepts of strategy planning and technology roadmaps, commercialization and technology transfer. They also gained an understanding of university research processes. This project prepared students for later application of these skills in real-world tasks, such as intellectual property transfer, market research and market development, and mergers and acquisitions (M&A). This project was an example of 'teaching by stealth' through the ecosystem (Levie, 2014) and experiential activities, by providing students with a problem regarding a technology and its transfer into commercialization, and allowing students to learn about technology transfer by engaging in it, rather than just taking a class in the commercialization of new products.

The goal of the analyses and recommendations was to provide HERL with a coherent, comprehensive guideline for commercializing their Smart Kitchen. With these recommendations, HERL can bring products to the markets that are beneficial to its target users, and also allows HERL and the University of Pittsburgh to reap the possible benefits of commercialization. A key measure of success of QoLT is the widespread use of the technologies that enhance the quality of life of people with disabilities and older individuals (Cooper, 2008). Our results may provide insights into potential pathways to commercialization success and adoption of the Smart Kitchen technologies by the targeted populations, and may also provide lessons for others involved in technology transfer. By examining multiple target populations, we were able to demonstrate that commercialization pathways may not be a single path, but may be dependent on a number of factors such as target population and institutions in the target space. Another lesson was that research projects moving toward commercialization may need to augment their staff and resources, either through the use of university technology transfer offices or through augmentation of projects with resources focused on outreach and commercialization.

REFERENCES

Anokhin, S., Wincent, J. and Frishammar, J. (2011). A conceptual framework for misfit technology commercialization. *Technological Forecasting and Social Change*, **78**(6), 1060–71.

Augusto, J.C. (2012). Smart homes as a vehicle for AAL. In J.C. Augusto, M. Huch and A. Kameas (eds), *Handbook of Ambient Assisted Living*. Amsterdam: IOS Press, pp. 387–8.

Ball, E.N. and Preston, K.G. (2014). University commercialization models: the University of Akron. *IEEE Computer*, **47**(8), 28–36.

Bauer, L.J. (2013). The role of the caregiver in supporting our service members and veterans. In *Supporting Families of Wounded, Injured, and Ill Veterans*, State of the Science Symposia Series, Uniformed Services University of the Health Sciences, Bethesda, MD.

Bauer, S.M. (2003). Demand Pull Technology Transfer Applied to the Field of Assistive Technology. *Journal of Technology Transfer*, **28**(3), 285–303.

Beach, S.R., Schulz, R., Matthews, J.T., Courtney, K. and Dabbs, A.D. (2014). Preferences for technology versus human assistance and control over technology in the performance of kitchen and personal care tasks in baby boomers and older adults. *Disability and Rehabilitation: Assistive Technology*, **9**(6), 474–86.

Borisoff, J.F. (2010). Small markets in assistive technology: obstacles and opportunities. In M.M.K. Oishi et al. (eds), *Design and Use of Assistive Technology: Social, Technical, Ethical, and Economic Challenges*. New York: Springer, pp. 105–13.

Carvalho, M., Fleury, A. and Lopes, A. (2013). An overview of the literature on technology roadmapping (TRM): contributions and trends. *Technological Forecasting and Social Change*, **80**(7), 1418–37.

Certificate Program in Leadership and Ethics Class of 2015. (2013). *Commercializing HERL's Smart Kitchen: Technology Transfer Pathways from the Lab to the Home*. Project deliverable. David Berg Center for Ethics and Leadership Certificate Program in Leadership and Ethics, College of Business Administration, University of Pittsburgh.

Chan, M., Estève, D., Escriba, C. and Campo, E. (2008). A review of smart homes – present state and future challenges. *Computer Methods and Programs in Biomedicine*, **91**(1), 55–81.

Chang, H. (2010). A roadmap to adopting emerging technology in e-business: an empirical study. *Information Systems and e-Business Management*, **8**(2), 103–30.

Cooper, R.A. (2008). Quality-of-life technology: a human-centered and holistic design. *IEEE Engineering in Medicine and Biology*, **26**(2), 10–11.

Cornell, (2012). Cornell University Disability Statistics Online Resource for U.S. Disability Statistics. http://www.disabilitystatistics.org (accessed 12 May 2014).

Datta, A., Reed, R. and Jessup, L. (2012). Factors affecting the governance of innovation commercialization: a theoretical model. *Journal of Business & Management*, **18**(1), 31–59.

Decker, R. (2000). Professional activism: reconnecting community, campus, and alumni through acts of service. In E. Tsang (ed.), *Projects that Matter: Concepts and Models for Service-learning in Engineering*. Washington, DC: American Association for Higher Education, pp. 53–7.

Ding, D., Telson, J., Krishnaswamy, K., Ka, H. and Cooper, R. (2014). Focus group evaluation on an overhead kitchen robot appliance. In *Proceedings of the Annual RESNA Conference*, http://www.resna.org/sites/default/files/conference/2014/Robotics/Ding.html (accessed August 3, 2015).

Faul, M., Xu, L., Wald, M. and Coronado, V. (2010). *Traumatic Brain Injury in the United States: Emergency Department Visits, Hospitalizations and Deaths 2002–2006*. Atlanta, GA: Centers for Disease Control and Prevention, National Center for Injury Prevention and Control.

Fenwick, D., Daim, T. and Gerdsri, N. (2009). Value Driven Technology Road Mapping (VTRM) process integrating decision making and marketing tools: case of Internet security technologies. *Technological Forecasting and Social Change*, **76**(8), 1055–77.

Franke, N., von Hippel, E. and Schreier, M. (2006). Finding commercially attractive user innovations: a test of lead-user theory. *Journal of Product Innovation Management*, **23**(4), 301–15.

Garcia, M.L. and Bray, O.H. (1997). *Fundamentals of Technology Roadmapping*, Sandia Report SAND97-0665. Albuquerque, NM: Sandia National Lab. http://prod.sandia.gov/techlib/access-control.cgi/1997/970665.pdf (accessed August 3, 2015).

Goldberg, M.R. and Pearlman, J.L. (2013). Best practices for team-based assistive technology design courses. *Annals of Biomedical Engineering*, **41**(9), 1880–88.

Graham, J. (2014). A shortage of caregivers. *New York Times*, 26 February. http://newoldage.blogs.nytimes.com/2014/02/26/a-shortage-of-caregivers (accessed August 3, 2015).

Graves, T.B., Collins, B.C., Schuster, J.W. and Kleinert, H. (2005). Using video prompting to teach cooking skills to secondary students with moderate disabilities. *Education and Training in Developmental Disabilities*, **40**(1), 34–46.

Gulbranson, C.A. and Audretsch, D.B. (2008). Proof of concept centers: accelerating the commercialization of university innovation. *Journal of Technology Transfer*, **33**(3), 249–58.

Harmon, R., Demirkan, H. and Raffo, D. (2012). Roadmapping the next wave of sustainable IT. *Foresight*, **14**(2), 121–38.

Holliday, P., Mihailidis, A., Rolfson, R. and Fernie, G. (2005). Understanding and measuring powered wheelchair mobility and maneuverability. *Disability and Rehabilitation*, **27**(16), 939–49.

Horsfall, D. and Maggs, A. (1986). Cooking skills instruction with severely multiply handicapped adolescents. *Journal of Intellectual and Developmental Disability*, **12**(3), 177–86.

Johnson, N., Davis, T. and Bosanquet, N. (2000). The epidemic of Alzheimer's disease: how can we manage the costs? *PharmacoEconomics*, **18**(3), 215–23.

Kohlbacher, F. and Hang, C.C. (2011). Applying the disruptive innovation framework to the silver market. *Ageing International*, **36**(1), 82–101.

Kohlbacher, F. and Herstatt, C. (2008). *The Silver Market Phenomenon: Business Opportunities in an Era of Demographic Change*. Berlin and Heidelberg: Springer.

Lane, J.P. (2003). The state of the science in technology transfer: implications for the field of assistive technology. *Journal of Technology Transfer*, **28**(3–4), 333–54.

Leahy, J.A. (2003). Paths to market for supply push technology transfer. *Journal of Technology Transfer*, **28**(3), 305–17.

Lee, J., Phaal, R. and Lee, C. (2011). An empirical analysis of the determinants of technology roadmap utilization. *R&D Management*, **41**(5), 485–508.

Lee, S. and Park, Y. (2005). Customization of technology roadmaps according to roadmapping purposes: overall process and detailed modules. *Technological Forecasting and Social Change*, **72**(5), 567–83.

Levie, J. (2014). The university is the classroom: teaching and learning technology commercialization at a technological university. *Journal of Technology Transfer*, **39**(5), 793–808.

Livingston, N.J. (2010). Community service in university curricula. In M.M.K. Oishi, et al. (eds), *Design and Use of Assistive Technology: Social, Technical, Ethical, and Economic Challenges*. New York: Springer, pp. 57–64.

Mahajan, H.P., Ding, D., Wang, J., Ni, S.X. and Telson, J. (2013). Towards developing a 'cueing kitchen' for people with traumatic brain injury. In *Proceedings of the Annual RESNA Conference*, http://www.resna.org/sites/default/files/legacy/conference/proceedings/2013/Robotics/Mahajan.html (accessed August 3, 2015).

Mangematin, V., O'Reilly, P. and Cunningham, J. (2014). PIs as boundary spanners, science and market shapers. *Journal of Technology Transfer*, **39**(1), 1–10.

Martin, B.C., McNally, J.J. and Kay, M.J. (2013). Examining the formation of human capital in entrepreneurship: a meta-analysis of entrepreneurship education outcomes. *Journal of Business Venturing*, **28**, 211–24.

Martin, M.J. (2007). University perspective on commercialization of IP. *Research-Technology Management*, **50**(5), 13–16.

McDevitt, V.L., Mendez-Hinds, J., Winwood, D. et al. (2014). More than money: the exponential impact of academic technology transfer. *Technology and Innovation*, **16**, 75–84.

Mechling, L.C. (2008). High tech cooking: a literature review of evolving technologies for teaching a functional skill. *Education and Training in Developmental Disabilities*, **43**(4), 474–85.

Miller, D.J. and Acs, Z.J. (2013). Technology commercialization on campus: twentieth century frameworks and twenty-first century blind spots. *The Annals of Regional Science*, **50**(2), 407–23.

Moehrle, M.G., Isenmann, R. and Phaal, R. (eds) (2013). *Technology Roadmapping for Strategy and Innovation: Charting the Route to Success*. New York: Springer.

Nath, V., Kumar, R., Agrawal, R., Gautam, A. and Sharma, V. (2013). Consumer adoption of green products: modeling the enablers. *Global Business Review*, **14**(3), 453–70.

National Center on Caregiving. (2005). *Selected Long-term Care Statistics*. San Francisco, CA: Family Caregiver Alliance. https://caregiver.org/selected-long-term-care-statistics (accessed August 3, 2015).

National Council on Disability. (2000). *Federal Policy Barriers to Assistive Technology*. Washington, DC: National Council on Disability.

O'Neal, T. (2005). Evolving a successful university-based incubator: lessons learned from the UCF technology incubator. *Engineering Management Journal*, **17**(3), 11–25.

Phaal, R., Farrukh, C. and Probert, D. (2004). Customizing roadmapping. *Research-Technology Management*, **47**(2), 26–37.

Phaal, R., Farrukh, C. and Probert, D. (2010). *Roadmapping for Strategy and Innovation: Aligning Technology and Markets in a Dynamic World*. Cambridge: Institute for Manufacturing, University of Cambridge.

Phan, P. (2014). The business of translation: the Johns Hopkins University Discovery to Market program. *Journal of Technology Transfer*, **39**(5), 809–17.

Phan, P.H., Siegel, D.S. and Wright, M. (2005). Science parks and incubators: observations, synthesis and future research. *Journal of Business Venturing*, **20**(2), 165–82.

Pigot, H., Lussier-Desrochers, D., Bauchet, J., Giroux, S. and Lachapelle, Y. (2008). A Smart Home to assist in recipe completion. In A. Mihailidis et al. (eds), *Technology and Aging*. Amsterdam: IOS Press, pp. 35–42.

Probert, D., Farrukh, C. and Phaal, R. (2003). Technology roadmapping – developing a practical approach for linking resources to strategic goals. *Proceedings of the Institution of Mechanical Engineers Part B Journal of Engineering Manufacture*, **217**(9), 1183–95.

Richey, J.M. and Grinnell, M. (2004). Evolution of roadmapping at Motorola. *Research-Technology Management*, **47**(2), 37–41.

Schoenborn, C.A. and Heyman, K.M. (2009). Health characteristics of adults aged 55 years and over: United States, 2004–2007. *National Health Statistics Reports*, **16**, 1–31. http://www.ncbi.nlm.nih.gov/pubmed/19697804 (accessed August 3, 2015).

Schulz, R. (ed.) (2013). *Quality of Life Technology Handbook*. Boca Raton, FL: CRC Press.

Schulz, R. and Beach, S.R. (2013). Who can benefit from quality of life technology? In R. Schulz (ed.), *Quality of Life Technology Handbook*. Boca Raton, FL: CRC Press, pp. 3–16.

Schulz, R., Beach, S.R., Matthews, J.T., Courtney, K.L. and Dabbs, A.J.D. (2012). Designing and evaluating quality of life technologies: an interdisciplinary approach. *Proceedings of the IEEE*, **100**(8), 2397–409.

Schulz, R., Beach, S.R., Matthews, J.T. et al. (2014). Willingness to pay for quality of life technologies to enhance independent functioning among baby boomers and the elderly adults. *The Gerontologist*, **54**(3), 363–74.

Seelman, K. (2013). Facilitators and barriers to technology uptake: organizational and societal perspectives. In R. Schulz (ed.), *Quality of Life Technology Handbook*. Boca Raton, FL: CRC Press, pp. 29–61.

Seelman, K.D., Collins, D.M., Bharucha, A.J. and Osborn, J. (2007). Giving meaning to quality of life through technology: cutting-edge research on aging-in-place technologies at Carnegie Mellon University/University of Pittsburgh. *Nursing Homes*, **56**(10), 40–2.

Sheth, J.N. and Ram, S. (1987). *Bringing Innovation to Market: How to Break Corporate and Customer Barriers*. New York: Wiley.

Siegel, D.S., Waldman, D.A., Atwater, L.E. and Link, A.N. (2004). Toward a model of the effective transfer of scientific knowledge from academicians to practitioners: qualitative evidence from the commercialization of university technologies. *Journal of Engineering and Technology Management*, **21**(1–2), 115–42.

Sindhav, B. (2011). Co-creation of value: creating new products through social media. *International Journal of Management Research*, **2**(1), 6–15.

Smialek, J. (2013). Boomers face caregiver shortage as U.S. offers new rules: jobs.

34 *Academic entrepreneurship*

Bloomberg News, 26 September. http://www.bloomberg.com/news/2013-09-26/
boomers-face-caregiver-shortage-as-u-s-offers-new-rules-jobs.html (accessed
August 3, 2015).
Sohlberg, M. and Mateer, C. (eds) (2001). *Cognitive Rehabilitation: An Integrative
Neuropsychological Approach*. New York: Guilford Press.
Som, A., Charanya, T., Linderman, S.W. and Siegel, J.S. (2014). Bridging the
gap between invention and commercialization in medical devices. *Nature
Biotechnology*, **32**, 1063–5.
Stanger, C.A., Anglin, C., Harwin, W.S. and Romilly, D.P. (1994). Devices for
assisting manipulation: a summary of user task priorities. *IEEE Transactions on
Rehabilitation Engineering*, **2**(4), 256–65.
Steinhardt, G. (2010). *The Product Manager's Toolkit: Methodologies, Processes
and Tasks in High-tech Product Management*. Berlin: Springer Verlag.
Stone, R.I. and Wiener, J.M. (2001). *Who Will Care For Us? Addressing the Long-
Term Care Workforce Crisis*. Washington, DC: The Urban Institute.
Stone, V.I. (2003). Systematic technology transfer: a case study in assistive technol-
ogy. *Journal of Technology Transfer*, **28**(3–4), 319–32.
Swamidass, P.M. (2013). University startups as a commercialization alternative:
lessons from three contrasting case studies. *Journal of Technology Transfer*,
38(6), 788–808.
Telson, J., Ding, D., McCartney, M. and Cooper, R.A. (2013). Preliminary
design of an overhead kitchen robot appliance. In *Proceedings of the Annual
RESNA Conference*, http://www.resna.org/sites/default/files/legacy/conference/
proceedings/2013/Robotics/Student%20Scientific/Telson.html (accessed August
3, 2015).
Title 28 CFR 35. (1991). Title 28 CFR Part 35 – Nondiscrimination on the Basis of
Disability in State and Local Government Services. Washington, DC: Department
of Labor. http://www.dol.gov/oasam/regs/cfr/28cfr/Part35/35toc.htm.
Tsang, E. (2000). Introduction. In E. Tsang (ed.), *Projects that Matter: Concepts
and Models for Service-learning in Engineering*. Washington, DC: American
Association for Higher Education, pp.1–12.
University of Pittsburgh. (2014). *Innovation Institute 2014 Annual Report*.
Pittsburgh, PA: University of Pittsburgh.
Vatananan, R.S. and Gerdsri, N. (2012). The current state of Technology
Roadmapping (TRM) research and practice. *International Journal of Innovation
and Technology Management*, **9**(4), 1250032-1–1250032-20.
Vincent, G.K. and Velkoff, V.A. (2010). *The Next Four Decades, the Older
Population in the United States: 2010 to 2050, Population Estimates and
Projections* (Current Population Reports). Washington, DC: US Census Bureau,
pp.25–1138.
Wagner, C. and Bremer, H. (2001). Regulatory and technology transfer. *Journal of
Rehabilitation Research and Development*, **38**(1 – Suppl.), S49–S51.
Wang, J., Ding, D., Mahajan, H.P., Filippone, A.B., Toto, P.E. and McCue,
M.P. (2013). Evaluation of different types of prompts in guiding kitchen tasks
for people with traumatic brain injury: a pilot study. *Proceedings of the Annual
RESNA Conference*, http://www.resna.org/sites/default/files/legacy/conference/
proceedings/2013/Outcomes/Student%20Scientific/Day.html (accessed August
5, 2015).
Webster, E. and Jensen, P.H. (2011). Do patents matter for commercialization?
Journal of Law and Economics, **54**(2), 431–53.

Wells, R., Phaal, R., Farrukh, C. and Probert, D. (2004). Technology roadmapping for a service organization, *Research-Technology Management*, **47**(2), 46–51.

Willyard, C.M. and McCless, C.W. (1987). Motorola's technology roadmap process. *Research Management*, **30**(5), 13–19.

Yiin, W. (2014). Technology geared to making life easier for elderly, disabled and caregivers. *Pittsburgh Post-Gazette*, 16 November. http://www.post-gazette.com/healthypgh/2014/11/16/Technology-geared-to-making-life-easier-for-elderly-seniors-disabled-and-caregivers-1/stories/201411160226 (accessed 5 August, 2015).

Zurcher, R. and Kostoff, R. (1997). Modeling technology roadmaps. *Journal of Technology Transfer*, **22**(3), 73–80.

Zywiak, W. (2013). *U.S. Healthcare Workforce Shortages: Caregivers*. Falls Church, VA: CSC.

PART I

Drivers of entrepreneurial activity

2. Poor opportunities in the academic labor market as a cause of spin-offs

Silvio Vismara and Michele Meoli

What's the point in killing yourself to be a productive researcher when finding an academic job is so hard? ('The productivity of PhDs. Lazy graduate students?' *The Economist*, 12 November 2014)

INTRODUCTION

The rate of establishment of academic spin-offs has proliferated in recent years and so has the literature on the subject (Shane, 2004b; Shane et al., 2015). A number of studies emphasize the impact of individual attributes and dispositions on academic entrepreneurship, highlighting how the motivations that induce researchers to create new ventures are wider than in other contexts and not driven solely by an entrepreneurial vision. For example, they may also be attracted by the prospect of enhancing their position (Meyer, 2003), or be motivated by a need for achievement (Roberts, 1991) or a desire of independence and challenge (Hessels et al., 2008). Other individual motives include seeking recognition by peers and ambition to develop a technology into a marketable product (Hayter, 2011; O'Gorman et al., 2008). The set of personal motivations proposed by the literature is thus diverse. Spanning monetary rewards to self-enhancing goals, these are, however, all 'positive' motivations. Nevertheless, the available evidence indicates that the post-entry performance of this type of firm is often weak (Colombo et al., 2011; Degroof and Roberts, 2004).

We extend the literature by investigating how the spin-off decision relates to contextual factors. The aim of this chapter is to add to the traditional view on the academic founders' incentives to spin-off by considering (1) at an individual level, the effects of lack of academic job positions and (2) at an organizational level, the moderating role of the structure of parent universities on the individual's decision. Accordingly, academic entrepreneurship is considered, rather than purely entrepreneurial, as responsive to shortcomings in the market for knowledge. Academics might indeed become entrepreneurs as a 'second-best solution.'

There are several motivations to spin-off and they may vary within the entrepreneurial team itself. Academic lifecycle models suggest that academics launch spin-offs late in their careers, after having developed their human capital (Shane, 2004a). The spin-off activity, however, typically involves more persons, with different status and function within the parent university (Pirnay et al., 2003) and often includes young members (Grimaldi et al., 2011). The incentives of young postdoctoral students, for instance, are very different from those of tenured professors. For the former, launching a spin-off may represent a compensatory solution to difficulties in the academic world. If this happens, we expect that the lack of academic job positions will positively influence the rate of creation of academic spin-offs.

Second, though ultimately propelled by individual drive, organizational factors may facilitate or inhibit the spin-off activity. Existing studies focus on the role played by the organization and resources of parent universities (Link and Scott, 2005; Siegel et al., 2003a; Siegel et al., 2003b) as well as local context support mechanisms and regional conditions (Audretsch et al., 2012; Fini et al., 2011; Meoli et al., 2013). Academic entrepreneurship is a form of university outreach or 'third mission.' Universities with a high level of research output can also be entrepreneurially successful, as there is evidence of such positive relationship at an individual level (Antonelli et al., 2011). On the contrary, universities that charge academics with high teaching loads will, *ceteris paribus*, offer a less supportive environment for academic entrepreneurship. We therefore argue that the teaching load, measured as student per faculty ratio, negatively moderates the positive relationship between lack of academic job positions and spin-off creation.

Third, the establishment of academic spin-offs is only one of the possible forms of business engagement that academics can choose. Alternatives include licensing, patenting, consulting and other personal-related activities with industrial partners. The motivations leading to the other choices among these possibilities are very different (Lockett et al., 2005). Among these, however, the creation of a firm is the one that entails the higher degree of freedom of activity. In this chapter, we posit that the inadequacy of administrative and bureaucratic procedures within a university impacts on the propensity to spin-off. When the support from the university to which they belong is inadequate, entrepreneurial academics, striving for better management of both cash and human resources, have higher incentives to opt for a spin-off solution rather than for alternative technology transfer means (for example, licensing). We therefore argue that an inadequacy in administrative support may positively affect the rate of creation of surrogate entities, in particular in the form of non-technology academic spin-offs.

The Italian system of higher education has been characterized, over the past 15 years, by different levels of career opportunities and administrative staff support (Donina et al., 2015), and is therefore suitable for testing our hypotheses. First, using a qualitative approach, we report evidence of how the decision to establish a spin-off is more frequent where and when there is lack of academic positions and how, in the case of non-technology spin-offs, this decision is further stimulated by organizational deficiencies. Further, with a longitudinal study of 559 spin-offs launched from 85 universities in the period 1999 to 2013, we test whether the rate of formation of spin-offs (number of spin-offs per year per university) is affected by the lack of academic job positions. Controlling for several university- and context-level factors, we find support for our hypotheses. Scarce possibilities of initial appointment in academic positions result in an increased propensity to undertake an entrepreneurial career through spin-offs. Such a relationship is negatively moderated by teaching load in technology spin-offs, and by administrative support in non-technology spin-offs.

The chapter is organized as follows. The following section develops the hypotheses of the chapter. The next section consists of a narrative description of two case studies that is interspersed with quotations from key informants and a discussion of how the heterogeneous nature of spin-offs affects the hypotheses presented in the previous section. This is followed by a description of the research design and then the results. The final section concludes the chapter.

HYPOTHESES DEVELOPMENT

Contrary to the traditional finding in entrepreneurship literature that age is negatively related to the probability of an individual becoming an entrepreneur, age is positively related to academic entrepreneurship (Levin and Stephan, 1991). This evidence has been explained in a lifecycle framework, where early stage scientists are focused on research and care more about scientific reputation, while becoming more sensitive to entrepreneurial opportunities as they mature (Wright et al., 2006). Furthermore, more experienced researchers are likely to have larger networks enabling them to find potential partners in the private sector. This means that age results in top academics having higher willingness and higher ability to establish academic spin-offs.

However, senior scientists typically do not embark on an entrepreneurial adventure alone. High-tech start-ups, and in particular academic spin-offs, are more often created by a team than by one lone entrepreneur (Roberts, 1991). Åstebro et al. (2012) find that recent graduates are likely to start a business within three years of graduation, and that the graduates' spin-offs are not of low quality. The primary role of young members in the progress of university spin-offs is confirmed by Clarysse and Moray (2004), who followed a sample of spin-offs from the idea phase until the post-start-up phase. It is therefore also important to devote attention to the decisions to become an entrepreneur by young academics and to understand under which circumstances they are more prone to do so.

The 'Survey of Doctorate Recipients' shows that the number of students willing to become faculty members is larger than the number of those who will actually find employment in that sector, suggesting imbalances in the scientific labor market (Roach and Sauermann, 2010). Moreover, while the number of PhD students is increasing, in many countries public support to universities is decreasing and it is evolving toward improvement of the efficiency of research organizations rather than increasing research expenditures (Mangematin, 2000). Under these conditions, an entrepreneurial career, through the foundation of an academic spin-off, can allow a doctorate holder the satisfactory exploitation of advanced knowledge in a certain field of expertise. Therefore, in some cases the spin-off may not be the first-best solution, but rather a compensatory, self-employment opportunity, in which young researchers engage in the absence of academic job positions. If this is the case, we expect that at a regional level, when academic job opportunities decrease, compared to the number of fresh graduates, the propensity to spin-off increases.

Based on these arguments, we add to the existing literature on factors leading individuals to found academic spin-offs by formulating the following hypothesis.

Hypothesis 1: A lack of academic job positions positively affects the rate of creation of academic spin-offs.

The rapid increase in university spin-offs has stimulated policy research concerned with explaining differences in spin-off rates across universities. Small universities will struggle to achieve success in their 'third mission,' on top of their teaching and research objectives, and their technology transfer activity, like other non-core activities, might be undersized (Swamidass and Vulasa, 2009). Small technology transfer offices (TTOs) will hardly be able to create a supportive environment for the establishment of spin-offs. Consistently, it is well established that the possibilities to create a spin-off are higher in universities with more resources and stronger TTOs

(Di Gregorio and Shane, 2003; Friedman and Silberman, 2003; Link and Scott, 2005; Siegel et al., 2003a).

In particular, while entrepreneurial academics are often also successful scientists (Antonelli et al., 2011), it is less plausible that an intense teaching activity will stimulate the creation of entrepreneurial ventures. *Ceteris paribus*, an academic with a high teaching load will have fewer possibilities to develop an independent activity as an entrepreneur to capitalize on their academic activity. We thus expect the rate of establishment of academic spin-offs to be lower when and where the teaching load is higher.

Hypothesis 2: A higher teaching load negatively moderates the relationship between lack of academic job positions and the rate of creation of academic spin-offs.

The support of TTOs is helpful in creating spin-offs and larger TTOs are better equipped to provide incubation services and coaching activities to prospective entrepreneurs. *Ceteris paribus*, the lower the administrative support granted by a university, the higher will be the aim of affiliated academics to establish a service-oriented spin-off. A scarce or virtually null support for in-house knowledge transfer activities will stimulate researchers to 'go out' and spin-off (Aldridge and Audretsch, 2011). By spinning-off, they can enjoy higher flexibility, at the expense of losing an anyway weak support from the university. Non-technology, often service-oriented, spin-offs might therefore represent a way to compensate for administrative inadequacy and, to some extent, function as a substitute for other forms of internally managed technology transfer activities. Accordingly, the inadequacy of administrative and bureaucratic procedures in a university is expected to negatively moderate the positive relationship between lack of academic job positions and the rate of creation of academic spin-offs.

Based on these arguments, we formulate the following hypothesis:

Hypothesis 3: A larger administrative support negatively moderates the relationship between lack of academic job positions and the rate of creation of academic spin-offs.

HETEROGENEITY IN ACADEMIC SPIN-OFFS

In this section, we highlight the highly heterogeneous nature of academic spin-offs and qualitatively show how different motivations can explain different trends in the rate of establishment of different types of spin-offs. We then provide a narrative description of two polar case studies of academic spin-offs, selected because they offer an extraordinary setting in which to observe the phenomenon under investigation, and show a close connection between real-life evidence and our hypotheses.

The nature of university spin-offs is heterogeneous and several papers distinguish technology spin-offs from others (Carayannis, 1998; Druilhe and Garnsey, 2004; Mustar et al., 2006; Roberts and Eesley, 2011). This focus on technology is coherent with the policy aim of fostering the commercialization of academic research, in particular in science and engineering, where the positive externality on the economy is expected to be larger (Bozeman, 2000). In a study of Massachusetts Institute of Technology (MIT) spin-offs, Roberts and Eesley (2011) find that technology-based companies have a disproportionate importance to their local economies, with respect to non-technology-based spin-offs, because they typically represent advanced technologies and usually sell to out-of-state and world markets. On the contrary, non-technology firms are common among academic spin-offs (Stankiewicz, 1994). Capital requirements and risk are low as they do not necessarily involve product or process innovations (Hindle and Yencken, 2004). A number of papers have proposed taxonomies to identify and classify the different types of spin-offs (for example, Carayannis, 1998; Druilhe and Garnsey, 2004; Mustar et al., 2006; Pirnay et al., 2003). Stankiewicz (1994) identifies consultancy and research and development (R&D) contracting spin-offs that generate lower wealth than product-oriented and technology asset-oriented mode spin-offs. It is therefore worthwhile fine-tuning our hypotheses on the basis of the type of academic spin-off. We first provide anecdotal evidence from two cases and then discuss the implications for our hypotheses with regard to technology versus non-technology spin-offs.

The first explanatory case is a technology-based spin-off founded in 2008 by a postdoctoral scholar with two professors. The company is rooted in a university research group with ten years of experience of applied research and with several industry collaborations, including co-patenting. After five years, the ownership structure of the company has not changed, while three other young researchers and an experienced manager have been hired. At the beginning, the difficulties in university recruitment played a relevant role in the decision to create this spin-off, as cited by the founder postdoc.

> In that period, I knew there were no possibilities for job positions at university within a commuting distance, and I did not want to relocate without concrete hopes to be able to come back in a not too distant future.

The lack of academic job positions was clearly among the motivations to establish this spin-off, as argued in our Hypothesis 1.

The second example is an academic spin-off created in 2004 from a team of four people, two academics and two young graduates.

> We [the academics] were frequently working with companies as consultants. Contracts were on behalf of the university, while we were burdened with bureaucracy and received virtually no support. With the spin-off, we still benefit from the affiliation with the university, but are much freer to manage the resources and cash flows of the business.

Now, ten years after the foundation, this spin-off is still governed by the founding team, with three temporary employees. They do not intend to grow though. The administrative inadequacy of the parent university is perceived by the founders as among the leading motivations to spin-off, as proposed in our Hypothesis 3.

This second case offers an example of how academics might be prone to create non-technology spin-offs in order to enjoy higher flexibility and to be freer to manage the human and cash resources. To some extent, this type of spin-off may replace TTOs. While the support of the parent university is particularly important for the establishment of spin-offs in high-tech sectors, non-technology spin-offs require less support from the parent university (Pirnay et al., 2003). Roberts and Malone (1996) argue that the support from a university is effective in some context, while low selectivity and low support strategies are the most effective in others. We posit that our Hypothesis 3 is expected to be supported mainly for the establishment of non-technology spin-offs. In these cases, a lower administrative support negatively moderates the relationship between lack of academic job positions and the rate of creation of non-technology spin-offs. On the contrary, the creation of technology spin-offs requires not only the resources from the parent university, but also a good stock of research that can be translated in an entrepreneurial venture. Academics with a lower teaching load will have more time to devote to research and the 'third mission'. We therefore expect our Hypothesis 2 to be valid in particular for technology spin-offs. A higher teaching load negatively moderates the relationship between competition for initial academic job positions and the rate of creation of technology spin-offs.

Table 2.1 summarizes our expectations of validity for our hypotheses on the creation of technology versus non-technology spin-offs and reports examples of the two types of spin-offs in our sample.

Table 2.1   Taxonomy and hypotheses

Type	Technology	Non-technology
Hp. 1	YES	YES
Hp. 2	YES	NO
Hp. 3	NO	YES
Example 1	Microtech University S. Anna of Pisa, 2000 Medical devices for micro-invasive surgery	Mint Publishing University S. Anna of Pisa, 2000 Services to support publishing and teaching activities in the juridical field
Example 2	Vetogene University of Milan, 2003 Genetic analysis for the control of pet genetic disorders	Ius University of Perugia, 2006 Training and legal support for local institutions
Example 3	In3diagnostic University of Torino, 2012 Diagnostic veterinary reagents	Wel.Co.Me. University of Bari, 2012 Consulting and education for social cooperatives and public institutions

RESEARCH DESIGN

Sample

Our sample is composed of spin-offs from Italian universities, founded from 1999 to 2013. We started from 1999 because the possibility for universities to create spin-off companies was defined in Italy in that year (Law 297/1999). Since then, public researchers can be involved in technology transfer projects while keeping their university position and wage. Using data from the Italian Ministry of Education, Universities and Research (MIUR), we identified 85 universities in Italy, excluding the 11 distance learning only universities. According to previous studies (for example, Bonardo et al., 2011; Fini et al., 2011), we defined an academic spin-off as a company with either a university or at least one academic among the founders. The dataset was built using information available from the websites of the universities, where TTOs are required to report the list of affiliated spin-offs. Overall, our sample is composed of 559 spin-offs established between 1999 and 2013 by the universities in our sample (54 universities are represented with at least one spin-off). Although we do not know the exact figure for the number of Italian academic spin-offs, our sample is similar to those of existing studies over the same time period (for example, Fini et al., 2009).

Spin-offs in our sample are classified as technology spin-offs if they are firms in high and medium-high technology sectors according to the Organisation for Economic Co-operation and Development (OECD) classification (OECD Science and Technology Scoreboard, 2001). Hence, firms in Aerospace, Computers, Electronics-communications, Pharmaceuticals, Scientific instruments, Motorvehicles, Machinery, Chemical and Transport equipment are considered as technology spin-offs. We classify all other spin-offs in our sample as non-technology spin-offs.

Table 2.2 reports the number of spin-offs per year in our sample, distinguishing technology and non-technology spin-offs. Out of 559 spin-offs, 416 are technology-based firms (74.4 percent), while 143 are non-technology (25.6 percent). There has been an increase in spin-off activity over time, with most of the spin-offs being created in the period 2004–09. A lower number of firms were established in the period 2010–13,

Table 2.2   Sample

Year	Spin-offs		Technology		Non-technology	
	No.	%	No.	%	No.	%
1999	15	2.7	13	86.7	2	13.3
2000	9	1.6	8	88.9	1	11.1
2001	7	1.3	6	85.7	1	14.3
2002	7	1.3	5	71.4	2	28.6
2003	31	5.5	23	74.2	8	25.8
2004	50	8.9	36	72.0	14	28.0
2005	43	7.7	34	79.1	9	20.9
2006	46	8.2	31	67.4	15	32.6
2007	78	14.0	54	69.2	24	30.8
2008	71	12.7	55	77.5	16	22.5
2009	57	10.2	43	75.4	14	24.6
2010	38	6.8	32	84.2	6	15.8
2011	40	7.2	28	70.0	12	30.0
2012	41	7.3	29	70.7	12	29.3
2013	26	4.7	19	73.1	7	26.9
Total	559	100.0	416	74.4	143	25.6

Note: The table reports the number of academic spin-offs founded in Italy from 1999 to 2013. Technology spin-offs are firms in high and medium-high technology sectors according to the OECD Science and Technology Scoreboard (2001) classification. All other spin-offs are classified as non-technology.

arguably due to the effects of the economic crisis. There is not a clear trend in the evolution of the type of spin-offs, as technology spin-offs account for 67 to 89 percent of the total number of spin-offs each year.

Model and Variables

To perform our longitudinal study, we use panel data negative binomial regressions, where the dependent variable is the total number of spin-offs (count) per university per year. We measure the effect of our independent variables on 1,275 university-year observations (85 universities observed for 15 years between 1999 and 2013). Our main explanatory variable is a proxy for the lack of opportunities for academic job positions in the local context, calculated as the ratio between the number of PhD students graduating per year in each university and the number of new positions as assistant professor offered by all universities in a given region. Given a certain amount of job positions, the higher the number of graduating PhD students in a certain year, the higher the lack of academic positions. Our analysis aims to test the significance of this variable in predicting the number of spin-offs per university per year as evidence in support of Hypothesis 1.

Hypotheses 2 and 3 are tested by considering two moderating effects for the lack of academic job opportunities. First, in order to test Hypothesis 2 we combine the lack of job positions with a measure of teaching load, namely the students to faculty ratio, measured as the number of overall students per professor. This indicator represents a good proxy for teaching resources in general and captures, on the one hand, the opportunities for student learning in classes; on the other hand, it proxies the teaching load for each faculty. An increase in the ratio indicates an increase in students per professor, in the quantity of teaching activities that each faculty has to perform and, more generally, the burdens limiting the possibilities to dedicate to other activities.

Further, in order to test Hypothesis 3, we combine the lack of academic positions with a measure of administrative support, namely the ratio between the number of technical and administrative staff and the number of academics year by year. This ratio indicates how many administrative units are available in a certain university per faculty. In a robustness analysis, we replace this indicator with TTO size, a variable counting the staff members in the TTO, in order to better measure the incidence of this service on spin-off creation.

In all our analyses, we make use of a set of controls classified into two groups, accounting for the specificities of the academic and the local context. The first category is composed of university-level control variables, and includes a measure of university size (number of students, including Bachelor, Master, PhD and specialization courses), and a measure of university patenting activity (number of patents), in addition to the three moderators mentioned above (teaching load, administrative support and TTO size). The second category groups regional-level control variables: it includes regional GDP growth, the regional patenting activity (number of patents at the regional level), a measure of the number of graduates in science, technology, engineering and mathematics (STEM) and regional R&D expenditure (regional R&D expenditure over regional GDP). In addition to all controls presented above, we include a set of dummy variables related to the macro regions, to take into account all potential unobservable differences between these areas.

Our sources of data for all control variables are the MIUR, the Conference of the Rectors of Italian Universities (CRUI) and the SCOPUS database for university data, while the data on the local context are collected from the Italian National Institute of Statistics (ISTAT). Details on the definition of the variables and their sources are reported in Table 2.3.

Table 2.4 reports the descriptive statistics and the correlation matrix for all variables, referring to the 1,275 university-year observations employed for our empirical analysis. At the regional level, there are on average 11.9 graduating PhD students per open position as assistant professors. The average teaching load is quantified in 33.5 students per faculty, while the administrative support shows that in Italy there have been almost 1.3 administrative staff per academic member. Italian universities enroll on average about 31,000 students. The average university has patented more than 4 patents per year, while the average TTO in Italy employees 4.4 persons. The number of graduates in science, technology, engineering and mathematics per thousand people is on average 10.6. R&D expenditures for public administrations, universities and private and public enterprises in Italy accounts for only 1.1 percent of the GDP.

RESULTS

Table 2.5 reports the estimates of negative binomial panel regressions on the total number of spin-offs, on the number of technology spin-offs and on the number of non-technology spin-offs created per year by the 85 Italian universities in our sample. In all models, we include all university-level and context-level control variables, as well as a set of dummies to control for macro-regional effects. The positive sign for the lack of academic positions in all models provides support for Hypothesis 1, both with reference to the full sample of spin-offs (coefficient = 0.684, $p < 0.01$) and

Academic entrepreneurship

Table 2.3   Variables definition

Variable	Definition	Source
Lack of academic job positions	Ratio between the number of graduating PhD students in a university and the number of positions open for assistant professorship at the regional level	MIUR
Moderating variables		
Teaching load	Ratio between the number of students and the number of faculty members	MIUR
Administrative support	Ratio between the number of technical and administrative staff members and the number of faculty members	MIUR
TTO size	Number of employees in TTOs	CRUI
Control variables		
University size	Number of students, including Bachelor, Master, PhD and specialization courses (logarithms are used in regressions)	MIUR
University patenting activity	Number of patents granted per year per university	SCOPUS
Regional GDP growth	Growth rate of regional gross domestic product	ISTAT
Regional patenting activity	Number of patents granted by the European Patent Office (per million people)	ISTAT
STEM graduates	Number of graduates in science, technology, engineering and mathematics between 20 and 29 years old (per thousand people)	ISTAT
R&D expenditure	Percentage of the R&D expenditures for public administrations, universities and private and public enterprises of GDP	ISTAT

Notes:
This table reports the definition of the variables and the data sources. MIUR is the Italian Ministry of Education, Universities and Research; CRUI is the Conference of the Rectors of Italian Universities; SCOPUS is an abstract and citation database by Elsevier; ISTAT is the Italian National Statistical Institute.
University-level control variables are measured per year and per university; context-level control variables per region per year.

to the subsamples of technology spin-offs (coefficient = 0.687, p < 0.01) and non-technology spin-offs (coefficient = 0.735, p < 0.01). The higher the number of PhD graduates per new academic position (at the regional level), the greater the probability for a university to create spin-offs. Administrative support and TTO size are statistically significant for the

Table 2.4 Descriptive statistics

	Mean	Std. dev.	1	2	3	4	5	6	7	8	9
1 Lack of academic job positions	11.9	13.7	1.000								
2 Teaching load	33.5	10.9	−0.138*	1.000							
3 Administrative support	1.3	0.9	−0.002	−0.173*	1.000						
4 TTO size	4.4	2.8	0.102*	−0.031	−0.056	1.000					
5 University size (000s)	31.2	27.5	0.090	0.295*	−0.458*	0.085*	1.000				
6 University patenting	4.7	7.4	0.192*	−0.189*	−0.112*	0.220*	0.353*	1.000			
7 Regional GDP growth	0.1	3.3	−0.121*	−0.003	−0.014	0.005	0.021	−0.046	1.000		
8 Regional patenting	71.1	55.4	0.010	−0.297*	−0.003	0.098*	−0.021	0.253*	0.034	1.000	
9 STEM graduates	10.6	4.6	0.219*	−0.385*	0.005	0.048	−0.017	0.347*	0.105*	0.458*	1.000
10 R&D expenditure	1.1	0.4	0.025	−0.277*	−0.038	0.093*	0.079	0.242*	−0.010	0.284*	0.609

Notes:
This table shows the descriptive statistics and the correlation coefficients for the sample of 1275 university-year observations (85 universities, observed for 15 years from 1999 to 2013).
* indicates significance at 5 percent level.

Academic entrepreneurship

Table 2.5   Lack of academic job positions

	Spin-offs	Technology	Non-technology
Lack of academic job positions	0.684***	0.687***	0.735***
	(0.123)	(0.126)	(0.198)
Teaching load	−0.123	−0.072	−0.625
	(0.429)	(0.423)	(0.981)
Administrative support	0.397**	0.430**	−0.538
	(0.187)	(0.236)	(0.371)
TTO size	0.184***	0.184***	0.116
	(0.056)	(0.054)	(0.075)
University size	0.405***	0.410***	0.253*
	(0.104)	(0.105)	(0.130)
University patenting activity	0.008	0.006	0.023
	(0.008)	(0.008)	(0.018)
Regional GDP growth	−0.468	−0.520	−0.212
	(0.628)	(0.630)	(1.001)
Regional patenting activity	0.003*	0.003*	−0.002
	(0.002)	(0.002)	(0.003)
STEM graduates	0.169***	0.164***	0.220***
	(0.024)	(0.024)	(0.054)
R&D expenditure	1.988***	1.884***	2.553***
	(0.344)	(0.342)	(0.671)
Constant	−5.027***	−5.136***	−2.497
	(1.189)	(1.197)	(1.528)
Observations	1275	1275	1275
Log-likelihood	−864.8	−849.5	−302.9

Notes:
This table reports the results of negative binomial panel regressions on the total number of spin-offs, on the number of technology spin-offs and on the number of non-technology spin-offs created per year by all Italian universities (excluding distance learning only institutions) over the period 1999–2013. Controls for the geographic area (North, Central, South) are included in all regressions.
***, ** and * indicate significance at the 1, 5 and 10 percent levels, respectively. Standard errors are in parentheses.

creation of spin-offs. When we look at the subsamples, however, the two coefficients are significant only for the creation of technology spin-offs, while there is no evidence with respect to non-technology spin-offs. Among the other university features, size matters in the creation of all types of spin-offs. The regional context also plays a role: in particular, the presence of STEM graduates enhances the probability of observing spin-offs, as well as a higher incidence of R&D expenditure on a regional budget.

Table 2.6   The moderating effect of teaching load

	Spin-offs	Technology	Non-technology
Lack of academic job positions	0.764***	0.777***	0.751***
	(0.116)	(0.119)	(0.199)
Lack of academic job positions × teaching load	−1.714***	−1.769***	−0.533
	(0.606)	(0.596)	(1.402)
Teaching load	−0.262	−0.212	−0.648
	(0.433)	(0.427)	(0.981)
Administrative support	0.314**	0.350*	−0.540
	(0.151)	(0.241)	(0.370)
TTO size	0.197***	0.197***	0.117
	(0.056)	(0.055)	(0.075)
University size	0.396***	0.403***	0.251*
	(0.104)	(0.105)	(0.129)
University patenting activity	0.010	0.008	0.024
	(0.008)	(0.008)	(0.018)
Regional GDP growth	−0.492	−0.549	−0.149
	(0.655)	(0.660)	(1.009)
Regional patenting activity	0.003	0.003	−0.003
	(0.002)	(0.002)	(0.003)
STEM graduates	0.180***	0.174***	0.222***
	(0.024)	(0.024)	(0.055)
R&D expenditure	1.984***	1.884***	2.549***
	(0.346)	(0.344)	(0.672)
Constant	−5.004***	−5.125***	−2.494
	(1.185)	(1.196)	(1.521)
Observations	1275	1275	1275
Log-likelihood	−861.8	−846.3	−302.9

Notes:
This table reports the results of negative binomial panel regressions on the total number of spin-offs, on the number of technology spin-offs and on the number of non-technology spin-offs created per year by all Italian universities (excluding distance learning only institutions) over the period 1999–2013. Controls for the geographic area (North, Central, South) are included in all regressions.
***, ** and * indicate significance at the 1, 5 and 10 percent levels, respectively. Standard errors are in parentheses.

Further, the regional patenting activity increases the probability of observing spin-off creation but, as one would expect, the result is not significant for non-technology spin-offs.

In Table 2.6, we focus on the moderating effect of the teaching load. Again, we report the results of our models estimated on the total number of spin-offs, on the number of technology spin-offs and on the number of non-technology spin-offs. The results show that the positive impact of lack of academic job positions on the creation of spin-offs is negatively moderated by professors' teaching load (coefficient = -1.714, $p < 0.01$). When we split the analysis between technology and non-technology spin-offs, however, we find that this evidence, in support of Hypothesis 2, is statistically significant only for technology spin-offs (coefficient = -1.769, $p < 0.01$). Indeed, the creation of technology spin-offs requires a good stock of research that can be translated in entrepreneurial ventures, and only academics with enough time to devote to research and technology transfer will be able to do so. This argument has a limited application to non-technology spin-offs (coefficient = -0.533, $p > 0.10$).

In Table 2.7, we investigate how the relationship between lack of job positions and spin-off creation is moderated by administrative support. Our results show that administrative support does not change the impact of the lack of job positions on spin-offs (coefficient = -0.002, $p > 0.10$) and on technology spin-off creation (coefficient = -0.011, $p > 0.10$), while it moderates negatively the effect on the creation of non-technology spin-offs (coefficient = -0.285, $p < 0.05$). The less the support given by the institution's administrative offices to the academic staff, the higher the probability that young scientists, looking for alternatives to academic job positions, might identify a non-technology business idea to be promoted as a spin-off, possibly replacing the deficiencies of the administrative staff. This result provides support for Hypothesis 3, although limited to the case of non-technology spin-offs.

The line of arguments on administrative inadequacy is further tested as follows. While our measure for administrative support captures the level of technical and administrative activity in a university, it does not necessarily identify the level of support in the specific field of technology transfer. A university might be characterized by a byzantine administration, and dedicate little effort to the commercialization of research, or it might leverage on the availability of a large staff for a proper activity of technology transfer. An important aspect within the organization of the university is, therefore, its TTO, which is in charge fostering the spin-off process. Spin-offs are, however, only one of the technology transfer related activities in which TTOs are involved, that range from industry cooperation in innovation to commercial licensing and seed capital investments (Lockett et al., 2005). Moreover, TTOs have to balance the objectives of different stakeholders (for example, university administration, faculty and industry). We argue that to fulfill their complex mission, the size of these TTOs matters.

Therefore, in order to test whether TTO efficacy, proxied by TTO size rather than administrative support, is a moderator for the lack of job

Table 2.7 The moderating effect of administrative support

	Spin-offs	Technology	Non-technology
Lack of academic job positions	0.685***	0.692***	0.811***
	(0.146)	(0.149)	(0.194)
Lack of academic job positions ×	−0.002	−0.011	−0.285**
administrative support	(0.188)	(0.188)	(0.127)
Teaching load	−0.123	−0.072	−0.631
	(0.429)	(0.423)	(0.986)
Administrative support	0.393**	0.430**	−0.600
	(0.197)	(0.187)	(0.374)
TTO size	0.184***	0.184***	−0.118
	(0.056)	(0.054)	(0.075)
University size	0.405***	0.410***	0.250*
	(0.104)	(0.105)	(0.128)
University patenting activity	0.008	0.006	0.024
	(0.008)	(0.008)	(0.018)
Regional GDP growth	−0.468	−0.519	−0.060
	(0.628)	(0.630)	(0.999)
Regional patenting activity	0.003*	0.003*	−0.003
	(0.002)	(0.002)	(0.003)
STEM graduates	0.169***	0.164***	0.224***
	(0.024)	(0.024)	(0.054)
R&D expenditure	1.988***	1.884***	2.559***
	(0.344)	(0.342)	(0.674)
Constant	−5.027***	−5.136***	−2.394
	(1.189)	(1.196)	(1.518)
Observations	1275	1275	1275
Log-likelihood	−864.8	−849.5	−301.9

Notes:
This table reports the results of negative binomial panel regressions on the total number of spin-offs, on the number of technology spin-offs and on the number of non-technology spin-offs created per year by all Italian universities (excluding distance learning only institutions) over the period 1999–2013. Controls for the geographic area (North, Central, South) are included in all regressions.
***, ** and * indicate significance at the 1, 5 and 10 percent levels, respectively. Standard errors are in parentheses.

positions, we re-ran the regressions presented in Table 2.7, after replacing administrative support with TTO size as moderator of lack of job positions. The results are provided in Table 2.8: again, the interaction is negative and statistically significant only for the creation of non-technology spin-offs (coefficient = −0.182, p < 0.05).

Table 2.8   The moderating effect of TTO size

	Spin-offs	Technology	Non-technology
Lack of academic job positions	0.627***	0.626***	0.790***
	(0.141)	(0.146)	(0.190)
Lack of academic job positions × TTO size	0.056	0.059	−0.182**
	(0.060)	(0.060)	(0.080)
Teaching load	−0.115	−0.064	−0.605
	(0.430)	(0.424)	(0.980)
Administrative support	0.450**	0.490**	−0.550
	(0.235)	(0.235)	(0.376)
TTO size	0.187***	0.188***	−0.108
	(0.056)	(0.055)	(0.076)
University size	0.409***	0.414***	0.261**
	(0.105)	(0.106)	(0.132)
University patenting activity	0.006	0.005	0.030
	(0.008)	(0.008)	(0.019)
Regional GDP growth	−0.404	−0.453	0.314
	(0.630)	(0.633)	(1.027)
Regional patenting activity	0.004**	0.004**	−0.003
	(0.002)	(0.002)	(0.003)
STEM graduates	0.167***	0.162***	0.229***
	(0.024)	(0.024)	(0.055)
R&D expenditure	2.006***	1.901***	2.593***
	(0.346)	(0.343)	(0.688)
Constant	−5.036***	−5.143***	−2.517
	(1.199)	(1.207)	(1.561)
Observations	1275	1275	1275
Log-likelihood	−864.3	−849	−300.4

Notes:
This table reports the results of negative binomial panel regressions on the total number of spin-offs, on the number of technology spin-offs and on the number of non-technology spin-offs created per year by all Italian universities (excluding distance learning only institutions) over the period 1999–2013. Controls for the geographic area (North, Central, South) are included in all regressions.
***, ** and * indicate significance at the 1, 5 and 10 percent levels, respectively. Standard errors are in parentheses.

As a further robustness check, we re-ran the negative binomial regressions including all moderators of lack of job positions, namely teaching load, administrative support and TTO size. The results, provided in Table 2.9, support the view that the three effects are valid also when jointly tested. These regressions show that the effects, even if related, do not completely

Table 2.9   Joint effects of the moderating variables

	Spin-offs	Technology	Non-technology
Lack of academic job positions	0.520***	0.530***	0.883***
	(0.142)	(0.145)	(0.214)
Lack of academic job positions × teaching load	3.791***	3.823***	2.960
	(0.856)	(0.856)	(3.038)
Lack of academic job positions × administrative support	0.661	0.648	−0.948***
	(0.607)	(0.504)	(0.283)
Lack of academic job positions × TTO size	0.099	0.104	−0.355***
	(0.083)	(0.084)	(0.114)
Teaching load	−0.399	−0.351	−0.443
	(0.444)	(0.441)	(0.995)
Administrative support	0.830**	0.900**	−0.699*
	(0.440)	(0.440)	(0.376)
TTO size	0.221***	0.222***	0.099
	(0.061)	(0.060)	(0.082)
University size	0.414***	0.422***	0.280**
	(0.111)	(0.112)	(0.142)
University patenting activity	0.007	0.005	0.029
	(0.008)	(0.009)	(0.019)
Regional GDP growth	−0.311	−0.367	−0.444
	(0.683)	(0.689)	(1.212)
Regional patenting activity	0.003*	0.003*	−0.002
	(0.002)	(0.002)	(0.004)
STEM graduates	0.179***	0.173***	0.215***
	(0.024)	(0.024)	(0.055)
R&D expenditure	2.103***	2.001***	2.624***
	(0.360)	(0.359)	(0.703)
Constant	−5.031***	−5.161***	−2.173
	(1.263)	(1.279)	(1.696)
Observations	1275	1275	1275
Log-likelihood	−855.6	−840	−296

Notes:
This table reports the results of negative binomial panel regressions on the total number of spin-offs created per year by all Italian universities (excluding distance learning only institutions) over the period 1999–2013. Controls for the geographic area (North, Central, South) are included in all regressions.
***, ** and * indicate significance at the 1, 5 and 10 percent levels, respectively. Standard errors are in parentheses.

overlap. This is of particular interest with respect to the role of administrative support and TTO size in the creation of non-technology spin-offs. While both deficiencies in the administrative and TTO activities enhance the opportunities to create non-technology spin-offs for graduating PhD students with no academic job positions, this evidence shows that these opportunities are diminished. For instance, an inefficient administration might provide the opportunity to create a spin-off for the management of cash flows, while an inefficient TTO might lead PhD students to create a firm to provide assistance to colleagues involved in technology transfer activities.

CONCLUSIONS

While a number of studies emphasize the impact of individual attributes and dispositions on academic entrepreneurship, researchers involved in creating new ventures may not be motivated solely by an entrepreneurial vision. Besides monetary rewards or self-enhancing goals, there might be other motivations, not necessarily positive, leading to the proliferation of academic spin-offs.

With a longitudinal study of 559 spin-offs launched from 85 Italian universities in the period 1999 to 2013, this chapter has investigated the 'dark side' of spin-off motivations. We extend the scope of determinants to consider the contingent effects of lack of academic career positions and of administrative inadequacies within the university system. Our results show, first, that a small number of career opportunities at a regional level, relative to the number of PhD graduates, increases the propensity to establish spin-offs. Academics might sometimes become entrepreneurs as a 'second-best solution,' when they do not feel they have opportunities to start an academic career at hand. Second, the teaching load moderates this relationship, especially with respect to technology spin-offs, because academics not too burdened with teaching activities have more possibilities to engage in the commercialization of technology research. Third, while a sufficient level of administrative support is generally required to boost spin-off activity, administrative inadequacy of the parent university moderates the impact of the lack of job positions leading to an increase in the number of non-technology spin-offs. Using spin-offs as surrogate TTOs, academics might be prone to create non-technology service-oriented spin-offs in order to enjoy higher flexibility and to be freer to manage human and cash resources.

We believe that our contribution directly affects potential academic entrepreneurs, academic managers and policy makers. First, we show

how potential entrepreneurs, through the foundation of an academic spin-off, can allow a doctorate holder satisfactory exploitation of her or his advanced knowledge in a certain field of expertise. Therefore, in some cases the spin-off may not be the first-best solution, but rather a compensatory, self-employment opportunity. Second, university managers here find evidence that a satisfactory spin-off activity is not necessarily related to an outstanding performance in the university 'third mission,' while there might be lack of opportunities for human resources, or administrative deficiencies, at the basis of such results. Third, our results are relevant for policy makers. While the attention on academic spin-offs has often been motivated by the potential ability to advance scientific knowledge as well as contribute to regional economic growth, we show how non-purely entrepreneurial motivations can be important determinants of the creation of academic spin-offs. In fact, our results are of interest for the stream of research highlighting the poor performance records of academic spin-offs (Bonardo et al., 2011; Degroof and Roberts, 2004). We indeed add some insights to understand the poor long-term growth of academic spin-offs that are often not driven by pure growth orientation. This ultimately casts doubts on the appropriateness of public incentives to establish spin-offs and on their short-term metrics.

We acknowledge that our analysis is not without limitations. First, the abnormal spin-off activity, especially observable in the non-technology field, may be specific to the Italian context that we chose for our analysis; and thus caution should be paid in generalizing the implications. Second, our analysis is limited to the observation of spin-off activity, but does not investigate the performance ability of spin-offs. Future research might investigate whether spin-off activity generated by lack of career opportunities and lack of administrative efficiency ultimately ends in growth, or simply limits the efficacy in solving contingent organizational limits by offering hybrid self-employment opportunities.

REFERENCES

Aldridge, T. and Audretsch, D. (2011). The Bayh-Dole Act and scientist entrepreneurship. *Research Policy*, **40**(8), 1058–67.

Antonelli, C., Franzoni, C. and Geuna, A. (2011). The organization, economics, and policy of scientific research: what we do know and what we don't know – an agenda for research. *Industrial and Corporate Change*, **20**(1), 201–13.

Åstebro, T., Bazzazian, N. and Braguinsky, S. (2012). Startups by recent university graduates and their faculty: implications for university entrepreneurship policy. *Research Policy*, **41**(4), 663–77.

Audretsch, D.A., Huelsbeck, M. and Lehmann, E.E. (2012). Regional competitiveness, university spillovers, and entrepreneurial activity. *Small Business Economics*, **39**(3), 587–601.

Bonardo, D., Paleari, S. and Vismara, S. (2011). The M&A dynamics of European science based entrepreneurial firms. *Journal of Technology Transfer*, **35**(4), 755–76.

Bozeman, B. (2000). Technology transfer and public policy: a review of research and theory. *Research Policy*, **29**(4), 627–55.

Carayannis, E.G. (1998). The strategic management of technological learning in project/program management: the role of extranets, intranets and intelligent agents in knowledge generation, diffusion, and leveraging. *Technovation*, **18**(11), 697–703.

Clarysse, B. and Moray, N. (2004). A process study of entrepreneurial team formation: the case of a research-based spin-off. *Journal of Business Venturing*, **19**, 55–79.

Colombo, M.G., Mustar, P. and Wright, M. (2011). Dynamics of science-based entrepreneurship, *Journal of Technology Transfer*, **35**(4), 1–15.

Degroof, J. and Roberts, E.B. (2004). Overcoming weak entrepreneurial infrastructures for academic spin-off ventures. *Journal of Technology Transfer*, **29**, 327–52.

Di Gregorio, D. and Shane, S. (2003). Why do some universities generate more start-ups than others? *Research Policy*, **32**(2), 209–27.

Donina, D., Meoli, M. and Paleari, S. (2015). Higher education reform in Italy: tightening regulation instead of steering at a distance. *Higher Education Policy*, **28**(2), 215–34.

Druilhe, C. and Garnsey, E. (2004). Do academic spin-outs differ and does it matter? *Journal of Technology Transfer*, **29**(3–4), 269–85.

Fini, R., Grimaldi, R. and Sobrero, M. (2009). Factors fostering academics to start up new ventures: an assessment of Italian founders' incentives. *Journal of Technology Transfer*, **34**(4), 380–402.

Fini, R., Grimaldi, R., Santoni, S. and Sobrero, M. (2011). Complements or substitutes? The role of universities and local context in supporting the creation of academic spin-offs. *Research Policy*, **40**(8), 1113–27.

Friedman, J. and Silberman, J. (2003). University technology transfer: do incentives, management, and location matter? *Journal of Technology Transfer*, **28**(1), 17–30.

Grimaldi, R., Kenney, M., Siegel, D.S. and Wright, M. (2011). 30 years after Bayh-Dole: reassessing academic entrepreneurship. *Research Policy*, **40**(8), 1045–67.

Hayter, C.S. (2011). In search of the profit-maximizing actor: motivations and definitions of success from nascent academic entrepreneurs. *Journal of Technology Transfer*, **36**, 340–52.

Hessels, J., Van Gelderen, M. and Thurik, R. (2008). Entrepreneurial aspirations, motivations, and their drivers. *Small Business Economics*, **31**, 323–39.

Hindle, K. and Yencken, J. (2004). Public research commercialisation, entrepreneurship and new technology based firms: an integrated model. *Technovation*, **24**(10), 793–803.

Levin, S.G. and Stephan, P.E. (1991). Research productivity over the life cycle; evidence for academic scientists. *American Economic Review*, **81**(4), 114–32.

Link, A.N. and Scott, J.T. (2005). Opening the Ivory tower's door: an analysis of the determinants of the formation of U.S. university spin-off companies. *Research Policy*, **34**(7), 1106–12.

Lockett, A., Siegel, D., Wright, M. and Ensley, M.D. (2005). The creation of spin-off firms at public research institutions: managerial and policy implications. *Research Policy*, **34**, 981–93.

Mangematin, V. (2000). PhD job market: professional trajectories and incentives during the PhD. *Research Policy*, **29**(6), 741–56.

Meoli, M., Paleari, S. and Vismara, S. (2013). Completing the technology transfer process: M&As of science-based IPOs. *Small Business Economics*, **40**(2), 227–48.

Meyer, M. (2003). Academic entrepreneurs or entrepreneurial academics? Research-based ventures and public support mechanism. *R&D Management*, **33**, 107–15.

Mustar, P., Renault, M., Colombo, M.G. et al. (2006). Conceptualising the heterogeneity of research-based spin-offs: a multi dimensional taxonomy. *Research Policy*, **35**, 289–308.

O'Gorman, C., Byrne, O. and Pandya, D. (2008). How scientists commercialise new knowledge via entrepreneurship. *Journal of Technology Transfer*, **33**, 23–43.

OECD Science and Technology Scoreboard (2001). *Science, Technology and Industry Scoreboard: Towards a Knowledge-based Economy*. Paris: OECD.

Pirnay, F., Surlemont, B. and Nlemvo, F. (2003). Toward a typology of university spin-offs. *Small Business Economics*, **21**(4), 355–69.

Roach, M. and Sauermann, H. (2010). A taste for science? PhD scientists' academic orientation and self-selection into research careers in industry. *Research Policy*, **39**, 422–34.

Roberts, E.B. (1991). The technological base of the new enterprise. *Research Policy*, **20**(4), 283–97.

Roberts, E.B. and Eesley, C.E. (2011). *Entrepreneurial Impact: The Role of MIT*. Hanover, MA: Now Publishers Inc.

Roberts, E.B. and Malone, D.E. (1996). Policies and structures for spinning off new companies from research and development organization. *R&D Management*, **26**(1), 17–48.

Shane, S. (2004a). *Academic Entrepreneurship: University Spinoffs and Wealth Creation*. Cheltenham, UK and Northampton, MA, USA: Edward Elgar.

Shane, S. (2004b). Encouraging university entrepreneurship? The effect of the Bayh-Dole Act on university patenting in the United States. *Journal of Business Venturing*, **19**(1), 127–51.

Shane, S., Dolmans, S.A., Jankowski, J., Reymen, I.M. and Romme, A.G. (2015). Academic entrepreneurship: which inventors do technology licensing officers prefer for spinoffs? *Journal of Technology Transfer*, **40**(2), 273–92.

Siegel, D.S., Waldman, D.A. and Link, A.N. (2003a). Assessing the impact of organizational practices on the productivity of university technology transfer offices: an exploratory study. *Research Policy*, **32**(1), 27–48.

Siegel, D.S., Westhead, P. and Wright, M. (2003b). Science parks and the performance of new technology-based firms: a review of recent U.K. evidence and an agenda for future research. *Small Business Economics*, **20**, 177–84.

Stankiewicz, R. (1994). Spin-off companies from universities. *Science and Public Policy*, **21**(2), 99–107.

Swamidass, P.M. and Vulasa, V. (2009). Why university inventions rarely produce income? Bottlenecks in university technology transfer. *Journal of Technology Transfer*, **34**(4), 343–63.

Wright, M., Westhead, P. and Ucbasaran, D. (2006). *Habitual Entrepreneurship*. Cheltenham, UK and Northampton, MA, USA: Edward Elgar.

PART II

Organizing for commercialization in the biopharmaceutical industry

3. When do biotechnology ventures pursue international R&D alliances?

Hakan Ener and Ha Hoang

INTRODUCTION

A key strategic question for technology entrepreneurs is how to commercialize a new product (Gans and Stern, 2003). Because of the worldwide market appeal of technology products, answering this question involves charting a path for access to international markets (Shan, 1990). Given the resource constraints faced by research and development (R&D)-intensive technology ventures, entrepreneurs have often taken a two-step path to access international markets. The first step has been to focus on early stage development of a product, during which time ventures would carry out projects either in-house or in collaboration with physically proximate partners (Whittington et al., 2009). Once these projects made progress, the second step would be to sign licensing agreements in order to hand over the promising products to larger companies that possess both complementary assets (such as a global sales force) and sufficient financial resources to market the product in countries around the world (Arora et al., 2001).

Licensing agreements between technology-based ventures and their licensees often allocate exclusive worldwide commercialization rights for the licensee, including in our research context, biotechnology (Somaya et al., 2011). This limits the potential international growth opportunities and financial returns for entrepreneurs because worldwide markets remain out of the venture's direct reach. Therefore, it is not surprising that some ventures have sought new ways to bring their products to markets around the world (Bloodgood et al., 1996).

An alternative route that we identified in the course of research on biotechnology ventures, a route that gained popularity especially by the early 1990s, is the formation of international alliances that begin with cross-border R&D collaboration (Rothaermel and Deeds, 2004) and evolve into commercialization alliances as product development milestones are met, with eventual marketing rights granted to a foreign partner in a predetermined geographic area. They may involve multiple partners, each of which typically has the exclusive commercialization rights for one region of the world (Somaya et al., 2011). Thus, they effectively allow each partner to exercise control over the product and collect profits in a specific market.

What makes these international collaborations even more interesting for entrepreneurs seeking rapid growth is that in heavily regulated industries such as biotechnology, international R&D alliances help to speed up product approvals abroad, as regulatory agencies typically approve locally developed products faster (Dranove and Meltzer, 1994). These benefits, combined with the learning benefits foreign partners can offer (Schildt et al., 2012), make international R&D alliances a particularly attractive choice.

In this chapter, our research question is: 'What drives some technology ventures to pursue this novel international path to commercialize their products while others choose not to pursue it?' We believe that this question is important for entrepreneurship scholars because decisions about how to commercialize a product are among the most fundamental choices entrepreneurs make about a new venture's business model, but the drivers of these decisions remain poorly understood (Gans and Stern, 2003).

In our theory, we argue that the choice to pursue a novel commercialization is driven by problemistic (that is, failure-induced) organizational search, a central construct in the behavioral theory of the firm, which arises following performance deviations relative to organizational aspirations (Greve, 2003).

We hypothesize that when a firm falls behind its aspirations in terms of successfully and rapidly developing new products, it is more likely to pursue the international R&D alliances route to product commercialization in order to bolster performance. In other words, we expect that when a venture fails in developing novel products, it is more likely to pursue a novel commercialization path in order to survive and grow.

In elaborating our search-based theory, we acknowledge that taking part in international R&D alliances involves both greater uncertainty (due to the inherent novelty of this commercialization path) and operational challenges that arise from cross-border collaboration with partners in distant locations (Autio et al., 2011; Bruneel et al., 2010). We therefore expect technology-based ventures to form international alliances cautiously. This suggests that international R&D alliances would comprise a relatively small proportion of firms' project portfolios, as is the case in our research context (see Data Sample section below). Furthermore, after a venture forms its first international R&D alliance, we expect it to diversify its international partner portfolio in subsequent projects in order to reduce dependence on the same foreign partner for commercializing multiple products.

We provide empirical support consistent with these insights in an analysis of newly initiated product development projects in the biotechnology industry. We draw upon our findings to argue that extant research on technology-based ventures has not adequately accounted for the performance feedback-driven organizational search process underlying their pursuit of novel commercialization paths, such as through their involvement in international R&D alliances. At the same time, the very limited amount of research that did incorporate performance feedback's impact on firms' international involvement (Wennberg and Holmquist, 2008) suffered from the methodological shortcomings identified in recent work by Sakhartov and Folta (2013). In particular, these authors recommended carrying out a series of steps, which we implement in our analyses that help researchers to discriminate between alternative explanations and alternative outcomes related to theory on organizational search. We are thus able to offer a robust explanation for when technology ventures pursue the international commercialization path with foreign R&D partners rather than persist with the dominant 'develop domestically and license out' route.

Theoretically, our research has implications for researchers to incorporate performance relative to aspirations as an independent construct in explaining technology ventures' pursuit of new commercialization paths. For entrepreneurial managers, our findings highlight the need to be proactive in seeking foreign partners since these partners may be initially reluctant to form an alliance with an underperforming venture.

THEORY AND HYPOTHESES

Several streams of research in entrepreneurship and technology management address the process of commercializing new products (Shane and Ulrich, 2004). A large body of this research is normative and aims to identify the practices that lead to better outcomes, such as faster development and lower cost (Krishnan and Ulrich, 2001). Despite our fine-grained understanding of factors that lead to the success of product development projects, few scholars have taken a broader view and examined what leads firms to follow a specific path for developing and commercializing products (Aggarwal and Hsu, 2009), which involves decisions about whether to do R&D in-house or not (Baum et al., 2000), and whether to share control of manufacturing and sales decisions with strategic partners (Katila et al., 2008).

An implicit assumption in research on ventures' commercialization strategies has been that resource constraints lead them to follow a strategy of external collaboration (Gans and Stern, 2003). For these firms, the typical commercialization path involves doing R&D and then licensing out a new product candidate by handing it over to a strategic partner, who then funds the completion of the product and proceeds to sell it around the world (Arora et al., 2001). A particularly relevant example is our research setting, the biotechnology industry in the United States, where ventures typically form alliances with nearby universities, research institutes or bio-technology companies in order to bring a therapeutic drug candidate to the testing phase (clinical trials), and proceed to license out the product and its associated intellectual property to large pharmaceutical firms that have the resources to fund the clinical trials, file for regulatory approval, manu-facture the product and sell it around the world (Rothaermel and Deeds, 2004). These licensing relationships with large pharmaceutical firms are arm's length contracts where an innovation is transferred between firms rather than being jointly created or sold (Aggarwal and Hsu, 2009).

While following the 'develop domestically and license out' path has paid off for many technology-based ventures, it has also imposed some con-straints on their growth. In exchange for accepting an up-front payment at the time of the alliance agreement – complemented by payments con-ditional on meeting project milestones and possibly eventual royalties on sales – ventures have yielded control over strategic decisions that impact products' eventual financial success: a recent large sample analysis of bio-technology ventures' alliance agreements showed that the licensee partner had the final say, on average, in about seven of the ten key decision areas in commercializing a new product spanning R&D, manufacturing and sales phases (Adegbesan and Higgins, 2011).

Faced with this prospect, some technology ventures have pursued a more novel collaborative approach for commercializing their products that would allow them to develop and sell their products internationally (Oviatt and McDougall, 2005). This approach involves engaging in international R&D alliances with foreign partners at an early phase of product develop-ment, and carrying out joint R&D (in more than one country), followed by manufacturing and sales by each partner in a predetermined geographic area rather than worldwide exclusivity. As Somaya et al. (2011) document, in alliances between partners from different countries firms have much greater freedom in deciding how to sell the product in their region of the world.

An additional benefit of collaborating internationally on R&D in technology-intensive industries relates to the likelihood and speed of clearing regulatory hurdles before a product can be launched. In heavily regulated industries such as biotechnology, evidence shows that regula-tory agencies are more favorable toward locally developed and produced products, and issue approvals more rapidly (Dranove and Meltzer, 1994). Thus, by involving foreign partners from key markets in the R&D phase of a project, firms can get products to market faster compared to following the dominant commercialization path.

These benefits complement the novel technical knowledge that foreign partners can offer in international R&D alliances (Colombo et al., 2009). Recent work in knowledge-based theory explains the formation of international R&D alliances as part of a strategy to access complex and often tacit technological knowledge held by foreign firms (Oxley and Sampson, 2004). According to this view, these are learning alliances whereby organizations from different countries agree to pool resources and knowledge in pursuing common goals (Khanna et al., 1998). Despite the operational challenges associated with collaborating across borders (Almeida et al., 2002) and safeguarding knowledge in unfamiliar legal contexts (Oxley and Sampson, 2004), an increasing number of firms have engaged in international R&D alliances in recent years in technology-intensive industries (Roijakkers and Hagedoorn, 2006).

We believe that understanding how managers perceive the potential benefits of international R&D alliances relative to its risks (outlined below) is crucial to developing a theory of when firms pursue this new path. The behavioral theory we apply to the international R&D alliance decision deals with the tendency of managers to search for novel – and potentially risky – strategic alternatives when performance falls relative to aspirations. This perspective suggests that managers' interest in international R&D partnerships may peak following setbacks in their ongoing product development activities as they seek to make up for time and resources lost in other projects that failed to make progress.

Search Behavior and International R&D Alliances

Our theory emphasizes problemistic search as a driver of international R&D alliance formation. We view international R&D alliances, whereby firms collaborate with foreign partners on product development in a bid to commercialize products internationally, as a risky but potentially rewarding decision that can boost performance. The risks stem from operational challenges and legal uncertainties around sharing valuable technological know-how across national borders. Scholars have found that success is often elusive when transferring knowledge across countries (Jensen and Szulanski, 2004) and getting foreign alliance partners to build knowledge collaboratively with limited direct contact (Almeida et al., 2002). Cross-country differences in terms of intellectual property protection enforcement may further increase the perceived risk of sharing know-how not only during the R&D phase, but also in relation to manufacturing and sales.

Cross-border R&D and joint commercialization with foreign partners also implies a greater financial burden for the technology venture itself, as it remains involved throughout the product's development. Technology ventures have been able to meet their financial needs through a combination of private (venture capital) and public equity funding following initial public offerings on the NASDAQ stock exchange (Pisano, 2006), enabling them to carry on developing products all the way to market launch rather than licensing them out earlier. However, deviating from the dominant commercialization strategy also exposes the firm to greater financial risk in cases where a product development project fails (Tyebjee and Hardin, 2004).

Organizational scholars explain risky managerial decisions by drawing on the problemistic search concept, which is central to the behavioral theory of the firm (Cyert and March, 1963). The necessity of search is influenced by an organization's performance relative to aspiration levels that are determined by its own track record and its relative success with respect to similar organizations that constitute a reference group (Greve, 2003). Hence, evaluation of a given performance outcome is less favorable as aspiration levels increase or when performance decreases. With performance below aspirations, organizations engage in problemistic search by undertaking new strategic actions to address the shortfall. For example, firms may enter unrelated product markets (Greve, 1998), less familiar strategic partners may be selected for interorganizational relationships (Baum et al., 2005) or foreign markets for exporting may be sought (Wennberg and Holmquist, 2008). This is because negative performance feedback makes it clear that current solutions are of diminishing value, thus managers will be prone to make choices that involve departure from prior strategies.

In terms of technology ventures' product commercialization choices, we expect problemistic search to arise when a firm's product development projects fail to make progress after following the dominant commercialization path of domestic development (either through an alliance or in-house) followed by licensing out. Because speed to market is crucial for success in technology-based products where patents protect first-movers (Schoonhoven et al., 1990), projects that fail to achieve intermediate milestones (such as prototyping or pilot testing) may result in significant loss. For firms that follow the dominant commercialization path, this is a serious setback as milestone-based payments fail to materialize and the collaboration may rapidly be terminated in line with the licensee's contractual rights (DiMasi, 2001).

Thus, when faced with lagging product development performance, we would expect managers to experiment with a novel commercialization path as they seek ways to make up for lost time and resources. We expect problemistic search to favor product development and commercialization decisions that promise greater rewards, even at the expense of greater risk. Based on the potential rewards and risks described above, we would expect more international R&D alliances to be launched, at any given level of total project activity (that is, controlling for the number of in-house projects and domestic alliances initiated concurrently):

Hypothesis 1: A firm will engage in more R&D projects involving foreign partners as its performance declines below aspirations.

Foreign Partner Choice: New versus Repeated Partnering

International R&D alliance agreements typically allow each partner to claim exclusive rights to commercialize the product in a specified geographic region but not worldwide (Somaya et al., 2011). For a US-based firm, this may mean that a European partner has the rights for Europe, while a partner in Japan may hold the rights for Asia. While such arrangements are advantageous in that they allow partners to have decision-making rights in markets that they are most familiar with, they also expose each partner to a risk of increasing mutual dependence (Gulati and Sytch, 2007): if the same firms collaborate on multiple projects over time, they may come to rely entirely on each other for their jointly created products' success in their respective geographic regions. Given the frequency with which patent and licensing disputes occur in technology-based industries (Agarwal et al., 2009) this is a cause for concern for both sides of the partnership.

The objective of alleviating partner dependence may be important enough for managers to be willing to forgo benefits that come with repeated partnerships, such as familiarity and trust (Gulati, 1995). One way to reduce partner dependence for access to international markets is to form subsequent alliances with new foreign partners. Following this strategy allows firms to continue benefiting from novel technical knowledge offered by international R&D alliances while distributing the risk associated with fluctuations in the partners' resources and ability to invest in joint projects (Vassolo et al., 2004). It is also important to note that the choice to partner with new foreign firms does not imply a trade-off in alliance performance, as research has shown that greater partner-specific experience does not have a positive impact on the outcomes of subsequent alliances (Hoang and Rothaermel, 2005).

Prior findings on the effects of problemistic search on alliance partner selection are consistent with our arguments. Scholars have found, for example, that when investment banks fail to meet their aspirations, they begin collaborating with new banks on future transactions (Baum et al., 2005). This may be partly driven by managers' interpretation that earlier collaborations are partly responsible for missing performance targets, as well as the expectation that further partnerships with the same partners may not yield novel knowledge beyond what has already been shared. Both of these factors suggest that when a firm with ongoing international R&D alliances fails to meet performance aspirations, subsequent international partners are likely to be new to the firm. Lavie and Rosenkopf's (2006) analysis of US-based software firms' alliance patterns have also shown that the tendency to partner with new firms has been increasing over time in this industry where almost 90 percent of firms have been involved in international alliances.

As Lavie and Miller (2008) show, greater diversity in international alliance partners can generate performance benefits for technology-based firms, and that managing a globally dispersed portfolio of strategic partners does not pose insurmountable challenges despite earlier arguments suggesting the contrary (Oxley and Sampson, 2004). Thus, we expect that negative deviations of product development performance compared to aspirations should bolster initiation of new projects with new international R&D alliance partners rather than reinforcing ties with existing foreign partners.

Hypothesis 2: Performing below aspirations will bolster alliance formation with new foreign partners rather than launching consecutive projects with existing foreign partners.

DATA SAMPLE

The dataset utilized in this chapter is a sample providing detailed project-level information on all R&D projects (in-house or alliance) initiated by publicly listed US biotechnology firms at any time after founding until 2001. Hagedoorn (1993) reports that biotechnology has the highest density of inter-firm alliance ties of any industry. Our dataset contains detailed information pertaining to the scope, timing, alliance partners and project outcomes associated with R&D projects conducted by firms in our sample.

We first selected a stratified random sample of 60 US-based firms out of a population of 315 biotechnology firms that went public on the NASDAQ stock exchange until 2001. Stratification was done as follows:

we ranked all firms in the population with respect to their compounded annual growth rate of non-operating income – a key indicator of resources provided by alliance partners (Powell et al., 1996) – over our sample period, and divided the population into quartiles. Such stratification helped us to avoid sampling on the dependent construct (alliance formation). We then randomly chose a quarter of our sample from the population of low growth ventures, half of our sample from the middle two quartiles and the remaining quarter of the sample from the top quartile.

Firms' projects were only included in the analyses if they involved human therapeutics (not diagnostics) in order to facilitate comparison across project outcomes in our sample. As some of our sample firms did not have enough projects dealing with human therapeutics, we ended with a sample of 52 firms that reflected a roughly equal proportion of low-medium-high growth in non-operating income growth as the originally selected 60 firms described above. A total of 1126 human therapeutics projects were conducted by these 52 biotechnology firms in the sample over a 23-year period (1979–2001). Out of these, 56 projects were international R&D alliances where one or more of the drug development phases (defined in the next section) were conducted outside the United States with a non-American partner firm. Not all of the firms in our sample initiated international alliances, thus we did not sample on the dependent variable.

An example that illustrates international R&D alliances in our sample comes from Genetics Institute, a company founded in 1980 in Cambridge, Massachusetts by two molecular biologists from Harvard University. For ten years, the company followed the dominant strategy of licensing out, and granted manufacturing and global marketing rights for several product candidates to Allied Health and Scientific Products Company, while it struggled to mount a competitive challenge to its larger and more successful rival Amgen. Then in 1991, trying a different approach, the company turned to Japan-based Yamanouchi Pharmaceutical Co. for a partnership to jointly develop and market a new therapy to alleviate blood clotting deficiencies that arise with chemotherapy in cancer patients. Two years after preclinical studies began in the United States the partners jointly began carrying out Phase 1 clinical trials in parallel in Japan and the United States. As the project showed promise in a number of related therapeutic indications (such as in the control of Crohn's disease) the partners began carrying out additional clinical trials in their respective countries until receiving US Food and Drug Administration (FDA) approval to market the product in 1998. The project completion time of seven years was faster than what the firm had been able to achieve in other projects, and the firm had maintained commercialization rights for North America, Europe and most of Asia except Japan, where its partner Yamanouchi held the rights. Genetics Institute rapidly proceeded to launch the product in the United States and Latin America, and its rival Amgen discontinued its development on a very similar therapy (IMS Health, 2001).

In our data, the national origin of each partner in an alliance was verified by inspecting company websites and publicly available data sources. Project data were obtained from Lifecycle, a proprietary database maintained by IMS Health, a pharmaceutical industry research firm. Lifecycle is commercially available and provides fine-grained data on R&D projects for a large number of pharmaceutical firms. IMS Health collects information globally from governmental agencies, industry conferences, patents and scientific publications, and contacts with scientists and managers within focal firms. To gather information on alliance projects over time, Lifecycle data were linked to alliance information obtained from various volumes of BioScan, an industry publication, and from a database from Recombinant Capital, a consulting firm specializing in the life sciences. BioScan and the Recombinant Capital database are two of the most comprehensive publicly available data sources documenting alliance activity in the global biotechnology industry. Both sources are fairly consistent and accurate in reporting alliances (their inter-source reliability was found to be greater than 0.90).

EMPIRICAL ANALYSES

The first hypothesis aims to explain the focal firm's count of new international alliances in a given year, while the second hypothesis explains the number of new foreign partners added to the focal firm's alliance portfolio. In both hypotheses, the unit of analysis is the firm-year. As a result, we aggregated the project-level data into a firm-level panel (unit of analysis: firm-year) before testing the hypotheses.

Dependent Variables

International alliances started by firm i in year t ('Count International Alliances'). This variable is a count measure that reflects whether one or more new drug development projects were initiated in collaboration with a foreign partner where part of the drug development project took place outside the United States. Thus, we identified international alliances as those where the preclinical and/or clinical development of a drug took place in more than one country as part of a formal collaboration between firms based in different countries. When a drug eventually received regulatory approval (as was the case with 17 international alliance projects in our sample), we inspected IMS Health data to verify that the market launch of the product was made not only in the United States but also in the country or region where the foreign alliances' partners were located.

International alliance with new foreign partner started by firm i in year t ('Count New Foreign Partners'). This variable is a count measure that reflects the addition of a new foreign partner to the firm's portfolio of international alliance partners in a given year (these foreign partners were either biotechnology firms or pharmaceutical firms in our sample). Note that this second dependent variable is related to the first one in that new foreign partners can be added to the firm's alliance portfolio only when a new international alliance is initiated. However, the converse is not always true: a new international alliance does not necessarily lead to partnering with a new foreign firm. Moreover, a new international alliance may lead to partnering with multiple new foreign firms, thus the correspondence between the two dependent variables is not one to one.

Independent and Control Variables

The main theoretical predictor is *attainment discrepancy*, which refers to the difference between an organization's actual performance and its aspiration level that is based on a comparison with peers (competitive aspirations) and the firm's own track record (historical aspirations). In order to calculate attainment discrepancy, we first constructed measures that capture the performance of a firm relative to its historical and competitive aspirations. Below, we first introduce our performance measure, and proceed with explaining how historical and competitive aspirations were each constructed in line with prior research (see Greve, 2003). Attainment discrepancy is then calculated as the difference between actual performance and the equally weighted combination of historical and competitive aspirations.

Annual project performance of the biotechnology firm. This variable provides a performance measure based on the biotechnology firm's ability to complete each of the drug development phases for all of its projects. We reviewed prior work in this industry that emphasizes performance as the ability of firms to proceed through discrete and uniform product development project phases (Chandy et al., 2006; Cockburn and Henderson, 2001; Danzon et al., 2005). In light of this research, we developed a novel coding scheme to reflect a firm's performance in drug development project phases.

The measure for the product development performance of a firm is aimed at capturing the pace of progress in the firm's portfolio of projects through Preclinical, Phase 1, Phase 2 and Phase 3 trials, obtaining US FDA approval and finally reaching the market. Progression through these stages indicates successively higher performance. We assigned 10 percentage points to the completion of each of the first five phases in a product development project (phases before market launch) while market launch adds the remaining 50 percent, reflecting its importance for the viability of a biotechnology firm (Pisano, 1996).

For each firm and each year, the incremental performance of ongoing projects was calculated, aggregated and averaged, thus reflecting the annual incremental performance of the firm in completing product development projects successfully. For instance, if a firm had two ongoing projects and one of the projects completed Phase 1 clinical trials in that year while the other project made no progress, the yearly project performance of the firm was calculated by adding 0.10 and 0, then dividing by 2, yielding 0.05. More generally, in years where a firm's product development projects made significant progress, this measure increased toward 1; when no progress was made the score remained close to zero.

Aspirations. We calculated two separate aspiration levels, in line with previous work (Greve, 2003). These measures constituted the basis for the main independent variable of this study, attainment discrepancy, which is the difference between performance and aspirations.

Historical Aspirations. In experimental research, scholars observed that a weighted average of historical performance data was incorporated into an aspiration level for the future (Lant, 1992). To capture this idea, we adopt an iterative measure of historical aspirations as follows:

$$HA_{t,i} = 0.5 * HA_{t-1,i} + 0.5 * P_{t-1,i} \qquad\qquad 3.1$$

where $HA_{t,i}$ refers to historical aspirations of firm i at time t and $P_{t-1,i}$ refers to the firm's performance in the most recent period $t - 1$. The parameter 0.5 is selected in order to provide an equal weighting between the firm's most recent performance and its prior aspirations. Robustness checks indicate that the results are not unique to this particular value and continue to hold when moderate values are chosen for a_1, as long as the value is not too close to either 0 or 1.

Competitive Aspirations. This variable provides the average annual project performance of the biotechnology firm's reference group within the previous year. The choice of a reference group is important in the formation of competitive aspirations: because firms compete in product markets specified in the approval decisions made by the US FDA, we defined the reference group on the basis of a firm's main product focus, where a reference group was comprised of all other firms in the sample whose product market focus is the same as the focal biotechnology firm. We used the longitudinal data to select the most frequent therapeutic category appearing in the firm's project records until that year. For example, if a firm had more product development projects in the cardiovascular product market than any other market since founding, then that firm was in the reference group composed of all other cardiovascular-focused firms. Over time as the firms' involvement in product markets evolved, the composition of the reference groups changed. At any given year, the average performance of firms in the reference group (excluding the focal firm) constituted the competitive aspirations of the firm (Greve, 2003), as indicated in the following equation:

$$Competitive\ Aspirations_{t,i} = \left(\sum_{i \neq j} P_{t,j} \right) / (N - 1) \qquad 3.2$$

where $P_{t,j}$ refers to the performance of each peer firm and N refers to the number of firms in the peer group. This variable is also standardized to facilitate comparison across firms.

Attainment Discrepancy

The difference between a firm's performance and its aspirations is referred to as attainment discrepancy (Lant, 1992). In order to create this measure, standardized historical and competitive aspirations were first combined into a single measure that captures the overall performance aspiration of the organization in a given year. We equally weighted the two types of aspirations in the following composite measure:

$$A_{t-1,i} = 0.5 * HA_{t-1,i} + 0.5 * CA_{t-1,i} \qquad 3.3$$

Attainment discrepancy was then calculated as the difference between last year's performance and aspirations:

$$AD_{t-1,i} = P_{t-1,i} - A_{t-1,i} \qquad 3.4$$

Above zero, this measure corresponds to positive performance feedback where performance exceeds aspirations, and vice versa. Since both hypotheses deal with the effects of performance below aspirations, we formed a spline function creating two separate variables. These variables can be expressed formally as follows:

$$AD - (above\ zero)_{t-1,i} = P_{t-1,i} - A_{t-1,i}\ if\ AD_{t-1,i} > 0, 0\ otherwise$$
$$AD - (below\ zero)_{t-1,i} = P_{t-1,i} - A_{t-1,i}\ if\ AD_{t-1,i} < 0, 0\ otherwise$$
$$3.5$$

Control Variables

In addition to this main theoretical predictor, we controlled for a variety of alternative factors that may influence the choice and timing of a firm's engagement in international R&D alliances. These are lagged one year (unless stated otherwise) to avoid simultaneity with the dependent variable.

We followed Sakhartov and Folta's (2013) suggestions for empirical model specification in testing hypotheses on the impact of performance relative to aspirations. The authors recommended specifying the relevant alternative outcomes (in our case, alternative to forming an international alliance). The project records in our sample showed that there are three ways in which firms initiate product development: as part of a domestic alliance (about two thirds of the projects in our sample), in-house (more than a quarter of projects) or as part of an international alliance (the remainder of projects in the sample). In order to isolate the impact of performance feedback on international alliance formation we included contemporaneous control variables for *Count Domestic Alliances* and *Count In-house Projects* since problemistic search may bolster project initiation in these categories as well. Such contemporaneous controls were lacking in prior work that highlighted the theoretical link between problemistic search and the international involvement of entrepreneurial firms (Wennberg and Holmquist, 2008), thus it was impossible to discriminate whether negative performance feedback led firms to look abroad more intensively than before (relative to alternative commercialization paths).

Furthermore, in line with Sakhartov and Folta's (2013) recommendation to account for the opportunity cost of alternative outcomes (in our case, engaging in domestic rather than international development), we created two measures. First, we calculated how fast the markets for pharmaceutical products grew during the past year in the rest of the world (outside the home country, United States) based on longitudinal data from PhRMA (2012), the largest industry association. We also computed the sample-wide cumulative ratio of international alliance projects that yielded products approved for market launch by the relevant governmental authorities in at least one country (updated yearly). Since increasing values of these measures should bolster the expected benefits from international alliances and make collaborations in foreign markets more attractive (increasing the opportunity cost of staying purely domestic), we expect a positive coefficient for these variables in our analyses. Again, we found that prior related work (Wennberg and Holmquist, 2008) did not incorporate the opportunity cost of staying domestic versus expanding internationally, hampering its ability to rule out profit-maximizing behavior (when firms seek to enter foreign markets if they offer higher expected returns, regardless of how well they do domestically) as the driver of observed outcomes.

The last variable we add to our analyses based on Sakhartov and Folta's (2013) suggestions is a proxy for switching costs between the alternative outcomes (purely domestic versus international alliances). Switching costs that make international alliances especially challenging arise from geographical distance as well as differences in business environments (including the legal framework governing intellectual property) between the home country and other countries (Zaheer and Hernandez, 2011). Based on the greater frequency of European and Japanese alliance partners within our sample of international alliances, we adopted two binary indicator variables in order to capture whether a focal firm in our sample had engaged in an alliance with any partners from these continents until the past year. Considering the geographic distance and legal differences (relative to the United States) in Europe and Japan, we expect switching costs for establishing subsequent partnerships to go down after establishing the first alliance in each of these regions, thus we expect a positive coefficient in our empirical tests of both hypotheses. Once again, we observed that prior related work did not adequately capture switching costs that arise when firms develop business in new foreign countries (Wennberg and Holmquist, 2008), and thus could not address the temporal interdependence of successive decisions to expand internationally.

Other firm-level controls include firms' technological capabilities, which can facilitate new alliances (both domestic and international). We obtained the patent application records for each of the sample firms, and counted the firm's issued patents per year (Deeds et al., 1998). We then weighted these patents by the number of citations received until 2002, and transformed the annually summed measure into its natural logarithm ('Annual Patent Applications'). A further control deals with whether a firm had any products on the market, which is a crucial event for firms in the biotechnology industry in order to send a signal to potential alliance partners regarding the firm's viability (Pisano, 2006). We therefore introduced a binary measure that changed from zero to one after a product was launched by the firm ('Product on Market'). Two other signals of the firm's prospects for survival that we control for are firm age and financial resources as proxied by current assets (in natural logarithm). Since alliance formation decisions may also be influenced by the phase of product development projects (Rothaermel and Deeds, 2004), we calculated the median phase of all ongoing projects by the focal firm, and assigned an ordinal value from zero to four (zero if the median phase was preclinical, one if the median phase was clinical trial Phase 1, and so on until the FDA registration phase).

Firms' involvement in the network of alliance relationships can also positively influence subsequent decisions (Coviello, 2006; Guler and Guillen, 2010): 'Alliance Centrality' is the yearly updated Bonacich eigenvector measure of centrality widely used in the network literature measured across all of the firm's alliances (domestic and international) and taking into account the indirect ties to partners' partners as well (Wasserman and Faust, 1994). Since competition may prompt firms to look for new growth areas beyond the domestic market (Porter, 1986), we counted the number of new firms that entered the firm's main product market ('Count New Rivals'). Finally, we incorporated a contemporaneous control with the count of all international alliances in the sample within the same year ('Sample-wide International Alliances') in order to account for industry-wide trends that may impact firms' tendency to form international alliances (Fernhaber et al., 2007).

Estimation

The dataset contained repeated observations for the same biotechnology firm across time, calling for a panel-based estimation technique. Since the dependent measures were count variables, we used negative binomial regressions to test the hypotheses after rejecting the Poisson specification due to overdispersion of the dependent variable. For both dependent variables, our tests of the panel model versus pooled regression models led us to choose the panel specification. We selected the appropriate panel estimation technique between random and fixed effects models through a Hausman test, which indicated that random effects panel regression is desirable (test statistic $p = 0.32$).

RESULTS

In order to assess multi-collinearity between our predictors we inspected correlations in Table 3.1 in addition to the variance inflation factors in the two statistical models that test the hypotheses. We found correlations to be low or moderate, and calculated a mean variance inflation factor of 1.16, considered unproblematic by conventional standards (Studenmund, 2001).

Before proceeding with hypothesis testing, we inspected the mean values for our dependent variables, which show that firms are cautious about deviating from the dominant commercialization path, with less than one international R&D alliance per firm initiated per year, on average. The average count of new foreign partners is higher than the average count of alliances, which reveals that international alliances often involve more than one foreign partner, consistent with our observation that partners from

Table 3.1 Descriptive statistics

	Mean	S.D.	Min	Max	(1)	(2)	(3)	(4)	(5)	(6)	(7)	(8)	(9)	(10)	(11)	(12)	(13)	(14)	(15)	(16)	(17)
1 Count International Alliances	0.07	0.27	0	2																	
2 Count New Foreign Partners	0.10	0.54	0	7	0.73																
3 Attainment Discrepancy Below Zero	-0.27	0.39	-2.66	0.00	-0.03	-0.11															
4 Attainment Discrepancy Above Zero	0.26	0.65	0	5.55	0.03	-0.01	0.28														
5 Count Domestic Alliances	0.41	1.34	0	16	0.09	0.01	0.10	0.01													
6 Count In-House Projects	0.75	1.55	0	14	0.01	-0.05	0.08	-0.02	0.21												
7 Sample-wide International Alliance Success	0.20	0.11	0.08	0.50	-0.04	0.00	0.12	-0.00	-0.09	-0.18											
8 Growth in Pharmaceutical Sales Abroad	0.08	0.08	-0.05	0.26	0.03	0.06	-0.05	0.04	0.02	0.03	0.11										
9 Alliance in Europe	0.13	0.33	0	1	0.10	0.04	0.02	0.03	0.20	-0.01	-0.03	0.07									
10 Alliance in Japan	0.09	0.28	0	1	0.05	0.02	-0.00	0.01	0.05	-0.05	0.03	0.03	0.49								

Table 3.1 (continued)

	Mean	S.D.	Min	Max	(1)	(2)	(3)	(4)	(5)	(6)	(7)	(8)	(9)	(10)	(11)	(12)	(13)	(14)	(15)	(16)	(17)
11 Annual Patent Applications	0.96	1.51	0	6.77	0.14	0.14	0.06	0.01	0.23	0.07	-0.13	0.14	0.29	0.24							
12 Portfolio Maturity	0.77	0.95	0	3	0.02	0.05	-0.15	0.28	-0.06	-0.12	-0.07	0.01	0.13	0.10	0.06						
13 Product on Market	0.08	0.28	0	1	-0.03	-0.03	0.01	0.03	0.04	-0.11	0.05	0.02	0.38	0.54	0.20	0.15					
14 Firm Age	8.60	6.05	1	33	-0.04	-0.04	0.07	0.01	0.11	-0.13	0.19	-0.06	0.41	0.29	0.26	0.24	0.29				
15 Current Assets	3.22	1.53	-1.77	7.63	0.07	0.07	0.18	0.04	0.21	0.08	0.12	-0.04	0.41	0.39	0.38	0.02	0.35	0.43			
16 Sample-wide International Alliances	2.55	2.15	0	8	0.13	0.08	-0.04	0.04	0.22	0.23	-0.38	0.23	0.14	0.07	0.22	0.06	0.05	-0.01	-0.05		
17 Count New Rivals	2.47	2.81	0	12	0.03	-0.02	-0.02	0.00	0.11	0.12	-0.45	-0.15	-0.04	-0.11	0.11	-0.09	-0.06	-0.23	-0.08	0.32	
18 Alliance Centrality	2.04	6.30	0.00	56.83	-0.01	-0.01	0.02	-0.05	0.08	0.01	0.08	-0.02	0.23	0.08	0.19	-0.00	0.09	0.21	0.36	-0.04	0.06

Note: Correlations greater than 0.08 in absolute value are significant at $\alpha = 0.05$.

Europe and Asia help firms in our sample to commercialize products in multiple international markets.

Results of the test for Hypothesis 1 regarding the international R&D alliance formation are presented in Table 3.2. Model 1 comprises only control variables, and reveals that firms with an active production of valuable patents are particularly active in forging international R&D partnerships. In contrast, the control variables related to the opportunity cost of international partnering are among those that are insignificant.

Model 2 adds the main theoretical predictor, attainment discrepancy (above and below zero indicated by separate variables in spline form) to the estimation. In line with Hypothesis 1, the coefficient of attainment discrepancy is significant and negative for values below zero. This implies that as performance declines below aspirations, firms initiate more international R&D alliances. Transforming the estimated coefficient into an expected count reveals that a standard deviation decrease in actual performance relative to aspirations results in 57 percent more international R&D alliances relative to when performance equals aspirations. It is important to point out that the results are not primarily driven by persistently underperforming, or 'lower quality' ventures, as several ventures in our sample had been able to launch products (and thus had high performance aspirations) before engaging in an international alliance for the first time.

Regression results in Model 2 also reveal that once firms perform above their aspirations, they remain within the dominant commercialization path, with no expected increase in international R&D alliance count. In contrast, when firms perform well (that is, when attainment discrepancy is above zero) there does not appear to be a significant deviation from the dominant commercialization path, which works well for these firms because it guarantees substantial payments as product development milestones are attained.

Hypothesis 2 on international R&D alliances with new foreign partners is tested in Model 4 of Table 3.2. In support of Hypothesis 2, the attainment discrepancy below zero variable is negative and significant. With a standard deviation decrease in performance below aspirations, the count of new foreign partners increases by 79 percent, which suggests that managers are eager to branch out of their international networks and avoid repeated partnerships abroad. Overall, our results are in line with our predictions that performance shortfalls relative to aspirations stimulate firms' tendency to search for international R&D alliances, and subsequently to avoid dependence on a single foreign partner.

Table 3.2   *Regression results*

		Model 1	Model 2	Model 3	Model 4
		Count International Alliances	Count International Alliances	Count New Foreign Partners	Count New Foreign Partners
Theoretical predictors	Attainment discrepancy below zero		−0.860**		−1.573***
			(0.524)		(0.510)
	Attainment discrepancy above zero		0.392		0.369
			(0.391)		(0.459)
Controls based on Sakhartov and Folta (2013)	Count domestic alliances	0.079	0.086	0.136	0.162
		(0.089)	(0.090)	(0.094)	(0.125)
	Count in-house projects	−0.044	−0.030	−0.407*	−0.418*
		(0.143)	(0.143)	(0.220)	(0.240)
	Sample-wide international alliance success	2.191	3.735	−5.766	−0.980
		(5.381)	(5.457)	(5.669)	(6.517)
	Growth in pharmaceutical sales abroad	1.545	1.826	0.879	2.213
		(2.780)	(2.843)	(2.816)	(2.884)
	Alliance in Europe	0.372	0.366	0.228	−0.699
		(0.592)	(0.582)	(0.573)	(0.662)
	Alliance in Japan	0.662	0.612	0.933	0.237
		(0.616)	(0.632)	(0.624)	(0.872)

Other firm-level controls	Annual patent applications	0.377**	0.395**	0.249	0.554**
		(0.178)	(0.179)	(0.182)	(0.243)
	Portfolio maturity	-0.208	-0.393	-0.245	-0.627*
		(0.257)	(0.300)	(0.248)	(0.343)
	Product on market	-0.867	-0.852	-1.287*	-0.699
		(0.804)	(0.809)	(0.772)	(1.042)
	Firm age	0.005	0.016	0.034	0.051
		(0.059)	(0.059)	(0.056)	(0.080)
	Current assets	0.012	0.028	0.106	0.164
		(0.233)	(0.234)	(0.221)	(0.284)
Other sample-level controls	Sample-wide international alliances	0.358***	0.386***	0.337**	0.431***
		(0.138)	(0.139)	(0.165)	(0.163)
	Count new rivals	-0.080	-0.069	-0.290**	-0.199*
		(0.098)	(0.097)	(0.122)	(0.111)
	Alliance centrality	-0.029	-0.033	-0.020	-0.043
		(0.038)	(0.039)	(0.034)	(0.039)
	Constant	10.387	10.069	-3.348*	10.208
		(578.4)	(1415.8)	(1.774)	(1004.2)
	Observations	365	365	365	365
	Number of firms	52	52	52	52

Note: Standard errors in parentheses. One-sided tests for main predictors, two-sided tests for others.* Significant at 10%; ** significant at 5%; *** significant at 1%.

85

DISCUSSION AND CONCLUSION

Our study addressed the question of when technology ventures pursue a novel alternative route to commercialize their products. The novel path we highlighted consisted of international alliances that begin with joint R&D and lead up to product launch in multiple markets where the partners operate. We hypothesized and found that the tendency of technology ventures to deviate from the dominant path of 'develop domestically and license out' increases with problemistic search as their product development performance declines relative to aspirations. Accordingly, underperforming firms had the greatest tendency to pursue international alliances to commercialize their new product candidates, but were cautious about relying excessively on foreign partners: the pattern was of increasing international diversity of alliance partners rather than reinforcing existing ties.

Until now scholars have largely overlooked the importance of performance relative to aspirations in shaping ventures' product commercialization decisions, viewing these choices as largely constrained by resources and capabilities (Zahra and Nielsen, 2002). However, as in our research context, even when resources constrain ventures to follow a collaborative path for commercializing their products, firms may pursue different strategies: while many follow the dominant pattern in the industry and license out their products and intellectual property, some seek foreign partners to co-develop products and sell them in multiple markets. It is worth reiterating that our finding holds while controlling for ventures' resource availability (in the form of current assets) as well as their technological capabilities reflected in patents. Thus, performance fluctuations relative to organizational aspirations yield a distinct mechanism that shapes when firms will pursue a commercialization path that is novel to an industry.

The theoretical contribution of our study is to explain why success in developing novel products may discourage firms' pursuit of a novel commercialization path. Given that ventures performing above aspirations in the product development domain were reluctant to experiment with the international alliance path, our explanation is that product development success diminishes the incentives for experimenting with a firm's commercialization strategy. In that sense, novel products and novel commercialization strategies appear to be substitutes in ensuring ventures' survival and growth.

It is theoretically interesting to speculate about alternative reasons that may drive high-performing technology ventures to avoid experimenting with a novel commercialization path. After all, high-performing ventures may stand to gain financially if rather than licensing out products they carried on developing them with a view toward obtaining commercial rights in one or more countries. Strategic conformity may be playing a strong role in the absence of a strong reason for change (Park, 2007). Equally important may be the fierce competition between technology ventures to be positioned as an R&D leader, which calls for specialization in early phases of product development and leaving subsequent commercialization activities to strategic partners. Scholars have also found that partners located near innovative technology ventures (for example, in the same city or state) have a significant advantage in making such alliance deals, as proximity facilitates effective transfer and monitoring of intellectual property (Whittington et al., 2009). Thus, high-performing ventures, especially those based in developed countries with large markets such as the United States, may be drawn to collaborate with spatially proximate partners as long as performance is above aspirations, resulting in a slow pace of internationalization (Oviatt and McDougall, 2005).

Our finding regarding when technology ventures increase the international diversity of their R&D alliance portfolios is another theme that contributes to theory in entrepreneurship. In prior research, scholars have theorized about why greater international diversity of R&D alliances may boost technology ventures' performance (Lavie and Miller, 2008), but not addressed ways in which diversity can emerge in the first place. In light of our finding that attainment discrepancy plays an important role in increasing the international diversity of alliances, we offer an interesting testable implication: since firms that perform above their aspiration levels are least likely to seek international diversity in alliance partners, they are likely to overlook opportunities for accessing new types of technological expertise in emerging regions around the world. This may lead to future competitive threats arising from foreign countries (Yamakawa et al., 2008).

To the best of our knowledge, our study is the first in drawing attention to the relevance of organizational aspirations – rather than entrepreneurs' personal aspirations – for understanding technology ventures' choices regarding the path to growth. Extant research has shown that personal aspirations matter a great deal in shaping decisions to launch ventures (Cassar, 2010) and remain involved in entrepreneurship (Gimeno et al., 1997). However, this research has developed largely in isolation from theory and findings on organizational aspirations (Greve, 2003). Our findings lend support to the idea that organizational aspirations begin forming a powerful influence early in the life of entrepreneurial ventures, even before products are commercialized: in fact, product development project milestones provide the earliest performance outcomes that allow comparison between ventures in an industry. Thus, we argue that organizational aspirations complement individual aspirations in explaining entrepreneurial behaviors.

Clearly, our findings will not be generally applicable to all contexts. As with any study set in the context of a single industry, our results come with some boundary conditions. First, product development projects in the biopharmaceutical industry have a uniform structure that cannot be directly applied to all technology-based industries in order to set aspiration levels and facilitate performance comparisons. Second, our focus on US-based technology ventures implies that their domestic market is big enough to ensure a sustainable future, and that looking for international partners and markets is not necessarily a strategic imperative for success. In contrast, for firms from smaller countries, international R&D alliances may be a necessary condition for product commercialization, which is consistent with empirical evidence that European companies have been extremely active in this field in the past decades (Narula and Duysters, 2004). We call for further research in other industries and countries to test the generalizability of our broader claim that firms are likely to deviate from their industries' dominant commercialization path as they underperform.

We believe that our study is the first to incorporate the methodological recommendations provided by Sakhartov and Folta (2013) in their constructive critique of prior research on problemistic search. Thanks to this feature of our research design, we were able to discriminate the impact of negative performance feedback on the pursuit of a novel product commercialization path involving international R&D partners, and made sure that the effects we identified are unique to this outcome (after controlling for any contemporaneous changes in domestic alliance formation and in-house projects). Moreover, we were careful to account for the opportunity cost of staying domestic versus going international, as well as the switching costs that arise when ventures search for new foreign partners. Thus, we believe that our research ruled out alternative theoretical explanations to the maximum extent possible.

Scholars can advance our problemistic search-based theory of novelty-seeking in product commercialization by explaining the choice of location for seeking foreign partners. We found that problemistic search results in looking for a novel commercialization path by partnering outside the firm's home country: but does this imply going further (for example, exploring geographically or culturally distant places) during periods of exceptionally strong negative performance feedback? Future research could take a multi-dimensional view of novelty in product development to fully reflect the choices that managers face.

As a practical implication, we highlight the need for entrepreneurial managers to be proactive about international product commercialization partnerships. Ventures that are underperforming in terms of product development success face a formidable challenge in finding international R&D partners, especially when the venture's survival is at stake (for example, if it has no revenues yet) and partners are risk-averse. We would advise underperforming ventures' managers to highlight the distinctive advantages they can offer to potential partners, for example, in terms of technological and market complementarities (Mitsuhashi and Greve, 2009; Rothaermel and Boeker, 2008), in order to bolster their chances of reaching an alliance agreement. While initiating an international R&D alliance is no guarantee for improving performance, a proactive approach for convincing potential partners to work together seems essential in order to pursue novel product commercialization strategies that would be impossible when working alone through in-house R&D.

In conclusion, we call on scholars to incorporate performance relative to aspirations as an independent construct in explaining technology ventures' pursuit of new-to-the-industry commercialization paths. These phenomena are crucial for understanding what drives strategic innovation and flexibility among technology ventures.

REFERENCES

Adegbesan, J.A. and Higgins, M.J. (2011). The intra-alliance division of value created through collaboration. *Strategic Management Journal* **32**(2), 187–211.

Agarwal, R., Ganco, M. and Ziedonis, R.H. (2009). Reputations for toughness in patent enforcement: implications for knowledge spillovers via inventor mobility. *Strategic Management Journal* **30**(13), 1349–74.

Aggarwal, V.A. and Hsu, D.H. (2009). Modes of cooperative R&D commercialization by start-ups. *Strategic Management Journal* **30**(8), 835–64.

Almeida, P., Song, J. and Grant, R.M. (2002). Are firms superior to alliances and markets? An empirical test of cross-border knowledge building. *Organization Science* **13**(2), 147–61.

Arora, A., Fosfuri, A. and Gambardella, A. (2001). *Markets for technology: The Economics of Innovation and Corporate Strategy*. Cambridge, MA: MIT Press.

Autio, E., George, G. and Alexy, O. (2011). International entrepreneurship and capability development – qualitative evidence and future research directions. *Entrepreneurship Theory and Practice* **35**(1), 11–37.

Baum, J.A.C., Calabrese, T. and Silverman, B.R. (2000). Don't go it alone: alliance network composition and startups' performance in Canadian biotechnology. *Strategic Management Journal* **21**(3), 267–94.

Baum, J.A.C., Rowley, T.J., Shipilov, A.V. and Chuang, Y.T. (2005). Dancing with strangers: aspiration performance and the search for underwriting syndicate partners. *Administrative Science Quarterly* **50**(4), 536–75.

Bloodgood, J.M., Sapienza, H.J. and Almeida, J.G. (1996). The internationalization of new high-potential US ventures: antecedents and outcomes. *Entrepreneurship Theory and Practice* **20**, 61–76.

Bruneel, J., Yli-Renko, H. and Clarysse, B. (2010). Learning from experience and learning from others: how congenital and interorganizational learning substitute for experiential learning in young firm internationalization. *Strategic Entrepreneurship Journal* **4**(2), 164–82.

Cassar, G. (2010). Are individuals entering self-employment overly optimistic? An empirical test of plans and projections on nascent entrepreneur expectations. *Strategic Management Journal* **31**(8), 822–40.

Chandy, R., Hopstaken, B., Narasimhan, O. and Prabhu, J. (2006). From invention to innovation: conversion ability in product development. *Journal of Marketing Research* **43**(3), 494–508.

Cockburn, I.M. and Henderson, R.M. (2001). Scale and scope in drug development: unpacking the advantages of size in pharmaceutical research. *Journal of Health Economics* **20**(6), 1033–57.

Colombo, M.G., Grilli, L., Murtinu, S., Piscitello, L. and Piva, E. (2009). Effects of international R&D alliances on performance of high-tech start-ups: a longitudinal analysis. *Strategic Entrepreneurship Journal* **3**(4), 346–68.

Coviello, N.E. (2006). The network dynamics of international new ventures. *Journal of International Business Studies* **37**(5), 713–31.

Cyert, R.M. and March, J.G. (1963). *A Behavioral Theory of the Firm*. Englewood Cliffs, NJ: Prentice-Hall.

Danzon, P.M., Nicholson, S. and Pereira, N.S. (2005). Productivity in pharmaceutical–biotechnology R&D: the role of experience and alliances. *Journal of Health Economics* **24**(2), 317–39.

Deeds, D.L., DeCarolis, D. and Coombs, J.E. (1998). Firm-specific resources and wealth creation in high-technology ventures: evidence from newly public biotechnology firms. *Entrepreneurship Theory and Practice* **22**(3), 55–73.

DiMasi, J.A. (2001). Risks in new drug development: approval success rates for investigational drugs. *Clinical Pharmacology and Therapeutics* **69**(5), 297–307.

Dranove, D. and Meltzer, D. (1994). Do important drugs reach the market sooner? *Rand Journal of Economics* **25**(3), 402–23.

Fernhaber, S.A., McDougall, P.P. and Oviatt, B.M. (2007). Exploring the role of industry structure in new venture internationalization. *Entrepreneurship Theory and Practice* **31**(4), 517–42.

Gans, J.S. and Stern, S. (2003). The product market and the market for 'ideas': commercialization strategies for technology entrepreneurs. *Research Policy* **32**(2), 333–50.

Gimeno, J., Folta, T.B., Cooper, A.C. and Woo, C.Y. (1997). Survival of the fittest? Entrepreneurial human capital and the persistence of underperforming firms. *Administrative Science Quarterly* **42**(4), 750–83.

Greve, H.R. (1998). Performance, aspirations, and risky organizational change. *Administrative Science Quarterly* **43**(1), 58–86.

Greve, H.R. (2003). *Organizational Learning from Performance Feedback: A Behavioral Perspective on Innovation and Change*. Cambridge: Cambridge University Press.

Gulati, R. (1995). Does familiarity breed trust? The implications of repeated ties for contractual choice in alliances. *Academy of Management Journal* **38**(1), 85–112.

Gulati, R. and Sytch, M. (2007). Dependence asymmetry and joint dependence in interorganizational relationships: effects of embeddedness on a manufacturer's performance in procurement relationships. *Administrative Science Quarterly* **52**(1), 32–9.

Guler, I. and Guillen, M.F. (2010). Home country networks and foreign expansion: evidence from the venture capital industry. *Academy of Management Journal* **53**(2), 390–410.

Hagedoorn, J. (1993). Understanding the rationale of strategic technology part-nering: interorganizational modes of cooperation and sectorial differences. *Strategic Management Journal* **14**(5), 371–85.

Hoang, H. and Rothaermel, F.T. (2005). The effect of general and partner-specific alliance experience on joint R&D project performance. *Academy of Management Journal* **48**(2), 332–45.

IMS Health. (2001). *Lifecycle R&D Focus*. London: IMS Health.

Jensen, R. and Szulanski, G. (2004). Stickiness and the adaptation of organiza-tional practices in cross-border knowledge transfers. *Journal of International Business Studies* **35**(6), 508–23.

Katila, R., Rosenberger, J.D. and Eisenhardt, K.M. (2008). Swimming with sharks: technology ventures, defense mechanisms and corporate relationships. *Administrative Science Quarterly* **53**(2), 295–332.

Khanna, T., Gulati, R. and Nohria, N. (1998). The dynamics of learning alliances: competition, cooperation and relative scope. *Strategic Management Journal* **19**(3), 193–210.

Krishnan, V and Ulrich, K.T. (2001). Product development decisions: a review of the literature. *Management Science* **47**(1), 1–21.

Lant, T.K. (1992). Aspiration level adaptation: an empirical exploration. *Management Science* **38**(5), 623–44.

Lavie, D. and Miller, S.R. (2008). Alliance portfolio internationalization and firm performance. *Organization Science* **19**(4), 623–46.

Lavie, D. and Rosenkopf, L. (2006). Balancing exploration and exploitation in alli-ance formation. *Academy of Management Journal* **49**(4), 797–818.

Mitsuhashi, H. and Greve, H.R. (2009). A matching theory of alliance formation and organizational success: complementarity and compatibility. *Academy of Management Journal* **52**(5), 975–95.

Narula, R. and Duysters, G. (2004). Globalisation and trends in international R&D alliances. *Journal of International Management* **10**(2), 199–218.

Oviatt, B.M. and McDougall, P.P. (2005). Defining international entrepreneurship and modeling the speed of internationalization. *Entrepreneurship Theory and Practice* **29**(5), 537–54.

Oxley, J.E. and Sampson, R.C. (2004). The scope and governance of international R&D alliances. *Strategic Management Journal* **25**(8–9), 723–49.

Park, K.M. (2007). Antecedents of convergence and divergence in strategic posi-tioning: the effects of performance and aspiration on the direction of strategic change. *Organization Science* **18**(3), 386–402.

PhRMA. (2012). *Pharmaceutical Research and Manufacturers of America, Industry Profile 2012*. http://www.phrma.org/sites/default/files/159/phrma_industry_profile.pdf (accessed 15 November 2012).

Pisano, G.P. (1996). *The Development Factory: Unlocking the Potential of Process Innovation*. Boston, MA: Harvard Business School Press.

Pisano, G.P. (2006). *Science Business: The Promise, the Reality & the Future of Biotech Business*. Boston, MA: Harvard Business School Press.

Porter, M.E. (1986). Changing patterns of international competition. *California Management Review* **28**(2), 9–40.

Powell, W.W., Koput, K.W. and Smith-Doerr, L. (1996). Interorganizational col-laboration and the locus of innovation: networks of learning in biotechnology. *Administrative Science Quarterly* **41**(1), 116–45.

Roijakkers, N. and Hagedoorn, J. (2006). Inter-firm R&D partnering in pharmaceutical biotechnology since 1975: trends, patterns, and networks. *Research Policy* **35**(3), 431–46.

Rothaermel, F.T. and Boeker, W. (2008). Old technology meets new technology: complementarities, similarities, and alliance formation. *Strategic Management Journal* **29**(1), 47–77.

Rothaermel, F.T. and Deeds, D.L. (2004). Exploration and exploitation alliances in biotechnology: a system of new product development. *Strategic Management Journal* **25**(3), 201–21.

Sakhartov, A.V. and Folta, T.B. (2013). Rationalizing organizational change: a need for comparative testing. *Organization Science* **24**(4), 1140–56.

Schildt, H., Keil, T. and Maula, M. (2012). The temporal effects of relative and firm-level absorptive capacity on interorganizational learning. *Strategic Management Journal* **33**(10), 1154–73.

Schoonhoven, C.B., Eisenhardt, K.M. and Lyman, K. (1990). Speeding products to market: waiting time to first product introduction in new firms. *Administrative Science Quarterly* **35**(1), 177–207.

Shan, W. (1990). An empirical analysis of organizational strategies by entrepreneurial high-technology firms. *Strategic Management Journal* **11**(2), 129–39.

Shane, S.A. and Ulrich, K.T. (2004). Technological innovation, product development, and entrepreneurship in management science. *Management Science* **50**(2), 133–44.

Somaya, D., Kim, Y. and Vonortas, N.S. (2011). Exclusivity in licensing alliances: using hostages to support technology commercialization. *Strategic Management Journal* **32**(2), 159–86.

Studenmund, A.H. (2001). *Using Econometrics: A Practical Guide*. Boston, MA: Addison Wesley.

Tyebjee, T. and Hardin, J. (2004). Biotech-pharma alliances: strategies, structures and financing. *Journal of Commercial Biotechnology* **10**(4), 329–39.

Vassolo, R.S., Anand, J. and Folta, T.B. (2004). Non-additivity in portfolios of exploration activities: a real options-based analysis of equity alliances in biotechnology. *Strategic Management Journal* **25**(11), 1045–61.

Wasserman, S. and Faust, K. (1994). *Social Network Analysis: Methods and Applications*. Cambridge: Cambridge University Press.

Wennberg, K. and Holmquist, C. (2008). Problemistic search and international entrepreneurship. *European Management Journal* **26**(6), 441–54.

Whittington, K.B., Owen-Smith, J. and Powell, W.W. (2009). Networks, propinquity, and innovation in knowledge-intensive industries. *Administrative Science Quarterly* **54**(1), 90–122.

Yamakawa, Y., Peng, M.W. and Deeds, D.L. (2008). What drives new ventures to internationalize from emerging to developed economies? *Entrepreneurship Theory and Practice* **32**(1), 59–82.

Zaheer, A. and Hernandez, E. (2011). The geographic scope of the MNC and its alliance portfolio: resolving the paradox of distance. *Global Strategy Journal* **1**(1–2), 109–26.

Zahra, S.A. and Nielsen, A.P. (2002). Sources of capabilities, integration and technology commercialization. *Strategic Management Journal* **23**(5), 377–98.

4. A technology credit scoring model for the biotechnology industry?

**So Young Sohn, Kyong Taek Lim and
Bo Kyeong Lee**

INTRODUCTION

Development in the biotechnology industry is largely based on the research-intensive small and medium-sized enterprises (SMEs) (Cooke, 2002; Mangematin et al., 2003). Major industrialized nations, such as the United States, England and Japan, are reallocating their investments from information technology industries to biotechnology industries. This change is directly associated with the need to resolve problems of human concern, such as health, environment, food and an aging society (Uzogara, 2000).

Many countries that have recognized the biotechnology industry as a high value-added sector have developed various supporting policies. According to Traore and Rose (2003), biotechnology research and development (R&D) expenditures in Canada increased from CAN$494 million in 1997 to CAN$827 million in 1999. The number of biotechnology firms increased from 282 to 358, a 27 percent growth over the two-year period. The federal government in Germany has started the *Bio Regio* program, a contest stimulating the creation of biotechnology clusters. Among 17 German regions, four winning regions have been supported with a total investment of €72 million (Kaiser and Prange, 2004). Taiwan has also identified biotechnology as one of its strategic industries since the early 1980s. The Taiwanese government greatly contributed to the biotechnology industry, and nearly 100 new biotechnology firms were established between 1997 and 2001 (Hsu et al., 2005). Since 2000, the South African government has also shown interest in supporting biotechnology and has initiated and supported the creation of biotechnological regional innovation centers (BRICs) to help foster industry growth. BRICs have received an initial sponsorship from the government of 450 million rands (US$75 million) (Cloete et al., 2006).

The biotechnology industry relies on the research-intensive sector of life sciences, which requires scientific knowledge, emerging technology, as well as equipment development. Therefore, innovation in biotechnology can be achieved through interaction among various organizations (Mangematin et al., 2003). As Kang and Park (2012) mentioned, this kind of diversity encourages the emergence of new SMEs. However, the SMEs in the biotechnology industry often encounter difficulties due to shortages of internal resources in affording the high costs of innovation and R&D activities. Under these circumstances, a technology credit guarantee funding scheme can help to support those biotechnology companies with high potential technology. For awarding a technology-based credit guarantee, an evaluation process is necessary to select proper biotechnology SMEs.

Sohn et al. (2005) were the first to develop a technology credit scoring model that relates technology factors composed of individual evaluation attributes to the loan defaults of fund recipients. Subsequently, many improved models have been developed and a modified model has been implemented by a Korean government agency. However, a credit scoring model that specifically addresses the biotechnology sector has not yet been developed.

The main purpose of this study is to develop technology credit scoring models that can be used to screen biotechnology industry firms for funding based on their technology attributes. The biotechnology industry is more regulated than others. In the biotechnology industry, industrial biotechnology and pharmaceutical development firms have very different risk profiles than others. Thus, we propose two different models: one for industrial biotechnology and another for pharmaceutical development firms, respectively. We utilize a logistic regression analysis based on technology-oriented, SME-specific and economic attributes for the technology credit scoring model. New technology credit scoring models are proposed to promote the biotechnology industry with consideration of risk management. This chapter is organized as follows. In the next section, we review previously published literature related to our study. In the third section, we introduce the data and variables used for the proposed credit scoring model. In the following section, logistic regression-based technology credit scoring models are proposed for industrial biotechnology and pharmaceutical development firms. In the final section, we discuss our study results and areas for further research.

LITERATURE REVIEW

In this section, we review the historical development of credit scoring models for firms, technology credit scoring models and characteristics of the biotechnology industry including industrial biotechnology and pharmaceutical development firms.

Credit Scoring Models

Scoring is a way to apply statistical modeling to a representative database and to generate a numerical score for each borrower or loan (Stanton, 1999). Altman (1968) was the first to introduce the discriminant-ratio model to the problem of corporate bankruptcy prediction using work capital, retained earnings, earnings before interest and taxes, market value equity, sales and total assets. Ohlson (1980) was the first to use the logistic model for bankruptcy prediction research (Hu and Ansell, 2007). Moreover, many other studies have examined financial accounting variables as predictor variables. For example, Mensah (1983) utilized short-term liquidity ratios, cash flow ratios, long-term solvency ratios, short-term capital productivity ratios, profit margin ratios, long-term capital productivity ratios, return on investment ratios, debt coverage and price-level ratios. Mensah (1983) constructed bankruptcy prediction models using multiple discriminant model and logit analysis. Casey and Bartczak (1985) used operating cash flow ratios to predict which firms would file for bankruptcy and conducted both a multiple discriminant model and conditional stepwise logit analyses using those variables. In addition, Jang and Chang (2008) found the evidence that government financial systems for SMEs have a significant influence on both product innovation and process innovation of SMEs.

However, the usefulness of financial ratio-based business failure prediction models has been questioned (Lussier, 1995). Furthermore, Gilbert et al. (1990) demonstrated that a financial ratio-based bankruptcy model estimated from a sample comprised of distressed firms also performs poorly, suggesting that the resolution of distress is influenced by non-financial factors. There are some studies that have included firm characteristics, such as the sizes or ages of firms, into their prediction models. Westgaard and Van der Wijst (2001) applied the age and size of a firm with financial factors into their prediction model based on logistic regression analysis. Bandyopadhyay (2006) used more firm characteristic variables for a prediction model of bankruptcy, including the age of the firm, group ownership, International Organization for Standardization (ISO) Quality Certification and industry characteristics, as well as six financial ratios. That study employed the logistic regression model to directly estimate the probability of default. Chi and Hsu (2012) suggested a hybrid approach to integrate a genetic algorithm into a dual scoring model (internal behavioral scoring and external credit bureau scoring model) to improve the performance of the credit scoring model. In the proposed scoring model, the authors used various input variables such as borrower characteristics, collateral characteristics, age, revolving balance and outstanding amount of cash cards. Furthermore, a firm's intangible asset can be used for the credit scoring model. In particular, since the value of a high-technology-based company is decided by the firm's technology and intellectual property, the technology credit scoring model can utilize that kind of information. We review the previous studies about the technology credit scoring model in the next subsection.

Technology Credit Scoring Models

With rapid growth of the knowledge-based society, technology competitiveness is considered a key factor and the demand for technological evaluation is rapidly increasing in both private and public sectors. Technology credit scoring models use a number of technology evaluation factors such as realism, capability, flexibility, use and cost and involve the subjective evaluation for each factor based on interval scores; the overall score of the technology is then computed through the addition or multiplication of individual scores (Souder, 1972).

Sohn et al. (2005) were the first to propose a technology credit scoring model that is used to give firms a guarantee for loan only based on their technology. They examined many attributes of the existing technology evaluation models and used factor analysis to resolve the problem of multicollinearity among evaluation attributes. The proposed scoring model considered the four main factors of management, technology, profitability and marketability of technology, and its detailed individual attributes are explained in Table 4.1. A new scoring model was developed by applying forward selection to factors in a logistic model for non-default.

Since the first attempt from Sohn et al. (2005), many advanced technology credit scoring models were introduced (Ju and Sohn, 2014a, 2014b; Kim and Sohn, 2007; Moon and Sohn, 2008a, 2008b, 2010, 2011; Moon et al., 2011; Sohn and Jeon, 2010; Sohn and Kim, 2007, 2012, 2013; Sohn et al., 2012).

The most comprehensive model (Moon and Sohn, 2010) utilizes not only technology-oriented attributes but also incorporates SMEs' characteristics and economic conditions.

Technology-oriented Attributes

In most cases of technology assessment, the following four areas are considered: management ability of the chief executive officer (CEO); the

Table 4.1   Technological attributes for scorecard

Factor	Abbrev.		Attribute	Scale
Management	KMA	v1	Knowledge management	5
	TEPS	v2	Technology experience	5
	MAS	v3	Management ability	5
	FSS	v4	Fund supply	5
	HRS	v5	Human resource	5
Technology	ETDS	v6	Environment of technology development	5
	OTDS	v7	Output of technology development (e.g., patents, certifications)	5
	NTS	v8	New technology development	5
	TSS	v9	Technology superiority	10
	TCS	v10	Technology commercialization potential	10
Marketability	MPS	v11	Market potential	5
	MCS	v12	Market characteristic	5
	PCS	v13	Product competitiveness	10
Profitability	SPS	v14	Sales schedule	10
	ASS	v15	Business progress (new) or Sales (old)	5
	PFS	v16	Return on investment (new) or Profitability (old)	5

Source: Sohn et al. (2005).

level of technology; the marketability of the technology; and the potential or realistic profitability of the technology (Moon and Sohn, 2010; Sohn et al., 2005). The firms that received credit guarantees were selected based on the results of a scorecard with the 16 summarized technology-oriented attributes, which are shown above in Table 4.1.

Those 16 attributes are the areas of evaluation. In the real application, each attribute is further detailed and assessed with pre-described criteria. Each of these 16 attributes are further detailed and evaluated using four to five measurable criteria in developing the scorecard. Of these 16 attributes, technological superiority, technological commercialization potential, product competitiveness and sales schedule were scaled on a ten-point scale, while the remaining attributes were scaled on a five-point scale. Without empirical data, those attributes that were evaluated on the ten-point scale were considered to be worth twice as much as those evaluated on the five-point scale. However, when establishing a technology credit scoring model, technology superiority, technology commercialization potential, product competitiveness and sales schedule need to be rescaled from a ten-point to the five-point scale in order to eliminate the pre-determined weight.

Table 4.2   Small and medium-sized enterprise-specific characteristics

Variable	Attribute	Explanation
C1	1. Stock market listed	KOSPI, KOSDAQ or other exchange = 1, or not = 0
C2	2. External audit	External audit = 1, or not = 0
C3	3. Foreign investment	Investment by foreigners = 1, or not = 0
C4	4. Professional manager	Separation between capital and administration = 1, or not = 0
C5	5. Venture company	Certified by SMBA[a] = 1, or not = 0
C6	6. INNO-Biz	Certified by SMBA[a] = 1, or not = 0
C7	7. Intellectual property	Having a patent, a utility model or other rights = 1, or not = 0
C8	8. Production stage	After pilot production stage = 1, or not = 0
C9	9. Joint company	Consortium = 1, or not = 0

Note: a.   Small and Medium Business Administration.

Source: Moon and Sohn (2010).

SME-specific Attributes

The nine firm-specific characteristics considered include whether the firm is stock market listed or not, whether it has had an external audit, whether it has received foreign investments, whether it has a professional manager, whether it is a venture company, whether it is an INNO-Biz firm, whether it has any intellectual property, whether it is in the production stage and whether it is a joint company. Such attributes of SMEs are potentially critical when predicting loan default in view of the fact that they represent stability, transparency and reliability of an SME. Table 4.2 lists the specific characteristics of SMEs to be considered for the credit scoring (Moon and Sohn, 2010).

Economic Attributes

Moon and Sohn (2010) considered nine types of economic indicator variables to capture the change in loan default probability according to the economic conditions at the time of the loan application. The nine economic indicator variables used were: the total business environment index; the SME economic situations index; the economic preceding index; the business survey index; the Korean Composite Stock Price Index (KOSPI); the SME operation index; the consumer price index; the

Table 4.3   Economic indicators

Variable name	Economic indicator
Eco1	Total business environment index
Eco2	SME economic situations index
Eco3	Economic preceding index
Eco4	Business survey index
Eco5	KOSPI (Korean Composite Stock Price Index)
Eco6	SME operation index
Eco7	Consumer price index
Eco8	National bond three-year earning rate
Eco9	Exchange rate between the won and the US dollar

Source: Moon and Sohn (2010).

national bond three-year earning rate; and the exchange rate between the won and US dollar. These variables were selected on the basis of a discussion with experts in related fields (for example, Korea Technology Credit Guarantee Fund, Small Business Corporation, Small and Medium Business Administration), along with variables identified by Ceylan and Ozturk (2004). Economic attributes that are continuously changing have a crucial impact on credit risk. SMEs are greatly affected by slight economic changes, in contrast to large corporations based on capital strength and technology. Table 4.3 lists the specific economic variables to be considered for the credit scoring.

Although Moon and Sohn (2010) extended the coverage of predictors, these previous studies did not provide a sectoral distinction for credit guarantee.

THE BIOTECHNOLOGY INDUSTRY

Biotechnology is becoming an important part of the industrial landscape of knowledge-intensive economies (Agarwal et al., 2007; Traore and Rose, 2003). Rapidly changing technology is often the primary basis for competition in the biotechnology industry. Firms have to sustain existing competitive advantages and establish new competencies in order to survive (Sen and Egelhoff, 2000). The biotechnology industry involves various sectors, some of which are more regulated than the others and some of which have very different risk profiles than the others. The biotechnology industry mainly consists of industrial biotechnology, pharmaceutical development firms and plant biotechnology firms.

Industrial biotechnology (also referred to as white biotechnology) is distinguished from red biotechnology aimed at the medical sector, and green biotechnology focusing on genetically modified crops. Industrial biotechnology uses biological systems for the production of chemicals, materials and energy (Soetaert and Vandamme, 2006). Advances in the industrial application of biology depend on the channeling of scientific know-how from the academic world, where this knowledge is mainly accumulated in the laboratories of university and public sector research institutes, into industry (Momma and Sharp, 1999). A firm's knowledge flow includes its geographic location, alliances with other institutions and organizations and R&D expenditures, while products in development and firm citations and patents are indicative of the knowledge stocks of a company (Deeds and Decarolis, 1999). In particular, firms with relatively higher levels of R&D intensity attribute their innovation performances to research-based innovation factors, such as increased research capabilities; research collaborations with universities, industry leaders and other biotechnology firms; and technology licensing.

Moreover, while R&D and scientific breakthroughs drive innovation in industrial biotechnology, market demand plays a critical role in business performance (Hall and Bagchi-Sen, 2002; Wolson, 2007). Industrial biotechnology is an industry in which even successful companies show negative profits over the short to medium term because the R&D costs for new products are so high (Stock et al., 1996). Although biotechnology SMEs possess high levels of technical skills, knowledge and experience, if they are faced with capital problems, firm management and maintenance become difficult.

The ability to access venture capital or government support is critically important to the innovation performance of a biotechnology firm (Hall and Bagchi-Sen, 2007). Generally, industrial biotechnology firms' growth relies on business supporters' and venture capitalists' investment on their innovation projects. Those firms aim for a worldwide market for their innovation. Moreover, initial public offerings (IPOs) enable initial investors to make profits that offset their initial risky investments (Mangematin et al., 2003). Funding from external institutions is a major source of support for biotechnology firms, which spend millions of dollars on R&D (Hall and Bagchi-Sen, 2002). Because it is an important issue for many industrial biotechnology firms to receive support from governments or venture capitalists, such firms need to develop and improve their unique technologies in order to attract investors.

Pharmaceutical development involves the design, discovery, development and marketing of new agents for the prevention, treatment and cure of disease. Pharmaceutical firms rely heavily on scientific research. Product innovation in the pharmaceutical sector is risky and time-consuming, with

R&D costs consuming a large proportion of sales revenues (DiMasi et al., 1991). Moreover, pharmaceutical development represents a high-technology industry in which the product development process is very long, research-intensive and protracted. Innovative projects in biomedical and pharmaceutical start-up firms have been associated with longer development times before product introduction; from six to nine years may be invested before successfully presenting a new product to the market (Green et al., 1995; Quintana-Garcia and Benavides-Velasco, 2004). Thus, it is important not only to acquire unique high-technology skills, but also to create and access other capabilities based on the intensive exploitation of existing technology in terms of management (Mangematin et al., 2003).

This innovation process in pharmaceutical technology leads to the competition and commercialization potential that are becoming increasingly important to high-technology companies (Kasch and Dowling, 2008). To develop technologies for the creation of a successful business in the pharmaceutical industry, a CEO's professional knowledge and experience and employees with knowledge of the pharmaceutical field are important. A CEO's prior experience, from industry exposure to industry-specific problems and solutions, for example, can affect his or her strategic decisions (Brockmann and Simmonds, 1997; Gunz and Jalland, 1996). In the pharmaceutical industry, a CEO's prior experience will enable early collaboration through reduced articulation uncertainty (Katila and Mang, 2003). Moreover, to help foster success in the pharmaceutical industry, many of the founders tend to hire people who have a background similar to their own (Lynskey, 2006).

During the 1990s, the red/green biotechnology distinctions began to dominate media coverage, public perception and regulation across Europe. By 1999, medical biotechnology (red) was treated much more favorably than agri-food biotechnology (green; Bauer, 2005), which refers to the color of plants and has become a metonymy for new crops and foods containing genetically modified ingredients. Green biotechnology is reportedly more risky and less beneficial than red biotechnology (Wenzel, 2006). In addition, capturing the full potential of green biotechnology, especially regarding quality improvement of output traits, is limited because of uncertain regional markets and limited access to food applications. Because of the limitation of marketability, food application and profitability, demand for technology credit scoring for green technology is limited. Thus, our study focuses on development of technology credit scoring for industrial and pharmaceutical biotechnology, distinguishing their special characteristics in terms of four attributes, that is, management, technology, marketability and profitability introduced above.

These characteristics play important roles as evaluation elements on lending decisions to biotechnology-based SMEs. Although they are known to have effects on business success, existing studies do not examine these factors in terms of prediction of loan default for biotechnology firms. In summary, pharmaceutical firms need more time to develop new products and they also wait for a long test period to confirm safety compared with industrial biotechnology firms. They need access to a continuous fund supply that is part of technology-oriented attributes to develop the new products. They also need to manage their knowledge during long-term R&D. Thus, management ability in fund supply and knowledge management can be considered important attributes. On the other hand, because the customers of industrial biotechnology firms are chemical, materials and energy firms, they require high-technology competitiveness and marketability in technology-oriented attributes. Therefore, important technology-oriented attributes will be different in each group. Based on the inference, we set up the hypothesis as follows.

Hypothesis: 'Management of technology'-oriented attributes would be associated with default of the technology-based loan of pharmaceutical firms, while technology and marketability attributes are associated with that of industrial biotechnology firms.

This hypothesis needs to be tested with consideration of individual firm characteristics and economic conditions at the time of loan application. Moon and Sohn (2010) have shown that some firm characteristics, such as whether it is stock market listed or not, if it has an external audit system and economic indicators such as domestic economy, business and operation factors are significant for the prediction of technology-based loan default. In this chapter, we use empirical data in order to test our hypothesis.

DATA AND VARIABLES

In this section, we introduce the data and variables used for the technology credit scoring models for the biotechnology industry. Technology-based SMEs are fundamental for economic growth and national competitiveness. The Korean government established a technology credit guarantee fund to support qualified technology-based SMEs to get a loan based not on typical collateral but on technology (Sohn et al., 2005). The attributes for the technology evaluation for credit guarantee include not only the characteristics of the technology itself but also the characteristics of a firm's owner in terms of the ability of management, level of technology, marketability of technology and technology profitability (or potential). The details are given in Table 4.1. The scale associated with individual attributes indicates the pre-determined weight in the scorecard. The general rule applied is that those firms with a score above 60 are qualified to receive a credit guarantee. The number of people who participated in the technology evaluation varied from one to four and a single score was derived via consensus. An evaluation by a single person is not good practice but has happened due to shortage of available experts to participate in the technology credit scoring.

We were able to obtain data on 3668 accepted manufacturing firms between 1999–2004, after eliminating those cases whose loan terms were still effective at the time of data collection. Those cases were omitted, as these firms could not be used for the estimation of the technology credit scoring model because their default results were censored.

Next, we chose biotechnology firms and the final sample consisted of 566 biotechnology firms, where 109 (19.26 percent) defaulted on their loans. These firms were then classified into industrial biotechnology firms and pharmaceutical development firms. Green biotechnology is usually applied to selection and domestication of plants via micro propagation or the design of transgenic plants. However, those firms included in our database were more associated with agricultural equipment, manufacturing technology or technology processing so we classified them into industrial biotechnology. In summary, we had a sample of industrial biotechnology consisting of 187 firms, where 31 (16.58 percent) of which defaulted on their loans. The rest of the sample consisted of a total of 379 pharmaceutical development firms and 78 (20.58 percent) defaulted.

With this data, we develop technology credit scoring models for industrial biotechnology and pharmaceutical development using logistic regression models. But before directly relating individual attributes to loan default, we apply factor analysis to eliminate potential multi-collinearity among many individual attributes.

Model for the Biotechnology Industry

In this subsection, we explain the exploratory factor analysis used to address potential multi-collinearity among multiple selection attributes and economic indicators. Next, we relate the resulting factors along with firm characteristics to loan defaults.

Factor analysis for technology attributes and economic indicators was performed to resolve the problem of potential multi-collinearity among explanatory variables that may lead to mathematical complication of singular matrices and possible errors in computation (Pasternak et al., 2001). As shown in Table 4.4, we performed factor analysis for technology-oriented

Table 4.4 Result of factor analysis for technology-oriented attributes in the biotechnology industry

	T1	T2	T3	T4	T5	T6	T7	T8	T9
V16	0.96654	−0.06715	−0.07748	0.04004	−0.02925	0.02873	−0.05887	0.00442	−0.05419
V15	0.96323	−0.09832	−0.06576	0.03261	0.00162	0.00948	−0.06937	−0.03581	−0.04756
V1	0.02485	0.91201	−0.04824	0.1007	−0.08257	0.03266	0.07769	0.05177	0.00384
V2	−0.19241	0.86643	0.04268	0.00265	0.09037	−0.0512	0.03367	−0.05786	0.05073
V5	0.01977	0.05658	0.75024	0.06904	−0.10681	0.136	0.21664	0.10889	0.08982
V3	−0.13733	−0.06113	0.73335	−0.09014	0.17544	−0.01453	0.04224	0.02793	0.20072
V9	0.1315	0.12387	−0.10188	0.75379	0.05269	0.06909	0.09709	0.17751	0.19331
V10	−0.26227	0.03095	0.49608	0.52348	0.20291	−0.04495	−0.30166	−0.07427	−0.32166
V13	0.02931	−0.09735	0.04003	0.51776	0.39711	0.36967	0.03179	0.01066	−0.01202
V6	−0.0605	0.33913	0.26633	0.44681	−0.26164	0.12767	0.4339	0.02635	0.00921
V8	−0.0323	−0.02569	−0.01604	0.1712	0.81192	−0.11255	0.15013	−0.03298	0.06624
V14	−0.00534	0.09102	0.23037	−0.11322	0.60472	0.47479	−0.10607	0.11988	−0.05321
V12	0.03065	−0.01491	0.04312	0.15543	−0.03034	0.87154	0.07894	−0.03337	0.0104
V7	−0.11876	0.07466	0.15286	0.0489	0.15473	0.0398	0.87465	−0.0018	−0.0671
V11	−0.03057	−0.00725	0.10487	0.13019	0.0171	−0.01219	0.00494	0.96583	0.01693
V4	−0.11173	0.05573	0.25165	0.12675	0.04702	−0.00565	−0.07373	0.01447	0.88934

Table 4.5   Results of factor analysis for economic indicators

	E1	E2	E3
ECO7	0.9742	−0.17488	0.06798
ECO3	0.91159	0.30134	−0.17517
ECO2	0.86011	−0.02465	−0.38998
ECO8	−0.83828	0.35013	−0.32874
ECO4	−0.16284	0.96829	−0.03177
ECO1	0.0549	0.93144	−0.12507
ECO5	−0.06773	0.79908	−0.499
ECO9	0.04802	−0.0559	0.90139
ECO6	0.14647	0.21744	−0.58551

attributes in the biotechnology industry. As a result of this analysis with varimax rotation, approximately 78 percent of the total variation in the original attributes was found to be explained by nine implied factors: business progress and return on investment (T1); knowledge and experience of the head manager (T2); management skill and personnel management (T3); technology competitiveness (T4); new technology development and sales schedule (T5); market characteristics (T6); output of technology development (T7); market potential (T8); and fund supply (T9).

The result of a factor analysis of the nine economic indicators is shown in Table 4.5, and three factors (E1, E2 and E3) accounted for 86 percent of the total variation. The factors were named as follows: E1 is the domestic economic factor, which is made up of ECO2, ECO3, ECO7 and ECO8; E2 is the business factor, which is made up of ECO1, ECO4 and ECO5; and E3 is the operation factor for the exchange rate factor, which is made up of ECO6 and ECO9.

For the technology credit scoring models of the industrial biotechnology and pharmaceutical development firms, nine technology-oriented attributes and three economic indicators were selected as candidate input variables, along with dummy variables representing the firm-specific characteristics shown in Table 4.2.

RESULTS OF LOGISTIC REGRESSION

In order to discern meaningful results from the logistic regression model for non-defaulting companies, we used the three groups of input variables described in the section on data and variables. In addition, we applied a stepwise variable selection scheme to obtain influential input variables

Table 4.6   *Stepwise logistic regression model for non-default for industrial biotechnology*

Parameter	DF	Estimate	Standard error	Wald chi-square	p value $> \chi^2$
Intercept	1	2.6276	0.4221	38.7543	< 0.0001
T4	1	0.5221	0.2770	3.5526	0.0595
T7	1	−0.5982	0.2623	5.2010	0.0226
T8	1	−0.9866	0.3470	8.0835	0.0045
E1	1	1.9529	0.4422	19.5009	< 0.0001

for the technology credit scoring model for industrial biotechnology and pharmaceutical development firms. For the stepwise selection process, we used a 10 percent significance level ($\alpha = 10\%$) as the inclusion threshold.

According to the results of the logistic regression, three factors from technology-oriented attributes representing technology competitiveness and marketability and one economic indicator were extracted for industrial biotechnology. On the other hand, two technology-related factors representing manager's knowledge and experience and fund supply, one economic indicator and two SME-specific characteristic factors were selected for pharmaceutical development. These results are given in Tables 4.6 and 4.7.

It is of note that industrial biotechnology and pharmaceutical development are not highly influenced by economic indicators except for variable E1 (domestic economic factor) in terms of their loan default. Promising SMEs should focus on developing new technology and, over the long term, they should aim to commercialize such developments independently. Nevertheless, SMEs based on high biotechnology generate most of their profits not through sales, but rather through technology transfer due to the slow speed of product commercialization.

As depicted in Table 4.6, an industrial biotechnology firm scoring high for T4 is likely to have low probability in loan default. Two technology factors, T7 and T8, are negatively related to non-defaulted loans. Firm's characteristics related to T4 play an important role in fostering the development of industrial biotechnology companies. Specifically, in the case of SMEs based on industrial biotechnology, the ability to develop technology represents a firm's competitiveness. Technology development skill generally tends to depend on technology superiority, commercializing ability, technology competitiveness and the environment of the technology development. Thus, improvements in developing technology ability based on these four attributes are required for firm success to pay back the loan.

Table 4.7   Stepwise logistic regression model for non-default for pharmaceutical development sector

Parameter	DF	Estimate	Standard error	Wald chi-square	P value > χ^2
Intercept	1	1.2146	0.2183	30.9549	< 0.0001
T2	1	0.5793	0.1692	11.7276	0.0006
T9	1	0.3910	0.1551	6.3572	0.0117
E1	1	1.0012	0.1860	28.9841	< 0.0001
C5	1	1.1266	0.3865	8.4940	0.0036
C9	1	0.8037	0.4542	3.1312	0.0768

Market potential (T8) is negatively related to non-defaulted loans, indicating that most of the SMEs in high market potential industries may be faced with disadvantageous situations because of the significant participation of larger companies (Moon and Sohn, 2010). Thus, SMEs with great market potential are also faced with a great deal of competition from other SMEs as well as from large firms because of the high entry threshold of the market.

Outputs of technology development (T7) such as patents and certifications have a negative relationship with the probability of non-defaulting on loans. Because most firms in industrial biotechnology are SMEs, small industrial biotechnology firms are burdened by high R&D, patent and certification cost. Moreover, continuous maintenance of the patents and certifications can generate problems in such firms. Although patents and certifications are beneficial for protecting technology, their high cost can contribute to financial problems such as defaulting on loans and even bankruptcy.

Table 4.7 shows the logistic regression model for non-default for the pharmaceutical development sector, where knowledge and experience of the head manager (T2) is positively related to non-defaulted loans. Because the pharmaceutical market is based on high technology, a CEO's knowledge and experience is an important factor in developing high technology. As a result, this experience and knowledge help keep companies competitive.

An outstanding fund supply ability (T9) is also positively related to the probability of firm success. Pharmaceutical SMEs mostly profit not through direct large-scale production, but through technology transfer. Because of this, if small biotechnology firms fall behind in the technology competition, it is difficult for them to assure revenue. Therefore, it is essential in this field to generate funds by developing innovative technology.

Further, status as a venture company (C5) is significantly related to increased probability of non-defaulted loans. If a pharmaceutical firm applying for a loan is certified as a venture firm by the Small and Medium Business Administration, it is more likely that it will receive financial support from governments or venture capitalists. Because their accounts have been audited by an external institution, the certification reflects open and healthy financial management.

In terms of SME-specific characteristics, being a joint company (C9) has a positive relationship with non-defaulting on loans. Pharmaceutical companies not only require substantial amounts of time to develop new products, but also require a high level of knowledge regarding innovation. Thus, it is beneficial for most pharmaceutical SMEs to cooperate with other firms that possess high-quality technology.

The domestic economic factor (E1) has a strong positive relationship with non-defaulting on loans in biotechnology and pharmaceutical development. Industrial biotechnology and pharmaceutical SMEs are more sensitive to changes in economic conditions than large companies. Because reduction of the market has a negative effect on the fund procurement, a limited fund supply has a negative impact on business growth.

For the industrial biotechnology firms, technology factors appeared to be more influential than the other factors, suggesting the importance of high technology. Industrial biotechnology SMEs are necessary to develop innovative procedures in order to reach a high level of technology. Therefore, it is essential to be equipped with high technology and sustain it.

In the case of pharmaceutical development, the logistic regression results show that technology management factors and SME-specific characteristics were the most influential indicators of success. To maintain business, it is necessary that the pharmaceutical technology is managed by a CEO who has sufficient knowledge and experience. Moreover, because most pharmaceutical firms are SMEs, fund supply management, certifications and joint efforts with other firms are important. The results of our logistic regression analyses support our hypothesis. The results also back up the idea that biotechnology firms should be considered differently from the others in terms of technology-based credit scoring.

We compared the performances of the proposed models to that of the existing scoring model (Moon and Sohn, 2010) using receiver operating characteristic (ROC) curves. The C statistic was defined as the area of the ROC curve which was the most widely used in the binary classification model after plotting the sensitivity versus 1-specificity. In terms of the area under the ROC curve (AUROC), the C statistic of the existing model applied to pharmaceutical development firms was 81 percent, while that of the proposed model was 84 percent, as shown in Figure 4.1.

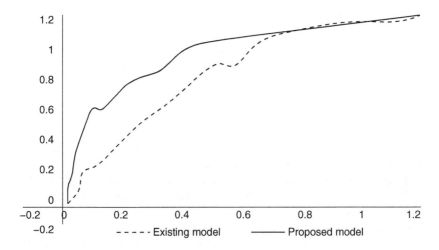

Figure 4.1   ROC curve of the proposed technology scoring model applied to industrial biotechnology

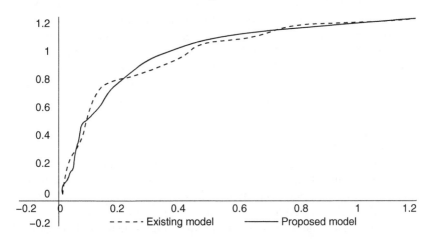

Figure 4.2   ROC curve of the proposed technology credit scoring model applied to pharmaceutical development

The C statistic for the existing model applied to industrial biotechnology firms was 69 percent, while that of the proposed model was 86 percent, as described in Figure 4.2. This demonstrates the superior performances of sectoral technology credit scoring models for industrial biotechnology and pharmaceutical development.

CONCLUSION

The biotechnology industry is an important part of the world economy and is an emergent sector. The roles of high-tech biotechnology SMEs are crucial. However, SMEs are experiencing funding problems despite their high technology. Thus, it is necessary to promote enterprises through various types of funding support. The technology credit scoring approach has been used to identify and support SMEs that have promising technology with market potential. However, a credit scoring model specializing in the biotechnology industry had not been proposed.

In this study, we developed technology credit scoring models for the industrial biotechnology and pharmaceutical development firms using the field data consisting of three groups of attributes: technology-oriented attributes; firm-specific characteristics; and economic indicators. Our research hypothesis was that management of technology-oriented attributes significantly influences the loan default of pharmaceutical firms while attributes of technology and marketability significantly influence that of industrial biotechnology firms. Our analyses confirmed this hypothesis.

According to the results, in order to maintain competitiveness in the pharmaceutical firms, a CEO's knowledge of corresponding technology is essential. Because high-level technology helps pharmaceutical firms sustain continuous growth, pharmaceutical enterprises need to be led by a CEO with sufficient technological knowledge. Additionally, the development of technology and commercialization require substantial time and costs. Therefore, the roles of government and funding institutions in supporting pharmaceutical SMEs are important. Small pharmaceutical development firms with venture certification are expected to benefit greatly from funding. To be certified as a venture company, it is necessary for pharmaceutical firms to increase R&D investment for the development of new proprietary technology. In order to remain innovative and competitive, pharmaceutical SMEs may seek to cooperate with other high-tech firms for a synergistic effect to produce high-quality and convergent technology.

In the case of industrial biotechnology, continuous R&D is required to strengthen a firm's capacity to develop competitive technology. Additionally, it is necessary to establish a business plan for the firm by reflecting on the prospect of future technology in the market. Typically, outputs of R&D activities such as patents and certifications are utilized not only to protect a new technology, but also to increase competitiveness. However, patents and certifications are positively related to the loan default for industrial biotechnology firms. This may be due to high R&D costs and costs involved in preparing and maintaining patents and certifications. Therefore, various monetary support programs to develop and maintain patents and certifications for industrial biotechnology SMEs are necessary. Additionally, the domestic economy is also a significant factor for the loan default for both industrial biotechnology and pharmaceutical development firms. Domestic economic conditions need to be considered by funding agencies when making lending decisions.

The main contribution of our study is suggesting new technology credit scoring models for the biotechnology industry. In the process of developing the model with technology-oriented attributes, we also consider SMEs' characteristics and the domestic economic condition. This study extends the technology credit scoring model in previous works (Moon and Sohn, 2010; Sohn et al., 2005) to the model of specific sectoral industry. Moreover, we compare the causes of default between pharmaceutical and industrial biotechnology firms. Most of all, we expect that our model provides transparency in funding support for the biotechnology industry.

Finally, it is essential for further analyses to use more recent biotechnology data in order to derive a more robust and accurate technology credit scoring model. In this chapter, we were only able to analyse the data available to us. Because the biotechnology industry is constantly developing and rapidly changing, our model should be modified when more recent data becomes available. Furthermore, it is possible to apply various methodologies other than logistic regression to develop a credit scoring model.

In this chapter, we examined the loan default. But neither the aspect of investment success nor innovation performances were considered. The success of technology-based funding should not be monitored simply in terms of loan payback but in terms of contribution to innovation. Currently, innovation performance data is not collected and managed by the governing agency under the Ministry of Finance. In view of the mission of the technology-based funding, the monitoring structure needs to be improved to accommodate innovation outcomes. Upon availability of such data, future studies can explore investment/innovation scoring models that relate individual attributes to investment/innovation performances. Overall these scoring models can be used as the basis for effective technology transfer.

REFERENCES

Agarwal, S.P., Gupta, A. and Dayal, R. (2007). Technology transfer perspectives in globalising India (drugs and pharmaceuticals and biotechnology). *Journal of Technology Transfer*, **32**(4), 397–423.

Altman, E.I. (1968). Financial ratios, discriminant analysis and the prediction of corporate bankruptcy. *Journal of Finance*, **23**(4), 589–609.

Bandyopadhyay, A. (2006). Predicting probability of default of Indian corporate bonds: logistic and Z-score model approaches. *Journal of Risk Finance*, **7**(3), 255–72.

Bauer, M.W. (2005). Distinguishing red and green biotechnology: cultivation effects of the elite press. *International Journal of Public Opinion Research*, **17**(1), 63–89.

Brockmann, E.N. and Simmonds, P.G. (1997). Strategic decision making: the influence of CEO experience and use of tacit knowledge. *Journal of Managerial Issues*, **9**, 454–67.

Casey, C. and Bartczak, N. (1985). Using operating cash flow data to predict financial distress: some extensions. *Journal of Accounting Research*, **23**(1), 384–401.

Ceylan, H. and Ozturk, H.K. (2004). Estimating energy demand of Turkey based on economic indicators using genetic algorithm approach. *Energy Conversion and Management*, **45**(15), 2525–37.

Chi, B.W. and Hsu, C.C. (2012). A hybrid approach to integrate genetic algorithm into dual scoring model in enhancing the performance of credit scoring model. *Expert Systems with Applications*, **39**(3), 2650–61.

Cloete, T.E., Nel, L.H. and Theron, J. (2006). Biotechnology in South Africa. *Trends in Biotechnology*, **24**(12), 557–62.

Cooke, P. (2002). Regional innovation systems: general findings and some new evidence from biotechnology clusters. *Journal of Technology Transfer*, **27**(1), 133–45.

Deeds, D.L. and Decarolis, D.M. (1999). The impact of stocks and flows of organizational knowledge on firm performance: an empirical investigation of the biotechnology industry. *Strategic Management Journal*, **20**(10), 953–68.

DiMasi, J.A., Hansen, R.W., Grabowski, H.G. and Lasagna, L. (1991). Cost of innovation in the pharmaceutical industry. *Journal of Health Economics*, **10**(2), 107–42.

Gilbert, L.R., Menon, K. and Schwartz, K.B. (1990). Predicting bankruptcy for firms in financial distress. *Journal of Business Finance & Accounting*, **17**(1), 161–71.

Green, S.G., Gavin, M.B. and Aiman-Smith, L. (1995). Assessing a multidimensional measure of radical technological innovation. *IEEE Transactions on Engineering Management*, **42**(3), 203–14.

Gunz, H.P. and Jalland, R.M. (1996). Managerial careers and business strategies. *Academy of Management Review*, **21**(3), 718–56.

Hall, L.A. and Bagchi-Sen, S. (2002). A study of R&D, innovation, and business performance in the Canadian biotechnology industry. *Technovation*, **22**(4), 231–44.

Hall, L.A. and Bagchi-Sen, S. (2007). An analysis of firm-level innovation strategies in the US biotechnology industry. *Technovation*, **27**(1), 4–14.

Hsu, Y.G., Shyu, J.Z. and Tzeng, G.H. (2005). Policy tools on the formation of new biotechnology firms in Taiwan. *Technovation*, **25**(3), 281–92.

Hu, Y.C. and Ansell, J. (2007). Measuring retail company performance using credit scoring techniques. *European Journal of Operational Research*, **183**(3), 1595–606.

Jang, W.S. and Chang, W. (2008). The impact of financial support system on technology innovation: a case of technology guarantee system in Korea. *Journal of Technology Management and Innovation*, **3**(1), 10–16.

Ju, Y.H. and Sohn, S.Y. (2014a). Updating a credit-scoring model based on new attributes without realization of actual data. *European Journal of Operational Research*, **234**(1), 119–26.

Ju, Y. and Sohn, S.Y. (2014b). Stress test for a technology credit guarantee fund based on survival analysis. *Journal of the Operational Research Society*, **66**(3), 463–75.

Kaiser, R. and Prange, H. (2004). The reconfiguration of national innovation systems – the example of German biotechnology. *Research Policy*, **33**(3), 395–408.

Kang, K.N. and Park, H. (2012). Influence of government R&D support and inter-firm collaborations on innovation in Korean biotechnology SMEs. *Technovation*, **32**(1), 68–78.

Kasch, S. and Dowling, M. (2008). Commercialization strategies of young biotechnology firms: an empirical analysis of the US industry. *Research Policy*, **37**(10), 1765–77.

Katila, R. and Mang, P.Y. (2003). Exploiting technological opportunities: the timing of collaborations. *Research Policy*, **32**(2), 317–32.

Kim, Y. and Sohn, S.Y. (2007). Technology credit scoring model considering rejected applicants and effect of reject inference. *Journal of the Operational Research Society*, **58**(10), 1341–7.

Lussier, R.N. (1995). A nonfinancial business success versus failure prediction model for young firms. *Journal of Small Business Management*, **33**(1), 8–20.

Lynskey, M.J. (2006). Transformative technology and institutional transformation: coevolution of biotechnology venture firms and the institutional framework in Japan. *Research Policy*, **35**(9), 1389–422.

Mangematin, V., Lemarié, S., Boissin, J.P. et al. (2003). Development of SMEs and heterogeneity of trajectories: the case of biotechnology in France. *Research Policy*, **32**(4), 621–38.

Mensah, Y.M. (1983). The differential bankruptcy predictive ability of specific price level adjustments: some empirical evidence. *Accounting Review*, **58**(April), 228–46.

Momma, S. and Sharp, M. (1999). Developments in new biotechnology firms in Germany. *Technovation*, **19**(5), 267–82.

Moon, T.H. and Sohn, S.Y. (2008a). Case-based reasoning for predicting multi-period financial performances of technology-based SMEs. *Applied Artificial Intelligence*, **22**(6), 602–15.

Moon, T.H. and Sohn, S.Y. (2008b). Technology credit scoring model for reflecting evaluator's perception within confidence limits. *European Journal of Operational Research*, **184**(3), 981–9.

Moon, T.H. and Sohn, S.Y. (2010). Technology credit scoring model considering both SME characteristics and economic conditions: the Korean case. *Journal of the Operational Research Society*, **61**(4), 666–75.

Moon, T.H. and Sohn, S.Y. (2011). Survival analysis for technology credit scoring adjusting total perception. *Journal of the Operational Research Society*, **62**(6), 1159–68.

Moon, T.H., Kim, Y. and Sohn, S.Y. (2011). Technology credit rating system for funding SMEs. *Journal of the Operational Research Society*, **62**(4), 608–15.

Ohlson, J.A. (1980). Financial ratios and the probabilistic prediction of bankruptcy. *Journal of Accounting Research*, **18**(1), 109–31.

Pasternak, H., Edan, Y. and Schmilovitch, Z. (2001). Overcoming multicollinearity by deducting errors from the dependent variable. *Journal of Quantitative Spectroscopy and Radiative Transfer*, **69**(6), 761–8.

Quintana-Garcia, C. and Benavides-Velasco, C.A. (2004). Cooperation, competition, and innovative capability: a panel data of European dedicated biotechnology firms. *Technovation*, **24**(12), 927–38.

Sen, F.K. and Egelhoff, W.G. (2000). Innovative capabilities of a firm and the use of technical alliances. *IEEE Transactions on Engineering Management*, **47**(2), 174–83.

Soetaert, W. and Vandamme, E. (2006). The impact of industrial biotechnology. *Biotechnology Journal*, **1**(7–8), 756–69.

Sohn, S.Y. and Jeon, H. (2010). Competing risk model for technology credit fund for small and medium-sized enterprises. *Journal of Small Business Management*, **48**(3), 378–94.

Sohn, S.Y. and Kim, H.S. (2007). Random effects logistic regression model for default prediction of technology credit guarantee fund. *European Journal of Operational Research*, **183**(1), 472–8.

Sohn, S.Y. and Kim, J.W. (2012). Decision tree-based technology credit scoring for start-up firms: Korean case. *Expert Systems with Applications*, **39**(4), 4007–12.

Sohn, S.Y. and Kim, Y.S. (2013). Behavioral credit scoring model for technology-based firms that considers uncertain financial ratios obtained from relationship banking. *Small Business Economics*, **41**(4), 931–43.

Sohn, S.Y., Moon, T.H. and Kim, S. (2005). Improved technology credit scoring model for credit guarantee fund. *Expert Systems with Applications*, **28**(2), 327–31.

Sohn, S.Y., Doo, M.K. and Ju, Y.H. (2012). Pattern recognition for evaluator errors in a credit scoring model for technology-based SMEs. *Journal of the Operational Research Society*, **63**(8), 1051–64.

Souder, W.E. (1972). A scoring methodology for assessing the suitability of management science models. *Management Science*, **18**(10), B-526–43.

Stanton, T.H. (1999). Credit scoring and loan scoring as tools for improved management of federal credit programs. *Financier (Burr Ridge)*, **6**(2/3), 24–41.

Stock, G.N., Greis, N.P. and Dibner, M.D. (1996). Parent-subsidiary communication in international biotechnology R&D. *IEEE Transactions on Engineering Management*, **43**(1), 56–68.

Traore, N. and Rose, A. (2003). Determinants of biotechnology utilization by the Canadian industry. *Research Policy*, **32**(10), 1719–35.

Uzogara, S.G. (2000). The impact of genetic modification of human foods in the 21st century: a review. *Biotechnology Advances*, **18**(3), 179–206.

Wenzel, G. (2006). Molecular plant breeding: achievements in green biotechnology and future perspectives. *Applied Microbiology and Biotechnology*, **70**(6), 642–50.

Westgaard, S. and Van der Wijst, N. (2001). Default probabilities in a corporate bank portfolio: a logistic model approach. *European Journal of Operational Research*, **135**(2), 338–49.

Wolson, R.A. (2007). The role of technology transfer offices in building the South African biotechnology sector: an assessment of policies, practices and impact. *Journal of Technology Transfer*, **32**(4), 343–65.

5. The dynamics of R&D inertia in the pharmaceutical chemicals industry

Srikanth Paruchuri

INTRODUCTION

Research and development (R&D) is a critical capability for firms in such research-intensive industries as pharmaceutical chemicals (Nerkar and Paruchuri, 2005; Teece et al., 1997). Despite this, our understanding of how such capabilities evolve vis-à-vis the external landscape is still limited. Although firms can change to improve their internal R&D processes, the technological landscape in which they compete is also actively changing. While prior scholars have examined the role of individuals and networks in shaping R&D capabilities (Paruchuri, 2010; Tsai, 2001), we still do not have a good understanding of how these changes are affected by the external environment.

Our investigation is guided by the theoretical argument between organizational ecologists and evolutionary theorists. Organizational ecologists, building on Stinchcombe (1965), originally considered organizations as stable, which is an outcome of selection mechanisms (Aldrich, 1979; Hannan and Freeman, 1977, 1984). Here, the mechanism of evolution for population ecologists is Darwinian, where changes in organizational populations occur only through selection, and those firms that survive this process display the most stable characteristics. Evolutionary theorists, on the other hand, assumed that organizations can and do evolve in response to environmental changes, so that the survivors are those most capable of exhibiting change (DiMaggio and Powell, 1983; Lawrence and Lorsch, 1967; Pfeffer and Salancik, 1978; Porter, 1980; Nelson and Winter, 1982). According to these researchers, organizations adapt to situations to improve their chances of survival and performance. Thus, the mechanism of evolution for these researchers is Lamarckian, where changes in organizational populations occur through adaptation *and* selection (that is, survivors are least stable).

Haveman (1992) reconciled these views by positing that core organizational change is beneficial only in response to radical changes in the environment. While such drastic environmental changes do occur, they are few and far between. Investigations of these competing views in an environment of non-radical or non-fundamental change – a more common context – remain less explored. To test this notion of organizational inertia under non-radical environmental change, we need to see if the rate of change in the core component (for example, R&D capabilities) of an organization matches the pace of change in the environment. In addition, the performance implications of such changes remain to be examined. Thus, my first goal is to explore this aspect of inertia by focusing on R&D within a large chemical firm competing in the pharmaceutical industry from 1980 to 1997, a period of relative stability in the technological environment.

Moreover, to shed further light on the change in R&D capabilities, this chapter also considers both the content and process of change, thereby addressing an existing gap in current organizational change research. Specifically, empirical research examining the process of change within organizations is scarce (Carroll and Hannan, 2000). Even more scarce is the research that examines both the content and process of organizational change (Barnett and Carroll, 1995; Rajagopalan and Spreitzer, 1997). This research requires an exploration of what has changed and the underlying mechanisms of that change. Thus, my second goal in this chapter is to fill this gap by exploring the content and the process of R&D capability change. I specifically examine the processes of change in two steps. First, I explore the role of inventors who are new to the organization's research and inventors who are embedded in organizational routines in bringing about changes in generating and sourcing knowledge. Second, I explore the process of assimilation of new inventors into organizational knowledge networks through their collaborations with inventors embedded in organizational routines.

RESEARCH AND DEVELOPMENT: A CORE COMPONENT IN THE PHARMACEUTICAL CHEMICALS INDUSTRY

The chemicals industry is one of the most important manufacturing industries that contribute heavily to the GDP of the United States. In 1993, the chemicals industry contributed 2.1 percent of the US GDP and about 11 percent of the total product of all manufacturing companies (Aboody and Lev, 2001). According to the American Chemistry Council (2004), chemicals are a $450 billion industry. Further, the chemicals industry employs over a million people and indirectly influences 36 million people who work in businesses that rely on chemical products. Additionally, chemicals exports constitute about 10 percent of US exports, and the chemicals industry was America's number one exporter in 2001. Furthermore, this industry directly influences diverse areas such as health, energy, farming, housing and communications. The focus of this case study is on the pharmaceutical chemicals industry.

The pharmaceutical chemicals industry has been a heavily research-driven industry. In fact, formal industrial R&D laboratories were first established by chemicals firms in the nineteenth century. Today, the industry has already developed more than 70000 different chemical substances generated by over a century of research (Gross, 1999). All the large firms in the chemicals industry, such as Air Products, Dow Chemical, DuPont, Union Carbide and so on, are known to have huge R&D departments. According to the National Science Foundation's (1996) Science and Engineering Indicators, the chemicals industry spent $16.7 billion on research, accounting for about 17 percent of the total non-federal research spending in the United States in 1993. This increased to around $29 billion by 2003. The chemicals industry employs more than 90000 people in research, and chemicals industry scientists account for one in seven patents filed in the United States (American Chemistry Council, 2004). This industry is heavily knowledge-oriented, and 43 percent of all workers in the industry are some sort of knowledge worker (American Chemistry Council, 2004). Further, firms in this industry are known by the innovations they have generated, and R&D thus forms a core component of these firms.

ORGANIZATIONAL INERTIA OR CHANGE IN R&D OF THE DOW CHEMICAL COMPANY

Dow Chemical was started by Herbert H. Dow on 18 May 1897 based on a plan to manufacture and sell bleach on a commercial scale (Whitehead, 1968). Soon after that, Dow diversified into agricultural chemicals in 1906. Over time, Dow diversified into multiple areas, and now supplies more than 3500 products to customers in 183 countries. The company has 180 manufacturing facilities in more than 37 countries. Its sales exceeded $33 billion, and it employed more than 46000 people in 2003.

R&D has been the primary driver of the expansion of firm business. Dow initiated a crash research program as early as 1915 and established its first basic research laboratory in 1919 (Brandt, 1997; Whitehead, 1968). Today, Dow is one of the big chemicals firms that spends large amounts of money on R&D and generates a large number of innovations. Specifically,

Dow spent around one billion dollars on R&D on average in each of the years from 1990 to 2004.[1] This annual R&D amount accounts for about 6 percent of the whole chemicals industry's annual R&D expenditure during that period. This emphasis on R&D has been a tradition of Dow Chemical right from its inception (Whitehead, 1968). The founder Herbert Dow was a researcher himself who was granted one of his initial patents in 1891. He understood the importance of research, and inculcated it into the organizational culture, as pointed out by senior Dow official Larry Wright: 'What made Dow a great company from the beginning was its culture of striving for innovation and improvement . . . the heritage that the founder gave us' (Brandt, 1997, p. 579).

Dow not only has a culture that values innovation, but R&D has been a core task of Dow Chemical. The importance of R&D can be seen from the Dow values statement espoused by Chief Executive Officer (CEO) Popoff in 1994 that 'We live our values by discovering science and developing technology' (Brandt, 1997, p. 603). The inclusion of a statement about innovation in Dow's core values statement also reflects the importance given to R&D (Brandt, 1997, p. 602). Further, the R&D department also holds large power in the firm, as reflected in the statement by another top ranking Dow employee, Mac Pruitt: 'Dow Chemical has been dominated primarily by research and development; they held the power in the company for many years' (Brandt, 1997, p. 579).

CONTENT OF CHANGE: LEADING, FOLLOWING OR INERTIA?

I examine how this core component of Dow Chemical changed (or not) over time with respect to the changes in the environment. The main function of R&D is to generate innovation. Innovation activities involve people and machinery, and their sequences are stored in the form of organizational routines (Nelson and Winter, 1982). These routines are also the mechanisms of continuity in organizations over time. The current innovation activities of the organization can be predicted by examining the activities of the organization in the recent past. Further, innovations are generated in the same areas in which the organization generated innovations in earlier periods (Helfat, 1994). However, organizations could change the focus of research and generate innovations in different areas. The changes in research focus on different areas constitute organizational change akin to the change in focus on different markets served by an organization (Singh et al., 1986).

Organizational ecologists posit that organizations cannot change the focus faster than changes occur in the environment. In contrast, adaptation theorists posit that some organizations can lead the changes in the environment; thus changes in the organization and environment could occur simultaneously (Nelson and Winter, 1982; Pfeffer and Salancik, 1978). Specifically, Pfeffer and Salancik (1978) posit that a leader who controls critical resources has the power required to lead changes in the environment. In the context of the chemicals industry, Dow Chemical, whose average annual research budget hovered around a billion dollars for the last decade and constituted about 6 percent of the chemicals industry's R&D budget, could be one of those leaders that could lead changes in the industry. If Dow Chemical is one of the innovation leaders in the chemicals industry, then Dow Chemical should lead the change in the chemicals industry. If this is true, then I expect that:

Hypothesis 1a: The changes in the research focus on different areas in the firm occur simultaneously with or before the changes in the research focus on different areas in the environment.

In contrast, if Dow Chemical is not an innovation leader but still responds to changes in the environment, then I expect that:

Hypothesis 1b: The changes in research focus in the organization will lag the changes in the environment.

However, if the R&D of Dow Chemical is an inertial component and does not respond to any changes in the environment, then I expect that:

Hypothesis 1c: The organizational changes in focus, if any, will be unrelated to either the concurrent or lagged environmental changes.

The other face of R&D function involves knowledge sourcing activities (Cohen and Levinthal, 1990), which are also carried out in routines (Nelson and Winter, 1982). Population ecologists posit that a focus on different areas of knowledge sourcing activities, similar to innovation activities, cannot change faster than the changes in the focus on different areas by the environment. However, an organization could be a leader in initiating these changes (Pfeffer and Salancik, 1978). If Dow Chemical is one of the leaders in the chemicals industry, I expect to see that:

Hypothesis 2a: The changes in the sourcing from different areas by the firm occur simultaneously or faster than the changes in the environment.

On the other hand, if Dow Chemical is not a leader but still responds to changes in environmental sourcing, then I expect that:

Hypothesis 2b: The changes in the organizational sourcing from different areas will lag the changes in sourcing by firms in the environment.

However, if Dow Chemical is inertial and does not respond to any changes in the environment, then I expect that:

Hypothesis 2c: The organizational changes in sourcing, if any, will be unrelated to either the concurrent or lagged changes in sourcing in the environment.

PERFORMANCE IMPLICATIONS

Organizational ecologists posit that there are detrimental performance implications when organizations change as fast as or faster than the environment (Hannan and Freeman, 1977, 1989). In contrast, adaptation theorists posit that organizations could change to adapt to or lead environmental changes (DiMaggio and Powell, 1983; Nelson and Winter, 1982; Pfeffer and Salancik, 1978). In fact, they propose that organizations should adapt or lead changes in the environment to improve their performance. If Dow Chemical turns out to be a non-inert organization, then I will be able to examine the performance implications to test which of these competing hypotheses holds. Thus, if assumption of inertia is apt then I expect to find that:

Hypothesis 3a: Dow Chemical performs poorly.

Alternatively, if the assumption of inertia is inappropriate then I expect to find that:

Hypothesis 3b: Dow Chemical performs well.

PROCESS OF CHANGE

Carriers of Change

Inventors carry out the innovation activities within the firm and form a significant part of the organizational innovation routines (Nelson and

Winter, 1982). Further, inventors are part of knowledge networks within and outside their firms, and the interaction of the inventors in those networks leads to the generation and transfer of knowledge (Allen and Cohen, 1969; Zucker et al., 1997). Thus, inventors are critical components of knowledge transfer mechanisms between and among different firms, and are causes of localization of knowledge in some geographic areas (Almeida and Kogut, 1999; Saxenian, 1990). Dow has historically accorded high importance to its inventors. For example, Dow Chemical had the R&D director report directly to the CEO when many firms did not even have an R&D division in the late 1930s (Brandt, 1997, p. 215).

The inventors within the knowledge network of the firm are embedded in and form a critical part of the established routines, and tend to carry out the R&D activities as they did before (Nelson and Winter, 1982). However, inventors who are new to the firm are not assimilated into the organizational routines and could allow a firm to move into new areas. These inventors influence R&D in two ways. First, they influence the sourcing of knowledge from new areas. Inventors who are embedded in firm routines and networks search locally to generate knowledge (Cyert and March, 1963; Nelson and Winter, 1982). This means that the inventors embedded in the firm routines source knowledge from the same domains as before. Inventors who are new to the firm, in contrast, are not embedded in the knowledge networks of the firm and hence could source knowledge from new domains. Second, inventors who are new to the firm could also generate knowledge in new areas. Inventors embedded in the organizational routines carry out their activities using the same methods and tools and generate innovations in the same areas (Nelson and Winter, 1982). Conversely, inventors who are new to the firm are less embedded in organizational routines, use methods different from the existing ones and bring change in the innovation activities leading to innovations in new areas. Thus, inventors who are new to the firm act as agents of change while inventors embedded in organizational routines lead to organizational inertia. Specifically, I expect that:

Hypothesis 4: The inventors who are new to the firm source more knowledge from areas new to the firm than inventors who are already embedded within the firm routine.

Similarly, I expect that:

Hypothesis 5: Inventors who are new to the firm generate more knowledge in areas new to the firm than inventors who are already embedded within the firm routines.

Assimilation of New Inventors into the Firm

Inventors new to the firm, who act as carriers of change, do not work as a separate unit. Rather, they are assimilated into the organizational network by collaborations with inventors embedded in the firm routines. Inventors who are new to the firm collaborate with inventors embedded within the firm routines to leverage the knowledge of the firm (Bouty, 2000; Levitt and March, 1988). These embedded inventors are part of the innovation routines of the firm, and hence hold tacit and explicit knowledge of the firm. Further, knowledge networks of embedded inventors underlie innovating routines of the firm (Nelson and Winter, 1982). However, various firm inventors are differently embedded and hold different amounts of organizational routine knowledge. Thus, inventors who are new to the firm seek some embedded inventors more than others to collaborate. I examine the knowledge networks of embedded inventors to understand the collaborations of inventors who are new to the firm with inventors embedded in organizational routines. I specifically examine the status and spanning of structural holes by embedded inventors.

Status is perceived as a signal of quality (Podolny, 1993). The high status inventors are considered to have better knowledge to generate innovations. Thus, these high status embedded inventors are perceived as holding significant parts of the innovating routines. Further, these high status embedded inventors are connected to other high status embedded inventors (Bonacich, 1987) and are perceived to have access to most others in the organizations. Thus, these inventors can quickly access different parts of the organizational routines. These two factors induce inventors who are new to the firm to collaborate with high status embedded inventors. For example, Podolny and Stuart (1995) showed that the status of firms influences the decision of other firms to enter the niche. Similarly, I expect that:

Hypothesis 6: The rate of collaboration of inventors new to the firm with embedded inventors increases with an increase in the status of the embedded inventors.

The other aspect of access concerns the structural holes in the organizational knowledge network (Burt, 1992). Inventors who span structural holes join the inventors who are otherwise not connected. These embedded inventors spanning structural holes thus become the linchpins in the knowledge networks of the firm. Further, these inventors have more and richer information than other embedded inventors as they are optimizing on their ties. Inventors who are new to the firm perceive these embedded inventors spanning structural holes as critical components of the organizational routines. Thus, I expect that:

Hypothesis 7: The rate of collaboration of inventors new to the firm with embedded inventors increases with an increase in the spanning of structural holes by embedded inventors.

RESEARCH DESIGN

Research Context

To investigate these hypotheses, I study changes in the R&D of Dow Chemical between 1980 and 1997. The year 1978 marks the beginning of the modern era at Dow (Brandt, 1997). Specifically, the recession of 1975 and the oil crisis were ending. This was also the time when Zoltan Merszei, who took the post of CEO and president in 1976, was forced to quit in 1978 because of poor management style and poor performance of the firm. To account for any pressures that might remain from these changes, I analyse the firm starting from 1980 to 1997. I end in 1997 because the strategy of the firm significantly changed starting in 1998. The firm, which focused on internal development until 1997, changed to a strategy of acquiring other firms in 1998 (McCoy, 2001). More importantly, this is also a period when there were no radical changes in the pharmaceutical industry. Specifically, the only radical change that took place prior to the observation period was the biotechnology revolution that started in the early 1950s. The next major step in this field was the invention of recombinant DNA by Cohen and Boyer in 1974. But many pharmaceutical and biotechnology firms had already started reacting to this technology by the early 1980s (Powell et al., 1996).

To examine the changes in the focus on different areas of research in Dow Chemical and the environment of Dow, I use patent data. Patents represent quantifiable and discrete innovations. Further, patenting is an important mechanism of protecting intellectual property rights in the chemicals industry. Thus, chemicals firms tend to patent all their innovations (Levin et al., 1987). Patents are classified into different three-digit technological classes by the United States Patents and Trademarks Office (USPTO). These classes represent technological areas of research. This classification system is similar to the Standard Industrial Classification (SIC) where a firm's operations are classified into different markets and industries. The changes in the relative significance paid to different areas can be examined from changes in patenting in and sourcing from different technological classes. This is similar to identifying changes in market focus by considering the sales in different markets.

DEFINING THE ENVIRONMENT OF DOW CHEMICAL

To be able to test the hypothesis of organizational inertia, I have to identify the relevant environment with respect to which changes in the organization are compared. One way of identifying the environment of the firm is to consider all of the firms in the same markets. This selection, however, leaves out many organizations such as research organizations and non-profit organizations that are doing research in the same areas. Since I am concerned with the research efforts of organizations, I consider all the firms that have generated innovations in the areas of the focal firm. But this selection raises an issue: Dow Chemical patented in more than 300 of the about 400 classes. This criterion includes almost all of the firms that ever patented in the environment; hence this would not be the appropriate environment.

To find a more appropriate environment, I computed the ratio of patents in the top ten classes to the overall number of patents filed by Dow Chemical during the period 1978 to 1997. The top ten classes accounted for 46 percent of the total patents. I defined the environment as consisting of the firms whose patents in the top ten Dow Chemical classes account for about 40 percent of their total patents;[2] 9789 entities satisfied this criterion. The validity of this criterion can be seen from the firms selected, which include all the known chemicals firms such as DuPont, American Home Products and so on. I have considered the patenting of all these firms in various technological areas as the environmental changes in research focus. There are a total of 4049 technological classes, most of which appear in multiple years.

To examine the hypothesis of organizational inertia in sourcing, I use information about the prior art listed on patents. Prior art represents the building blocks of the patent (Fleming, 2001). I analyse the change in sourcing by examining the sourcing of the 'prior art' citations from different technological classes. The environment consists of the same set of firms as the earlier analysis. Thus, I consider sourcing from different technological areas of all these firms as constituting environmental changes in sourcing. There are a total of 5981 technological classes from which knowledge was sourced, many of which appear in multiple years.

To examine the hypothesis about the performance implications of change, I further refined the sampling. Specifically, I included only those firms in the environment that have at least 50 patents[3] in their patent portfolio. The reason for including this minimum cumulative patenting criterion is to ensure that the performance of Dow Chemical is matched with the firms that have research programs rather than with firms that might have randomly generated some patents. This yielded a total of 279 firms.

ANALYTICAL TECHNIQUES AND DEPENDENT VARIABLES

Content of Change

To examine the hypothesis of change in knowledge generation, I examine the patenting of the organization and compare it with patenting in the environment. More specifically, I examine the patenting of the organization in the classes in which entities in the environment patented. That is, the risk set for the analysis consists of all technology classes in which entities in the environment have patented during 1980 to 1997. The dependent variable is the number of patents generated by Dow Chemical in each of these classes. Because this is a count variable, the family of Poisson models are more suited than the regressions based on the assumption of normal distribution of data. However, since the data can consist of over-dispersion, I use the negative binomial model, which takes into account this over-dispersion (Cameron and Trivedi, 1998). Further, some of the classes are repeated in several years. Thus, these observations are not independent of each other. This correlation among different observations decreases the variance of the estimates and makes the covariates more significant. To account for this, I use the generalized estimation equation method (White, 1980).

There is one additional issue with the data. Since the risk set consists of all of the classes in which the firms in the environment patented, there are some classes in which Dow Chemical never patented. So the value of the dependent variable for these classes is always zero. Thus, this creates two sets of classes: one in which Dow Chemical patented at some point and the other in which Dow Chemical never patented. The negative binomial regressions do not distinguish between these two sets. Zero-inflated negative binomial (ZINB) regression models account for this difference. However, I have to examine the appropriateness of using these ZINB models over negative binomial models for the data. The fit of models to the data can be examined by the Vuong statistic (Vuong, 1989). If the test statistic is positive and significant, it indicates that ZINB models are better suited than negative binomial regressions. If the test statistic is negative and significant, it indicates that negative binomial models are better suited than ZINB models.

To examine the hypothesis of organizational inertia in sourcing, I use a similar analytical technique as the above. The risk set consists of all the classes from which firms in the environment sourced their prior art. The dependent variable is the number of 'prior arts' citations sourced from these classes by the firm. The data structure for sourcing is similar to the above data structure and, hence, I examine the Vuong statistic to choose between the ZINB and negative binomial models (Vuong, 1989).

Performance Implications

Earlier researchers have typically used survival or economic performance to examine performance implications. Since I am examining the changes within a unit, these measures are not the most appropriate, as they are influenced by processes beyond the core component of the firm. The more appropriate performance measure for R&D is the patent citations (Podolny and Stuart, 1995; Trajtenberg, 1990). The more an innovation is used to generate other innovations, the more impact it is perceived to have on development of knowledge. Thus, the more citations the firm receives, the better the performance of the firm's R&D. I measure the performance variable as the number of citations received by the firm on all of its patents in each year. Since this is a count measure, I use the distribution of Poisson family. However, considering the assumption in Poisson models of mean equal to variance, I use negative binomial regression that relaxes this restrictive assumption (Cameron and Trivedi, 1998).

Carriers of Change

To examine the hypothesis that the new inventors act as carriers of change by patenting in new areas, I coded whether each patent is in a class in which Dow Chemical had not patented in the five years prior to the patent.[4] Thus, the value of the dependent variable is coded as one when the patent falls in a new area and zero when it falls in one of the prior classes. I use the logistic regression to analyse the probability that the patent falls in a new area.

To examine the hypothesis that the inventors new to the firm act as carriers of change by sourcing from new areas, I counted the number of new areas from which 'prior art' citations are sourced. Specifically, I coded whether each 'prior art' citation of a patent is sourced from an area in which Dow Chemical had sourced in the five years prior to the focal patent. If the citation is sourced from one of the earlier classes, then it is coded as zero; otherwise, it is coded as one. The dependent variable is the number of new areas from which the prior art is sourced on each patent. To account for the over-dispersion in the data, I use the negative binomial model specification to analyse the data. Further, since the same areas appear in multiple years, I also use the generalized estimation equation method to estimate the correct standard errors based on the areas (White, 1980).

Collaborations by New Inventors

To examine the hypotheses that the rate of collaboration of new inventors increases with increase in the status and spanning of structural holes of embedded inventors, I examine the productive collaborations that resulted in patents. I counted the number of new inventors on each patent. I identified a new inventor as someone who had never patented with Dow Chemical prior to the focal patent. Since the data on inventors is available from 1975, the left censoring in the data is reduced. Thus, the dependent variable is the number of new inventors on each patent, which is suited for the family of Poisson specifications. I use the negative binomial model to account for the over-dispersion in the data.

INDEPENDENT VARIABLES

Content of Change

The change of patenting in different areas is examined with respect to the changes in the environment. If Dow Chemical is leading the changes in the environment, we should see that the changes in the environment and changes in the organization occur concurrently. I explore this hypothesis by examining the patenting of all the firms that constitute the environment in different technological classes. Thus, the independent variable is the count of the patents generated in different classes by all the organizations in the environment, measured in the same year as the dependent variable. Similarly, I use the number of 'prior arts' sourced by all the organizations in the environment from different classes in the same year as the dependent variable to examine changes in organizational sourcing.

In contrast, if Dow Chemical was reacting or responding to the changes in the environment, concurrent year environmental changes will not be significantly related to the changes in the organization. But the organizational changes will be related to the changes in the environment with some lag. I examine this by using one-year lagged independent variables. Thus, to examine the organizational changes in a particular year, I measure the environmental changes in the prior year and use this measurement as an independent variable in this analysis. Specifically, I use the number of patents that were generated in different classes by all the organizations in the environment in the prior year as the independent variable in the patenting change analysis, and I use the number of 'prior arts' sourced by all firms in the environment from different classes in the prior year as the independent variable to examine the changes in sourcing.

Performance Implications

To examine the performance of R&D of Dow Chemical, I include dummy variables for each of the firms other than Dow. Each dummy variable represents a firm and is coded as one for that firm and zero otherwise. If Dow Chemical is performing better than others, most of these dummy variable coefficients will be negative and significant. Alternatively, if Dow Chemical is not performing well, most of these dummy variable coefficients will be positive and significant. Inclusion of these dummies makes the model a fixed-effects model.

Carriers of Change

To examine the hypothesis that new inventors act as carriers of change, I examine all the innovations generated by the firm. I use the number of inventors new to the firm on each innovation as an independent variable in the analysis. I code the inventors who have patented with Dow Chemical for the first time as the new inventors. While these inventors could be working in the firm for some time before they generated innovation, their contribution to generating knowledge is captured by patenting because of their presence in the chemicals industry where all innovations are patented. Similarly, to examine the hypothesis that the inventors new to the firm are carriers of change in sourcing, I measure the number of new inventors on each innovation in the same way.

Collaborations by New Inventors

To examine the hypotheses that inventors new to the firm collaborate with embedded inventors who have high status and who span structural holes, I measure the status and spanning of structural holes by old inventors on teams that generated innovations. I consider co-patenting as a tie between inventors and use a five-year window to create the network measures. Following earlier researchers, I measure the status of an inventor as a Bonacich power measure, where the beta is set to three quarters of the inverse of maximum Eigen value (Podolny, 1993). I also calculate constraint-based and redundancy-based structural holes measures developed by Burt (1992) using UCINET VI (Borgatti et al., 2002). For each team that generated innovation, I use the average status and average spanning of structural holes by embedded inventors in the team as the independent variables. The hypotheses will be supported if these variables have a significant positive coefficient in the analyses.

CONTROL VARIABLES

In the content of change analysis, I control for the research activities of the organization in the prior years. Specifically, I control for the patenting done by Dow Chemical in the risk set of classes in the five-year window prior to the current year. Since organizations continue to carry out the same activities over time, I expect this to have significant positive or inverted U-shape relation with the current activities of the firm (Helfat, 1994). Similarly, I also control for the previous activities of all firms in the environment by including the prior patenting by these firms. Specifically, I include the number of patents generated by these firms from 1978 to the year prior to the observation of the environmental change. That is, when the independent variable is the concurrent change in the environment, I use the patenting by these firms until the previous year as a control variable. When the independent variable is the one-year lagged change in the environment, I use the patenting by these firms until the year before the prior year as a control.

I use similar controls in the analysis of change in sourcing. Specifically, I control for the sourcing patterns of Dow Chemical in the five-year window before the current year to capture the prior activities of the firm. I also control for the prior sourcing by the firms in the environment by including the number of patents sourced from each class by all firms in the environment up to the year of observation of the environmental change variable.

In the analysis of performance implications of change, I include several control variables to account for factors that influence performance. Specifically, I include the cumulative patents of each firm until the beginning of the current year to account for the possibility that more patents lead to more citations. I also include the cumulative number of internal citations received by each firm until the beginning of the current year to account for the possibility that internal citations might drive external citations. Additionally, I include the number of internal citations in the current year to account for the saliency of the process by which internal citations drive external citations. Further, I also include the cumulative number of citations to account for the quality of the patents generated by firms (Podolny and Stuart, 1995). Finally, I also include a time trend control variable.

In the analysis of inventors new to the firm acting as carriers of change, I include the total number of inventors of each innovation and the total number of 'prior art' citations used to generate the innovation as control variables (Fleming, 2001). In the analysis of new inventors patenting in new areas, I also include the number of new 'prior art' citations used to generate an innovation as a control variable (Cohen and Levinthal, 1990). The logic behind including this variable is that sourcing from some areas leads to patenting in the same or similar areas. Thus, the output will also be in new areas if the 'prior art' was sourced from new areas.

While the several control variables described so far are included only in the specified analysis, the following control variables are included in all analyses other than performance analysis. Organizational size could influence the content and process of change (Baum and Singh, 1994). So I included two size variables, sales and total number of employees, measured in the prior year as controls in the analysis. I gathered this information for Dow Chemical from the Compustat database. Because the changes in the organization could arise from other changes in the organization such as changing emphasis on R&D over time, I included the R&D expenditure of the firm in the current year as a control in the analysis. Another change at the organization level is the change in the CEO (Finkelstein and Hambrick, 1996; Singh et al., 1986; Wiersema and Bantel, 1992; Zajac, 1990). So I include a dummy variable CEO change that is coded as one in the year of the change and zero in other years. Further, since the change in CEO could take time to have an effect on the organization (Finkelstein and Hambrick, 1990), I also include a CEO change clock that is set to zero in the year of the CEO change and is incremented by one each year after that until there is another CEO change (Amburgey et al., 1993). Finally, to control for any trend that might exist over the years in the direction of research, I included a time trend variable as a control. This variable takes on the value of the year the innovation was generated as indicated by the year of patent application.

RESULTS

Content of Change

The descriptive statistics and simple correlations of the variables for the one-year lag and concurrent change in patenting content analyses are presented in Tables 5.1a and 5.1b respectively. The correlation between the two size variables, sales and employees, is high as expected. Results of estimations with only either variable in the models are similar to the ones presented here.

Table 5.2 presents the results of the content of patenting change analysis. The Vuong statistic that examines the better fit of data between the negative binomial and the ZINB was more than 20, and significant for both one-year lag change analysis and concurrent change analysis. This positive significant statistic indicates that the zero-inflated models are better suited for the data. Hence, I present the estimates of the ZINB regressions. Models 1a through 6a examine the one-year lag patenting changes. That is, these models test the hypothesis that the changes in the organizational patenting lag the changes in the environment by a year. Model 1a includes only the control variables. I included the variables prior organizational patenting in model 3a and one-year lagged environmental change in model 4a. Both of these variables have an inverted U-shape relation with the organizational changes. However, when I included both variables in the same model, model 5a, estimates for one-year lagged environmental change become insignificant. To examine if there is a linear relationship of environmental change with organizational change rather than an inverted U-shape, I include only the environmental change term in the analysis in model 6a, and the coefficient is still insignificant. Thus, these results indicate that the changes in organizational patenting are not lagging the changes in the environment. Hypothesis 1b is not supported.

The other hypothesis, Hypothesis 1a, states that the organizational changes occur at the same pace as the changes in the environment. To examine this hypothesis, a similar set of analyses for concurrent changes in organization and environment are presented in models 1b through 6b. The estimates for the prior organizational patenting and concurrent environmental changes entered separately in models 3b and 4b show that they have an inverted U-shape relationship with organizational changes. When both the variables are included in a single model, both variables continue to have a significant inverted U-shape relation with the organizational changes. Finally, I entered only a linear term for concurrent changes in the environment in model 6b, and it is also significant. These results indicate that the changes in organizational patenting are occurring simultaneously with environmental changes. Thus, Hypothesis 1a could not be rejected.

Similar analyses examining the changes in the content of sourcing change are presented in Table 5.4. The descriptive statistics and simple correlations for one-year lagged changes in sourcing and concurrent changes in sourcing are presented in Tables 5.3a and 5.3b respectively. The Vuong statistic is positive and significant, indicating ZINB models are appropriate. The results

Table 5.1a Descriptive statistics and simple correlations for the analysis of one-year lagged changes (N = 4047)

	Mean	S.D.	1.	2.	3.	4.	5.	6.	7.	8.	9.
1. Organizational change	1.34	3.93									
2. Lagged external change	0.03	0.11	0.45	1							
3. Prior org. patenting	0.67	1.82	0.92	0.51	1						
4. Prior external patenting	1.84	2.10	0.24	0.23	0.28	1					
5. R&D expenses	0.80	0.31	-0.04	0.03	0.02	0.14	1				
6. Change of CEO	0.12	0.32	-0.01	0.00	0.00	0.02	-0.06	1			
7. CEO change clock	3.61	2.44	0.04	-0.01	0.02	-0.06	0.15	-0.54	1		
8. Size – sales	1.53	0.40	-0.08	0.04	-0.02	0.18	0.79	0.05	-0.18	1	
9. Size – no. of employees	5.48	0.67	0.03	-0.01	0.03	-0.05	0.29	-0.12	0.32	-0.12	1
10. Time trend	1988.8	5.18	-0.08	0.04	-0.02	0.18	0.72	0.17	-0.19	0.94	-0.36

Note: All correlations with magnitude greater than |0.03| are significant at p < 0.05 level.

Table 5.1b Descriptive statistics and simple correlations for the analysis of concurrent changes in organization and environment (N = 4049)

	Mean	S.D.	1.	2.	3.	4.	5.	6.	7.	8.	9.
1. Organizational change	1.35	3.93									
2. Concurrent external change	0.03	0.11	0.43								
3. Prior org. patenting	0.66	1.80	0.85	0.50							
4. Prior external patenting	1.87	2.14	0.25	0.22	0.29						
5. R&D expenses	0.80	0.31	-0.04	0.03	0.05	0.14					
6. Change of CEO	0.11	0.32	-0.01	0.02	0.01	0.07	-0.07				
7. CEO change clock	3.66	2.45	0.04	-0.02	0.01	-0.05	0.16	-0.53			
8. Size – sales	1.52	0.40	-0.08	0.04	0.02	0.16	0.79	0.04	-0.17		
9. Size – no. of employees	5.48	0.66	0.03	0.00	0.02	-0.01	0.30	-0.12	0.32	-0.11	
10. Time trend	1988.7	5.13	-0.07	0.04	0.02	0.16	0.73	0.16	-0.18	0.94	-0.35

Note: All correlations with magnitude greater than |0.03| are significant at p < 0.05 level.

Table 5.2 *Analysis of organizational change in the patenting content*

Model no.	One-year lagged changes						Concurrent changes					
	1a	2a	3a	4a	5a	6a	1b	2b	3b	4b	5b	6b
External change				7.09***	−0.268	0.120				8.51***	1.38*	0.370*
				(1.63)	(0.424)	(0.093)				(1.55)	(0.769)	(0.223)
(External change)²				−2.73***	0.234					−4.91***	−0.672+	
				(0.660)	(0.204)					(1.06)	(0.473)	
Prior org. patenting			0.578***		0.585***	0.573***			0.547***		0.504***	0.533***
			(0.037)		(0.041)	(0.038)			(0.039)		(0.047)	(0.040)
(Prior org. patenting)²			−0.021***		−0.021***	−0.021***			−0.020***		−0.019***	−0.019***
			(0.002)		(0.002)	(0.002)			(0.002)		(0.002)	(0.002)
Prior external patenting	0.210***	0.617***	0.070	0.249*	0.069	0.066	0.220***	0.611***	0.080	0.221*	0.058	0.065
	(0.059)	(0.128)	(0.048)	(0.112)	(0.048)	(0.048)	(0.058)	(0.128)	(0.053)	(0.115)	(0.055)	(0.054)
(Pr. extern. patenting)²		−0.059***	−0.003	−0.020+	−0.003	−0.003		−0.055***	−0.003	−0.015	0.001	−0.00
		(0.01)	(0.006)	(0.012)	(0.006)	(0.00)		(0.014)	(0.006)	(0.012)	(0.007)	(0.007)
R&D expenses	0.612*	0.574*	0.188	0.498*	0.185	0.195	0.734***	0.374	0.049	0.519+	0.114	0.089
	(0.266)	(0.268)	(0.226)	(0.273)	(0.22)	(0.226)	(0.258)	(0.282)	(0.281)	(0.288)	(0.279)	(0.281)
CEO change	0.208*	0.190*	0.059	0.173*	0.060	0.062	0.132	0.287**	0.071	0.166+	0.074	0.069
	(0.095)	(0.094)	(0.087)	(0.094)	(0.08)	(0.086)	(0.095)	(0.110)	(0.109)	(0.098)	(0.105)	(0.108)

CEO change clock	0.032**	0.030**	0.003	0.030*	0.003	0.004	0.028**	0.033**	0.011	0.036**	0.013	0.012
	(0.010)	(0.011)	(0.013)	(0.012)	(0.013)	(0.013)	(0.010)	(0.011)	(0.014)	(0.012)	(0.014)	(0.014)
Size – sales	-0.415*	-0.087	0.056	-0.409	0.050	0.042	-0.135	-0.071	0.281	-0.321	0.214	0.255
	(0.227)	(0.254)	(0.280)	(0.282)	(0.284)	(0.283)	(0.224)	(0.240)	(0.312)	(0.265)	(0.309)	(0.31)
Size – employees	-0.114	-0.217*	-0.100	-0.140	-0.092	-0.09	-0.210*	-0.094	-0.111	-0.143	-0.116	-0.117
	(0.085)	(0.092)	(0.080)	(0.100)	(0.081)	(0.081)	(0.085)	(0.093)	(0.097)	(0.094)	(0.096)	(0.097)
Time trend	-0.062*	-0.073**	-0.073*	-0.066*	-0.072*	-0.072*	-0.097***	-0.069*	-0.106**	-0.080*	-0.106**	-0.108**
	(0.026)	(0.027)	(0.031)	(0.030)	(0.030)	(0.030)	(0.027)	(0.030)	(0.035)	(0.031)	(0.036)	(0.036)
Intercept	125*	146**	144*	134*	143*	144*	194***	139*	211**	160*	211**	215**
	(52.5)	(55.5)	(60.9)	(61.1)	(61.3)	(61.2)	(54.2)	(60.4)	(71.3)	(63.3)	(71.5)	(71.7)
Wald Chi2	62.0	101.3	849.1	138.5	897.5	867.4	71.37	114.7	698.1	228.7	820.55	817.4

Note: *** p < 0.001; ** p < 0.01; * p < 0.05; + p < 0.10; significance of all independent variables are one-tailed test and all control variables are two-tailed tests. Numbers in parentheses are robust standard errors.

135

Table 5.3a   Descriptive statistics and simple correlations for the analysis of one-year lagged changes in sourcing (N = 5981)

	Mean	S.D.	1.	2.	3.	4.	5.	6.	7.	8.	9.
1. Organizational change	8.65	31.83									
2. Lagged external change	1.21	4.57	0.57								
3. Prior org. sourcing	3.52	12.00	0.88	0.64							
4. Prior external sourcing	12.77	14.57	0.19	0.24	0.24						
5. R&D expenses	0.80	0.31	0.03	0.06	0.08	0.24					
6. Change of CEO	0.12	0.32	0.02	0.01	0.01	0.06	-0.07				
7. CEO change clock	3.61	2.44	0.02	-0.03	-0.01	-0.14	0.16	-0.54			
8. Size – sales	1.53	0.40	0.01	0.10	0.07	0.39	0.78	0.04	-0.18		
9. Size – no. of employees	5.47	0.67	0.02	-0.06	0.00	-0.24	0.30	-0.12	0.33	-0.13	
10. Time trend	1988.8	5.18	0.02	0.10	0.08	0.42	0.71	0.16	-0.20	0.94	-0.37

Note: All correlations with magnitude greater than |0.03| are significant at p < 0.05 level.

Table 5.3b Descriptive statistics and simple correlations for the analysis of concurrent changes in sourcing (N = 5981)

	Mean	S.D.	1.	2.	3.	4.	5.	6.	7.	8.	9.
1. Organizational sourcing	8.60	31.70									
2. Concurrent external change	1.17	4.55	0.56								
3. Prior org. sourcing	3.48	11.93	0.88	0.60							
4. Prior external sourcing	13.41	14.92	0.22	0.23	0.24						
5. R&D expenses	0.80	0.31	0.03	0.06	0.08	0.26					
6. Change of CEO	0.11	0.32	0.02	0.05	0.01	0.17	-0.07				
7. CEO change clock	3.66	2.45	0.01	-0.04	-0.01	-0.12	0.15	-0.54			
8. Size – sales	1.53	0.40	0.01	0.09	0.07	0.37	0.78	0.05	-0.19		
9. Size – no. of employees	5.48	0.66	0.02	-0.03	0.00	-0.11	0.30	-0.11	0.32	-0.13	
10. Time trend	1988.7	5.16	0.02	0.09	0.08	0.39	0.72	0.17	-0.20	0.94	-0.36

Note: All correlations with magnitude greater than |0.03| are significant at p < 0.05 level.

Table 5.4 Analysis of organizational change in sourcing content

	One-year lagged changes					Concurrent changes				
Model no.	1a	2a	3a	4a	5a	1b	2b	3b	4b	5b
External change				0.269***	0.037*				0.256***	0.039*
				(0.047)	(0.018)				(0.047)	(0.019)
(External change)²				−0.001***	−0.000*				−0.002***	−2.8e-4
				(3.2e-4)	(0.000)				(0.0003)	(1.4e-4)
Prior org. sourcing			0.130***		0.121***			0.133***		0.123***
			(0.009)		(0.009)			(0.009)		(0.009)
(Prior org. sourcing)²			−0.001***		−0.001***			−7.9e-4***		−7.6e-4***
			(7.6e-5)		(7.5e-5)			(7.7e-5)		(7.6e-5)
Prior external sourcing	0.049***	0.099***	0.027***	0.032*	0.025***	0.048***	0.090***	0.019**	0.026*	0.017**
	(0.009)	(0.016)	(0.006)	(0.013)	(0.007)	(0.009)	(0.015)	(0.006)	(0.013)	(0.006)
(Pr. external sourcing)²		−9.4e-4***	−2e-4	−2.9e-4*	−1.8e-4		−7.5e-4**	−2.4e-5	−1.2e-4	−5.7e-6
		(1.7e-4)	(8.9e-5)	(1.5e-4)	(0.4e-5)		(1.6e-4)	(7.8e-5)	(1.4e-4)	(8.1e-5)
R&D expenses	0.654*	0.580*	−0.208	0.291	−0.174	1.05***	0.636*	0.145	0.694+	0.204
	(0.297)	(0.305)	(0.364)	(0.392)	(0.372)	(0.297)	(0.326)	(0.386)	(0.379)	(0.397)

CEO change	0.285**	0.228*	0.126	0.131	0.12	0.048	0.194	0.030	0.047	0.017
	(0.103)	(0.10)	(0.122)	(0.149)	(0.124)	(0.107)	(0.11)	(0.122)	(0.144)	(0.123)
CEO change clock	0.025*	0.023*	0.000	0.011	0.000	0.010	0.017	-0.004	0.013	-0.004
	(0.011)	(0.012)	(0.013)	(0.013)	(0.013)	(0.011)	(0.012)	(0.013)	(0.015)	(0.013)
Size – sales	-0.779***	-0.538*	-0.382	-0.833*	-0.442	-0.471*	-0.404	-0.346	-0.704*	-0.402
	(0.273)	(0.299)	(0.323)	(0.377)	(0.326)	(0.272)	(0.299)	(0.325)	(0.360)	(0.327)
Size – employees	0.079	-0.052*	0.135	0.091	0.139	-0.207*	-0.103	0.011	-0.104	0.003
	(0.100)	(0.103)	(0.117)	(0.135)	(0.118)	(0.101)	(0.109)	(0.122)	(0.131)	(0.123)
Time trend	-0.044	-0.060+	-0.020	-0.023	-0.024	-0.092*	-0.074*	-0.051	-0.061	-0.050
	(0.036)	(0.035)	(0.040)	(0.04)	(0.041)	(0.038)	(0.037)	(0.042)	(0.046)	(0.043)
Intercept	91.4	121+	57.6	47.7	5.5	187*	150*	104	124	101
	(73.0)	(70.9)	(81.9)	(96.0)	(83.2)	(76.3)	(75.1)	(85.1)	(93.2)	(86.5)
Wald Chi2	84.2	88.2	532.7	130.5	547.9	75.9	92.5	523.8	123.0	530.0

Note: *** p < 0.001; ** p < 0.01; * p < 0.05; + p < 0.10; significance of all independent variables are one-tailed test and all control variables are two-tailed tests.

Table 5.5   Performance implications of change descriptive statistics and
simple correlations

Variable	Mean	S.D.	(1)	(2)	(3)	(4)	(5)
1. Citation performance	70.66	181.25					
2. Cumulative patenting	178.95	448.44	0.95				
3. Cumulative cites	350.31	1126.16	0.94	0.92			
4. Cumulative internal cites	79.54	314.16	0.94	0.91	0.96		
5. Current internal cites	13.97	46.73	0.89	0.85	0.77	0.85	
6. Year trend	1989.41	5.63	0.25	0.21	0.27	0.21	0.15

Note: All correlations are significant at $p < 0.01$ level; $N = 4691$.

of organizational changes in sourcing with respect to one-year lagged environmental changes are presented in models 1a through 5a. The variables prior sourcing of the firm and one-year lagged environmental sourcing are entered into models separately in models 3a and 4a respectively, and both terms are entered into the same model in model 5a. The estimates show that these variables have an inverted U-shape relation with the organizational sourcing not only in separate models, but also when entered in the same model. Thus, these results support Hypothesis 2b, which states that the organizational changes in sourcing responded to environmental changes.

The results for the concurrent changes in organization and environment sourcing are presented in models 1b through 5b. The prior sourcing patterns and concurrent changes in the environment are entered into models 3b and 4b respectively, and both variables are entered into the single model in model 5b. The estimates show that these variables have an inverted U-shape relation with the organizational sourcing not only in separate models, but also when entered in the same model. Thus, these results indicate that organizational changes in sourcing are also occurring concurrently with the changes in the environment. The two sets of results on organizational sourcing indicate that changes in organizational sourcing are very closely aligned with changes in sourcing by organizations in the environment.

Performance Implications of Change

The results of the negative binomial regression are presented in Table 5.6, and the descriptive statistics and the simple correlations are presented in Table 5.5. The results show that while there are 31 firms whose performance is similar to Dow Chemical's, only five firms are performing better than Dow Chemical in citation rates. Considering the total sample of

Table 5.6   Negative binomial analysis of citation performance

Variable	Model 1
Cumulative patenting	0.002
	(0.0003)***
Cumulative cites	−0.0006
	(4.3e-5)***
Cumulative internal cites	0.0002
	(0.0001)***
Current internal cites	0.0046
	(0.0006)***
Year trend	0.2127
	(0.0027)
Firm dummies	5 dummies are positive and significant
	31 dummies are non-significant
	Others are negative and significant
Log likelihood	−18 510.3
N	4691

Note: S.E. are in parentheses; *** $p < 0.01$.

279 firms, Dow is performing in the top 3 percent (tied for sixth position among 279 firms) or in the top 8 percent (ranked at 22, that is, median of the 32 tied ranks from 6 to 38). Either way, Dow Chemical is among the top 10 percent of the firms in the distribution of performance. Thus, this result along with earlier results of change rejects the assumption of inertia. Thus, Hypothesis 3b could not be rejected.

Carriers of Change

The results of the analyses for new inventors as carriers of change are presented in Table 5.8, and the simple descriptive statistics and correlations of variables in the analyses are presented in Table 5.7. Models 1 and 2 examine the role of new inventors in sourcing knowledge from new areas, while models 3, 4 and 5 examine the role of new inventors in patenting in new areas. Model 1 contains only the control variables, and model 2 includes the number of new inventors on the team along with control variables. The results show that the number of new inventors is only weakly related ($p < 0.10$) to the organizational sourcing from new domains. Models 4 and 5 are step models that examine the role of sourcing from new areas and the number of new inventors on patenting in new areas. The results indicate that sourcing from new areas increases the probability of patenting in new

Table 5.7 *Descriptive statistics and simple correlations for carriers of change analyses*

	Mean	S.D.	1.	2.	3.	4.	5.	6.	7.	8.	9.	10.
1. No. of prior art from new areas	0.81	1.78										
2. Patent in new class	0.02	0.15	0.07									
3. Number of new inventors	0.41	0.75	-0.02	0.07								
4. Team size	2.26	1.32	-0.05	-0.01	0.37							
5. Total prior art	10.26	13.20	0.24	0.02	0.01	0.23						
6. CEO change	0.11	0.31	0.00	0.02	0.02	0.08	0.07					
7. CEO change clock	3.92	2.52	0.01	-0.01	-0.02	-0.09	-0.04	-0.54				
8. R&D expenses	0.76	0.30	-0.03	0.02	0.04	0.25	0.18	-0.04	0.03			
9. Size – sales	1.43	0.38	-0.07	0.02	0.04	0.31	0.22	0.02	-0.17	0.86		
10. Size – employees	5.54	0.55	0.03	0.01	-0.01	-0.05	-0.03	-0.20	0.14	0.34	0.12	
11. Time trend	1988	4.60	-0.07	0.02	0.05	0.33	0.24	0.18	-0.16	0.81	0.92	-0.16

Note: All correlations with magnitude greater than |0.03| are significant at $p < 0.05$ level.

Table 5.8   Analysis of new inventors as carriers of change

	Sourcing from new areas		Patenting in new areas		
Type of analysis	Negative binomial		Logistic regression		
Model no.	1	2	3	4	5
Intercept	373.8***	37.08***	154.2	122.4	88.23
	(84.26)	(84.28)	(294.8)	(304.0)	(305.1)
No. of prior art from new areas				.1386***	0.6196***
				(0.0305)	(0.0944)
New inventors		0.0692+			0.1400***
		(0.0517)			(0.0297)
Team size	−0.1306***	−0.1462***	−0.1071	−0.0779	−0.2965***
	(0.0310)	(0.0314)	(0.0719)	(0.0706)	(0.0613)
Total prior art	0.0806***	0.0811***	0.0076**	0.0016	0.0049
	(0.0021)	(0.0021)	(0.0027)	(0.0059)	(0.0053)
CEO change	0.1328	0.1352	0.7668+	0.7377	0.7019
	(0.1628)	(0.1633)	(0.4624)	(0.4751)	(0.4746)
CEO change clock	0.0014	0.0015	0.0252	0.0312	0.0262
	(0.0156)	(0.0155)	(0.0643)	(0.0666)	(0.0661)
R&D expenses	1.407***	1.388***	1.3996	1.0961	0.9475
	(0.4001)	(0.4008)	(1.0667)	(1.0915)	(1.1146)
Size – sales	0.2838	0.2855	0.3222	0.4327	0.425
	(0.3761)	(0.3734)	(1.3229)	(1.3675)	(1.3664)
Size – employees	−0.2667*	−0.2613*	−0.2161	−0.1837	−0.1427
	(0.1232)	(0.1231)	(0.4573)	(0.4688)	(0.4636)
Time trend	−0.1886***	−0.1867***	−0.0797	−0.0638	−0.0466
	(0.0424)	(0.0425)	(0.1485)	(0.1531)	(0.1537)
Log likelihood	−2633.7	−2632.4	−575.6	−568.5	−554.4

Note: *** $p < 0.001$; ** $p < 0.01$; * $p < 0.05$; + $p < 0.10$; significance of all independent variables are one-tailed test and all control variables are two-tailed tests. Numbers in parentheses are robust standard errors.

areas, and the number of new inventors on a team increases the probability of patenting in new areas. Thus, new inventors not only increase sourcing from new areas, but also increase the probability of patenting in new areas.

Collaborations by New Inventors

The results of the analysis of collaborations by new inventors are presented in Table 5.10, and the descriptive statistics and simple correlations of variables for this analysis are presented in Table 5.9. The average

Table 5.9 Descriptive statistics and simple correlations for collaborations analysis

	Mean	S.D.	1.	2.	3.	4.	5.	6.	7.	8.	9.	10.
1. New inventors	0.41	0.75										
2. Status of old inventors	1.14	1.15	0.34									
3. Efficient structural holes	0.73	0.53	0.34	0.38								
4. Constraint structural holes	0.60	0.53	0.35	0.32	0.71							
5. Team size	2.26	1.32	0.37	0.44	0.15	0.17						
6. CEO change	0.11	0.31	0.02	0.06	-0.02	-0.02	0.08					
7. CEO change clock	3.92	2.52	-0.02	-0.09	0.02	0.00	-0.09	-0.54				
8. R&D expenses	0.76	0.30	0.04	0.27	0.02	-0.01	0.25	-0.04	0.03			
9. Size – sales	1.43	0.38	0.04	0.35	0.01	-0.01	0.31	0.02	-0.17	0.86		
10. Size – employees	5.54	0.55	-0.01	-0.05	0.04	0.02	-0.05	-0.20	0.14	0.34	0.12	
11. Time trend	1988	4.60	0.05	0.35	0.00	-0.02	0.33	0.18	-0.16	0.81	0.92	-0.16

Note: All correlations with magnitude greater than |0.03| are significant at $p < 0.05$ level.

Table 5.10 Collaborations by new inventors analysis

Model no.	1	2	3	4	5	6	7	8
Intercept	145*	137*	34.2	44.4	48.9	56.0	16.5	39.4
	(62.1)	(70.0)	(47.1)	(55.6)	(44.0)	(53.7)	(49.9)	(59.0)
Status of old inventors		0.209***			0.101***	0.125***	−0.340***	0.016
		(0.018)			(0.014)	(0.011)	(0.046)	(0.031)
Efficient structural holes			0.796***		0.730***		0.197**	
			(0.047)		(0.044)		(0.067)	
Constraint structural holes				0.662***		0.592***		0.363***
				(0.033)		(0.034)		(0.068)
Status efficient structural hole							0.342***	
							(0.025)	
Status constraint structural hole								0.114***
								(0.022)
Team size	0.355***	0.422***	0.381***	0.392***	0.349***	0.356***	0.442***	0.394***
	(0.021)	(0.031)	(0.025)	(0.026)	(0.025)	(0.027)	(0.029)	(0.030)
CEO change	0.121+	−0.065	−0.084	−0.051	−0.108	−0.071	−0.108	−0.087
	(0.066)	(0.119)	(0.076)	(0.093)	(0.070)	(0.092)	(0.094)	(0.101)

Table 5.10 (continued)

Model no.	1	2	3	4	5	6	7	8
CEO change clock	0.003	−0.014	−0.023**	−0.016+	−0.024**	−0.016	−0.027**	−0.014
	(0.011)	(0.013)	(0.008)	(0.010)	(0.008)	(0.010)	(0.010)	(0.011)
R&D expenses	0.633**	0.678**	0.426*	0.456*	0.479*	0.488*	0.362+	0.429+
	(0.201)	(0.253)	(0.204)	(0.237)	(0.190)	(0.229)	(0.196)	(0.242)
Size − sales	0.093	−0.235	−0.267	−0.261	−0.316+	−0.330	−0.368+	−0.396+
	(0.251)	(0.298)	(0.179)	(0.210)	(0.177)	(0.213)	(0.214)	(0.232)
Size − employees	−0.190*	−0.177+	−0.107	−0.091	−0.122+	−0.100	−0.083	−0.070
	(0.094)	(0.104)	(0.074)	(0.093)	(0.069)	(0.092)	(0.078)	(0.099)
Time trend	−0.074*	−0.070*	−0.018	−0.023	−0.026	−0.029	−0.009	−0.021
	(0.031)	(0.035)	(0.024)	(0.028)	(0.022)	(0.027)	(0.025)	(0.030)
Log likelihood	−3872.9	−2892.6	−2751.4	−2791.1	−2734.3	−2767.7	−2677.2	−2759.1

Note: *** $p < 0.001$; ** $p < 0.01$; * $p < 0.05$; + $p < 0.10$; significance of all independent variables are one-tailed test and all control variables are two-tailed tests. Numbers in parentheses are robust standard errors.

status of embedded inventors on the team is included in model 2, and the estimates are positive and significant. This result indicates that the rate of collaboration of new inventors with embedded inventors of the organization increases with an increase in the average status of the old inventors on the team. The two types of spanning of structural holes measures are included in models 3 and 4. The estimates of both structural holes variables are positive and significant, indicating that the rate of collaboration of new inventors with embedded inventors increases with an increase in the average spanning of the structural holes of embedded inventors on the team. The two types of structural holes measures along with the status measure are included in models 5 and 6, and the results continue to hold. The interaction of the status measure with the spanning of structural hole variables are presented in models 7 and 8. These interaction terms are positive and significant, indicating that the status and the spanning of structural holes of embedded inventors positively interact to increase the rate of collaboration by new inventors.

DISCUSSION

This exploration of the assumption of inertia is motivated by the paucity of empirical research examining such an important assumption. To examine the differences that still exist on organizational inertia between population ecologists, on the one hand, and adaptation theorists, on the other, I empirically examined an organization in the context in which organizations are supposed to be inertial. I focused on the core component of a firm under conditions of non-fundamental changes in the environment (Hannan and Freeman, 1989; Haveman, 1993). Specifically, R&D is a core component in the chemicals industry because of the importance of R&D for the identity and survival of chemicals firms. The organizational inertia assumption was explored by examining the relative changes in the R&D focus of Dow Chemical with the changes in the environment in a relatively stable period of the environment.

The results of the change of patenting content analysis showed that Dow Chemical was leading the changes in the environment. The changes in the organizational patenting were related to the concurrent changes in the environment, and not related to the lagged changes in the environment. This implies that the pattern of changes in organizational patenting was similar to the concurrent pattern of change in the environment. Similarly, I found that Dow Chemical adapted to sourcing changes in the environment. These results indicate that Dow Chemical was changing concurrently with the environment in both patenting and sourcing. These findings imply that organizations can change and adapt to the environment. Further, I found that citation performance of R&D of Dow Chemical was within the top 10 percent of the sample that I analysed.

These results run counter to the population ecologists' assertion that an organization's core components, which represent the identity of the firm, cannot beneficially change as fast as the environment (Carroll and Hannan, 2000; Hannan and Freeman, 1989). These results show that changes in the core components of an organization do not necessarily have detrimental performance effects when these changes are as fast as the environmental changes. These results also suggest that organizations can develop strategies to gainfully conform to the institutions (DiMaggio and Powell, 1983; Meyer and Rowan, 1977), form mergers (Monteverde and Teece, 1982; Williamson, 1975), form joint ventures (Harrigan, 1985), change top managers (Hambrick and Mason, 1984) and develop capabilities internally (Nelson and Winter, 1982). Furthermore, organizations need not only respond, but could also lead changes in the environment (Nelson and Winter, 1982; Pfeffer and Salancik, 1978).

Another implication of these findings is with respect to the momentum of change. When organizations are in a dynamic environment where change is expected from them, organizational change need not mean a loss of either reliability or accountability. Specifically, Hannan and Freeman (1977) suggest that organizations that are reliable and accountable will gain resources for survival. Thus, organizations become institutionalized in their goals and routinized in their activities, which make them inertial. However, organizational change could be a goal that is institutionalized and activities for change routinized, giving rise to reliability and accountability of the organizational change (Nelson and Winter, 1982). For example, many organizations such as Xerox, 3M and General Electric have not only been constantly innovative in their processes, but have the activities of this change routinized. Earlier research also supports this perspective. Specifically, Kelly and Amburgey (1991) and Amburgey et al. (1993) found that the probability of subsequent change increases after an organizational change. These findings along with the findings in this chapter suggest that the organization that is oriented toward change gains momentum in change, and this momentum in change could reach a stage where the changes in the organization could be as fast as the changes in the environment. Furthermore, this momentum of change need not have detrimental effects on organizational performance. Stated differently, organizations with constant change might be selected in, and static organizations might be selected out.

Exploring the process of change, I found that the inventors new to the firm are the carriers of change in R&D at Dow Chemical. Specifically,

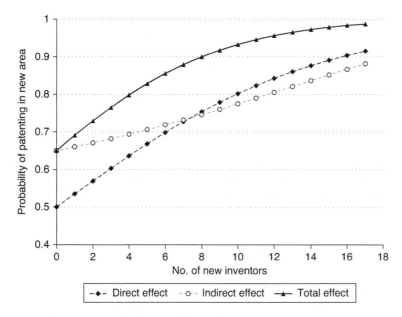

Figure 5.1 *Direct and indirect effects of new inventors on patenting in new areas*

inventors carry out the innovative routines of the firm (Nelson and Winter, 1982). Thus, the old inventors' activities tend to reinforce the prior activities of the organizations. Inventors new to the firm, on the other hand, are carriers of change by drawing from new domains and patenting in new areas. These results suggest that new inventors not only directly influence patenting in new areas, but also influence patenting in new areas indirectly through their sourcing. Specifically, new inventors source from new areas, and sourcing from new areas is related to patenting in new areas. Thus, new inventors influence patenting in new areas directly {probability $= e^{(newinvs*0.1400)}/[1 + e^{(newinvs*0.1400)}]$} and indirectly {probability $= \exp(0.6196*e^{(0.0692*newinvs)})/[1 + \exp(0.6196*e^{(0.0692*newinvs)})]$}. These independent effects and the combined effect of new inventors on patenting in new areas are shown in Figure 5.1.

Finally, I also explored collaborations by new inventors to leverage the knowledge and routines of the firm. Specifically, I found that the new inventors collaborated more with embedded inventors of high status and embedded inventors who spanned structural holes. High status inventors form a significant part of the knowledge networks underlying the organizational routines, and hence provide attractive collaborating options for new inventors (Podolny, 1993). Similarly, inventors spanning structural holes form linchpins of organizational routines and hold critical components of the organizational routines, and hence provide attractive collaborating options for new inventors (Burt, 1992). The results indicate that not only do these two measures directly influence the rate of collaborations by new inventors, but they also interact positively to influence the rate of collaborations. One implication of these findings is regarding the 'gatekeepers' (Allen and Cohen, 1969; Tushman and Scanlan, 1981). Specifically, earlier researchers have examined the position of inventors who act as gatekeepers in the organization in understanding the sourcing of external knowledge. The results in this chapter complement those studies by showing that the inventors who have high status and who span structural holes act as gatekeepers in inducing the new inventors into the organizational activities.

LIMITATIONS AND CONCLUSIONS

This chapter has some limitations that could become avenues for future research. Specifically, I focused on a single organization. While this focus is beneficial to understanding the issue in depth, it also creates limitations on the external validity of the findings. Dow Chemical might have some idiosyncratic characteristics. Though several indicators such as sales, employees and R&D expenses show that it is a firm typical of large and old chemical firms, the idiosyncratic characteristics of change might not be captured by these indicators. Future studies could examine ways to capture these idiosyncratic characteristics among firms and relate these to the concept of inertia. Again, because these findings are based on one firm, I cannot make a statement about organizational inertia in general (Hannan and Freeman, 1984). Rather, I have shown that one organization does not have inertia. However, organizational inertia might be a dominant characteristic in organizational populations.

The second limitation of this study arises from the use of patent data. This data only captures the innovations that are patented. Since the firm and the firms in the environment belong to the chemicals industry, most innovations are patented (Levin et al., 1987). However, this data does not capture the information about inventors who attempted but did not generate innovations. Given that the R&D function is concerned with knowledge creation and sourcing, excluding those inventors who did not generate innovations does not pose a serious threat to the findings of the study. However, future studies could go into the firm and get access to a firm roster of inventors and overcome this issue.

Even with these limitations, this chapter makes a significant contribution to organizational studies. Specifically, this chapter examines a core assumption of organizational inertia that differentiates various organizational theories into two different camps. Because of this assumption, these camps explain the process of organizational evolution differently and have diverging implications for managers. This chapter empirically showed by analysing an organization in depth that organizations can adapt to or even lead environmental changes. Further, this chapter shows that even the core components of organizations, which represent the identity, can change in the context of non-fundamental environmental changes as fast as the environment. Additionally, this chapter empirically explored both the content and process of change, thereby filling a major gap that exists in organizational change research (Barnett and Carroll, 1995; Rajagopalan and Spreitzer, 1997). I hope that these findings lead to a more complete understanding of inertia and the variety of organizational change processes.

NOTES

1. Data gathered from Compustat database.
2. I have used several different criteria such as the ratio of a firm's patents in the top ten Dow classes of their total patents equal to 30 percent and 50 percent. The results for analysis with these different criteria are consistent with the ones presented in the chapter.
3. Other criteria such as 30 and 40 minimum patents yielded similar results.
4. I have also used other time windows such as three and four years. The results are consistent with the ones presented here.

REFERENCES

Aboody, D. and B. Lev (2001). 'R&D productivity in the chemical industry.' Working Paper, New York University.

Aldrich, H.E. (1979). *Organizations and Environments*. Englewood Cliffs, NJ: Prentice Hall.

Allen, T.J. and S. Cohen (1969). 'Information flow in R&D labs.' *Administrative Science Quarterly*, **14**, 12–19.

Almeida, P. and B. Kogut (1999). 'Localization of knowledge and the mobility of engineers in regional networks.' *Management Science*, **45**, 905–17.

Amburgey, T.L., D. Kelly and W.P. Barnett (1993). 'Resetting the clock: the dynamics of organizational failure.' *Administrative Science Quarterly*, **38**, 51–73.

American Chemistry Council. (2004). http://www.americanchemistry.com (accessed 10 December 2004).

Barnett, W.P. and G.R. Carroll (1995). 'Modeling internal organizational change.' *Annual Review of Sociology*, **21**, 217–36.

Baum, J.A. and J.V. Singh (eds) (1994). *Evolutionary Dynamics of Organizations*. New York: Oxford University Press.

Bonacich, P. (1987). 'Power and centrality: a family of measures.' *American Journal of Sociology*, **92**, 1170–82.

Borgatti, S.P., M.G. Everett and L.C. Freeman (2002). *UCINET VI*. Columbia: Analytic Technologies.

Bouty, I. (2000). 'Interpersonal and interaction influences on informal resource exchanges between R&D researches across organizational boundaries.' *Academy of Management Journal*, **43**(1), 50–66.

Brandt, E.N. (1997). *Growth Company: Dow Chemical's First Century*. Michigan, MI: Michigan State University Press.

Burt, R.S. (1992). *Structural Holes: The Social Structure of Competition*. Cambridge, MA: Harvard University Press.

Cameron, A.C. and P.K. Trivedi (1998). *Regression Analysis of Count Data*. New York: Cambridge University Press.

Carroll, G.R. and M.T. Hannan (2000). *The Demography of Corporations and Industries*. Princeton, NJ: Princeton University Press.

Cohen, W.M. and D.A. Levinthal (1990). 'Absorptive capacity: a new perspective on learning and innovation.' *Administrative Science Quarterly*, **35**, 128–52.

Cyert, R.M. and J.G. March (1963). *A Behavioral Theory of the Firm*. Englewood Cliffs, NJ: Prentice Hall.

DiMaggio, P.J. and W.W. Powell (1983). 'The iron cage revisited: institutional isomorphism and collective rationality in organizational fields.' *American Sociological Review*, **48**, 147–60.

Finkelstein, S. and D.C. Hambrick (1990). 'Top management team tenure and organizational outcomes: the moderating role of managerial discretion.' *Administrative Science Quarterly*, **35**, 484–503.

Finkelstein, S. and D.C. Hambrick (1996). *Strategic Leadership – Top Executives and their Effects on Organizations*. Minneapolis, MN: West Publishing Company.

Fleming, L. (2001). 'Recombinant uncertainty in technological search.' *Management Science*, **47**, 117–32.

Gross, R. (1999). 'Growing through innovation.' *Chemical Engineering News*, 25 October, p. 5.

Hambrick, D.C. and P.A. Mason (1984). 'Upper echelons: the organization as a reflection of its top managers.' *Academy of Management Review*, **9**, 193–206.

Hannan, M.T. and J. Freeman (1977). 'The population ecology of organizations.' *American Journal of Sociology*, **82**, 929–64.

Hannan, M.T. and J. Freeman (1984). 'Structural inertia and organizational change.' *American Sociological Review*, **49**, 149–64.

Hannan, M.T. and J. Freeman (1989). *Organizational Ecology*. Cambridge, MA: Harvard University Press.

Harrigan, K.R. (1985). *Strategies for Joint Ventures*. Lexington, MA: Lexington Books.

Haveman, H.A. (1992). 'Between a rock and a hard place: organizational change and performance under conditions of fundamental environmental transformation.' *Administrative Science Quarterly*, **37**, 48–75.

Haveman, H.A. (1993). 'Organizational size and change: diversification in the savings and loan industry after deregulation.' *Administrative Science Quarterly*, **38**, 20–50.

Helfat, C. (1994). 'Evolutionary trajectories in petroleum firm R&D.' *Management Science*, **40**(12), 1720–47.

Kelly, D. and T.L. Amburgey (1991). 'Organizational inertia and momentum:

a dynamic model of strategic change.' *Academy of Management Journal*, **34**, 591–612.

Lawrence, P.R. and J.W. Lorsch (1967). *Organization and Environment: Managing Differentiation and Integration*. Boston, MA: GSBA, Harvard University.

Levin, R.C., A.K. Klevorich, R.R. Nelson and S.G. Winter (1987). 'Appropriating the returns from industrial research and development.' *Brookings Papers on Economic Activity*, **3**, 783–831.

Levitt, B. and J.G. March (1988). 'Organizational learning,' in W.R. Scott (ed.), *Annual Review of Sociology*, **14**, 319–40.

McCoy, M. (2001). 'Dow Chemical.' *Chemical and Engineering News*, **79**(25), 21–5.

Meyer, J.W. and B. Rowan (1977). 'Institutionalized organizations: formal structure as myth and ceremony.' *American Journal of Sociology*, **83**, 340–63.

Monteverde, K. and D.J. Teece (1982). 'Supplier switching costs and vertical integration in the automobile industry.' *Bell Journal of Economics*, **12**, 206–13.

National Science Foundation. (1996). *U.S. Science and Engineering in a Changing World*. Arlington, VA: National Science Foundation.

Nelson, R.R. and S.G. Winter (1982). *The Evolutionary Theory of Economic Change*. Cambridge, MA: Belknap Press of Harvard University Press.

Nerkar, A. and S. Paruchuri (2005). 'Evolution of R&D capabilities: the role of knowledge networks within a firm.' *Management Science*, **51**(5), 771–85.

Paruchuri, S. (2010). 'Intraorganizational networks, interorganizational networks, and the impact of central inventors: a longitudinal study of pharmaceutical firms.' *Organization Science*, **21**(1), 63–80.

Pfeffer, J. and G.R. Salancik (1978). *The External Control of Organizations*. New York: Harper & Row.

Podolny, J.M. (1993). 'A status-based model of market competition.' *American Journal of Sociology*, **98**, 829–72.

Podolny, J.M. and T.E. Stuart (1995). 'A role-based ecology of technological change.' *American Journal of Sociology*, **100**, 1224–60.

Porter, M. (1980). *Competitive Strategy: Techniques for Analyzing Industries and Competitors*. New York: Free Press.

Powell, W.W., K.W. Koput and L. Smith-Doerr (1996). 'Interorganizational collaboration and the locus of innovation: networks of learning in biotechnology.' *Administrative Science Quarterly*, **41**(1), 116–45.

Rajagopalan, N., and G.M. Spreitzer (1997). 'Toward a theory of strategic change: a multi-lens perspective and integrative framework.' *Academy of Management Review*, **22**(1), 48–80.

Saxenian, A.L. (1990). 'Regional networks and the resurgence of Silicon Valley.' *California Management Review*, **33**, 89–113.

Singh, J.V., R.J. House and D.J. Tucker (1986). 'Organizational change and organizational mortality.' *Administrative Science Quarterly*, **31**, 587–611.

Stinchcombe, A.L. (1965). 'Social structure and organizations,' in J.G. March (ed.), *Handbook of Organizations*. Chicago, IL: Rand McNally, pp. 142–93.

Teece, D.J., G. Pisano and A. Shuen (1997). 'Dynamic capabilities and strategic management.' *Strategic Management Journal*, **18**, 509–33.

Trajtenberg, M. (1990). 'A penny for your quotes: patent citations and the value of inventions.' *RAND Journal of Economics*, **21**, 172–87.

Tsai, W. (2001). 'Knowledge transfer in intraorganizational networks: effects of network position and absorptive capacity on business unit innovation and performance.' *Academy of Management Journal*, **44**(5), 996–1004.

Tushman, M.L. and T. Scanlan (1981). 'Boundary spanning individuals: their role in information transfer and their antecedents.' *Academy of Management Journal*, **24**(2), 289–305.

Vuong, Q.H. (1989). 'Likelihood ratio tests for model selection and non-nested hypotheses.' *Econometrica*, **57**, 307–33.

White, H. (1980). 'A heteroskedasticity-consistent covariance matrix estimator and a direct test for heteroskedasticity.' *Econometica*, **48**, 817–30.

Whitehead, D. (1968). *The Dow Story: The History of the Dow Chemical Company*. New York: McGraw-Hill.

Wiersema, M.F. and K.A. Bantel (1992). 'Top management demography and corporate strategic change.' *Academy of Management Journal*, **35**, 91–121.

Williamson, O.E. (1975). *Markets and Hierarchies: Analysis and Antitrust Implications*. New York: Free Press.

Zajac, E.J. (1990). 'CEO selection, succession, compensation, and firm performance: a theoretical integration and empirical analysis.' *Strategic Management Journal*, **11**, 313–33.

Zucker, L.G., M.R. Darby and M.B. Brewer (1997). 'Intellectual human capital and the birth of U.S. biotechnology enterprises.' *American Economic Review*, **88**, 290–306.

6. How corporate governance affects innovation in the pharmaceutical industry

Phillip H. Phan, Gideon Markman and David Balkin

INTRODUCTION

To date, research on the relationship between board structure and per-formance remains inconclusive (cf. Certo et al., 2001; Daily et al., 2000; Dalton et al., 1999; Hill and Snell, 1989). Partially, this stems from a sample selection bias in which, for example, studies using *Fortune 500* firms report results that are inherently biased in favor of successful firms (cf. Daily and Dalton, 1992; Van de Ven et al., 1999; Zahra, 1996). Theoretically, perfor-mance is a multidimensional construct impacted by such multilevel factors as strategy, structure and environment. Hence, because the link between governance and performance is at best tenuous, researchers now look for mediating and/or moderating constructs, one of which is innovation, to improve the explanatory power of their models. Following in the tradition of this literature, we therefore ask whether corporate governance matters to innovation productivity. Although this question has been asked in various ways in previous studies, and the answer may seem obvious, our review of the literature suggests that it has not been completely answered, and the answers are equivocal. Hence, we believe there is still a contribution to be made in answering this question.

While specific studies of governance-innovation models may not gen-eralize well because they have to deal with heterogeneity in govern-ance systems, innovation patterns and technological specialization across countries, industries and time periods, taken as a whole they provide a guide for further theorizing. As such, there is now a growing body of research on the link between corporate governance and innovation (for example, Baysinger et al., 1991; Hill and Snell, 1988, 1989; Jensen, 1993; Markman et al., 2001; Mizruchi, 1983; Zahra, 1996). In this chapter, we build on this stream of research to test a longitudinal model linking corporate governance to innovation in the pharmaceutical industry. In the tradition of Hill and Snell (1988) and Hill and Hansen (1991), Lacetera (2001) investigated the relationships between various corporate govern- ance variables and research and development (R&D) intensity in a sample of large US-based pharmaceutical firms. They found that governance mattered in the input decisions (R&D spending) related to innovation. We contribute to this growing and important literature by testing a theo- retically robust model with multidimensional measures of innovation, specific operationalizations of ownership and control based on the extant literature and theoretically relevant measures of performance in a panel dataset. In our review of the literature it became obvious that to build good theoretical models in this domain requires a high level of specificity on the innovation process, which can only be achieved by focusing on an industrial context. This is because innovation, as an activity, varies consid- erably across industries and time periods.

Starting with Berle and Means (1932) and progressing to Mizruchi (1983) and Fama and Jensen (1983), agency theory has rightly been con- cerned with the issue of value appropriation. However, Jensen (1993) makes the point that value appropriation cannot be understood absent value creation. Theoretically, our contribution is to suggest one way that the positive branch of agency theory can be formulated to answer ques- tions of value creation. Empirically, our contribution is to offer a multidi- mensional operationalization of the innovation construct, which can guide future research.

THEORY AND HYPOTHESES

In the context of the decision to invest in innovation, agency theory assumes that shareholders are risk neutral because they can diversify their investment risks in a portfolio of stocks with uncorrelated betas. Therefore, they prefer managers to undertake risky investment in innovation because the potential returns can be disproportionate to the size of the investment. The corollary is that because investors can attenuate the variance of their investment by portfolio diversification, they benefit from investments with high mean-variance cash flows such as those expected from investment in innovation.

The normative view of agency theory (Eisenhardt, 1989) considers the problem of managerial-shareholder relationships as one of value appro- priation. Because expenditures on innovation are discretionary it can also be viewed as a form of value appropriation in that such expenditures can lead to waste on managerial pet projects. Further in any one firm, individual investors bear a fraction of the costs of innovation failure while for executives, the risks of a loss to reputation and thus the future value of their income streams can be substantial. Therefore, it is likely that managers will try to protect the value of their future cash flows from employment by attenuating the overall risk of their strategic decisions (Hill and Phan, 1991).

Empirically, it is difficult to determine, *a priori*, which R&D expenditures are wasteful and which are wealth producing (that is, efficient). However, the research in technology management suggests that those R&D expenditures that lead to patents (identifiable, defensibly intellectual property) are more likely to be valuable because a patent can be traded, exploited to create new products and markets or optioned out. More importantly, a firm that has built up a robust portfolio of patents is more likely to find a market for its intellectual property since the presence of a portfolio signals a competency in R&D. Furthermore, we can ascertain, *ex post*, whether R&D expenditures were efficient if they lead to the creation of actual products, processes and services for which there is a market value.

Innovation expenditures that have to be sustained over a period of time to yield results, and for which success or failure directly drives the market value of the firm are strategic and hence the purview of the board of directors (Jensen, 1993). Whenever discretionary expenditures are substantial relative to the revenues of the firm and if they can significantly alter the firm's future revenue streams, agency theory argues that boards should be involved in the decision control process (cf. Casper and Matraves, 2003; Chung et al., 2003; Gugler, 2003; Jensen, 1993; Jensen and Meckling, 1976; Wright and Kroll, 2002). Indeed, the Sarbanes-Oxley Act of 2002[1] embeds language that suggests the board's *de jure* obligation is to be knowledgeable about the firm's strategy. This is because boards are privy to inside information not accorded to stock analysts and are therefore able to act before the damage from misallocated investments becomes too costly to reverse (Aldrich et al., 1998; Miyajima et al., 2002; Mizruchi, 1983). Also, the board has legal powers to discipline and enforce decisions that may not be in management's personal interests.[2] Boards have a choice as to the way the firm can innovate by the type of expenditures they approve. Innovation can be acquired from the outside through licensing, alliances and mergers or it can also be developed internally through R&D processes.

Innovation in the Pharmaceutical Industry

We chose the pharmaceutical industry because the principal method of value creation involves discretionary expenditures in innovation, over which the board of directors has direct oversight. Firms in our sample are engaged in manufacturing, fabricating or processing of *in vivo* diagnostic substances and pharmaceutical preparations (except biological) of drugs for human or veterinary use. The greater part of the products of these firms are intended for internal consumption, such as ampoules, tablets, capsules, vials, ointments, medicinal powders, solutions and suspensions.

The innovation cycle in the pharmaceutical industry begins with R&D investment, which contributes to a firm's intellectual property portfolio through patent registrations, and concludes with the creation of tangible new products (drugs, measurement and delivery devices), which generates the cash flow to fuel the next innovation cycle. Value is created at different stages of the innovation process. R&D investments increase the firm's knowledge absorptive capacity (Markman et al., 2001). It forms the basis for an R&D capability that can be quantified as a patent-protected discovery or a new product introduction. Large pharmaceutical companies also engage in the trading and licensing of patent rights as a way of realizing the cash value of their intellectual property portfolios. Such intellectual property portfolios can become platforms for joint ventures and strategic alliances for exploration into new technological corridors and therapeutic categories. In short, because R&D increases a firm's knowledge absorptive capacity it also expands its strategic options and enhances the underlying economic value of its organizational assets.

Therefore, a pharmaceutical firm is better analysed as a portfolio of intellectual property assets in different stages of maturity. The process of R&D is complex, costly, risky and it requires a sustained mobilization of human and financial resources over a long period of time before offerings reach the market. The innovation process in the pharmaceutical industry is characterized by escalating costs, unanticipated obstacles and technological dead-ends that can derail once-promising projects (Tushman and Rosenkopf, 1992). For example, at any one time Pfizer reports more than 75 projects – including potential new products as well as potential new indications or formulations for existing products – in various development stages. According to the International Federation of Pharmaceutical Manufacturers and Associations (IFPMA), it is not uncommon for R&D to take up to 10–15 years and over $800 million to research and develop a single new medicine. During the R&D process, more than 8000 compounds are tested, of which only one is developed into a potent and safe drug.

Drug discovery, then, is seldom a one-shot project. In order for economic value to be realized at each stage of the innovation cycle continual and cumulative investments must be made. The decision to register and later defend patents involves additional resources. The decision to commercialize a discovery also involves substantial expenditures in product development, distribution, marketing and sales. Radical new products and therapies have no track record for the capital market to evaluate and therefore hints of unsuccessful drug trials can jolt the stock price, which makes it costly for the firm to raise funds to keep projects going. A clinical trial may be interrupted for a number of reasons including a decision to abandon an area of research in the wake of a corporate takeover, an unsuccessful legal battle with a competitor or the failure of a drug trial phase. In summary, the discretionary and economically meaningful nature of each stage of the innovation process implies a significant monitoring role for the board of directors.

Innovation and Corporate Governance

To optimize the use of financial, human and organizational capital, pharmaceutical firms must continuously engage in innovation. The empirical evidence suggests that investors favor firms that strive to be best in one or few value creation activities over those that are stretched across a wide range of activities (Ruef and Scott, 1998). Firms that tightly focus their R&D dollars can outspend their competitors in specific knowledge areas, although investments into narrow technological corridors might be difficult to reverse. While this increases a firm's exposure to the risk of loss, it can also lead to sustainable resource-based competitive advantages.

Our review of the literature alludes to an empirical question on the extent of the board involvement in questions of R&D spending. Traditional innovation management models do not consider the role of the board. One view is that innovation is a managerial activity, which is delegated to management by the board of directors. Thus, specific decisions on where to innovate are left to management. Another view suggests that innovation is a value creating activity that is routinely considered by the board through its resource allocation function (Casper and Matraves, 2003; Chung et al., 2003; Gugler, 2003; Jensen, 1993; Wright and Kroll, 2002). At the corporate level, firms can choose to create value by innovation, restructuring and leveraging competencies through mergers. With respect to innovation, firms can choose to innovate internally through an R&D program and/or acquire intellectual property through alliances and mergers. Although the end result is the same – the commercialization of intellectual property for profit – the paths are quite different and may even be complementary. More importantly, because these corporate-level expenditures are discretionary, having to do with the exploration of new opportunities, the board of directors is nominally responsible for their approval. Frequently, the time horizon over which rents can be expected from a pharmaceutical R&D project may exceed the average executive's tenure, making it impossible to recover the returns on the risks he is taking today. Hence, the board can play a role in creating the right incentives to drive innovation. At minimum, the board has to approve the annual budget and strategic plan submitted by management and is therefore de facto involved in the allocation of resources to R&D activities.

The question, then, is what types of governance variables are most relevant to the question of managerial risk taking? A careful review of the available evidence (for example, Baysinger et al., 1991; Casper and Matraves, 2003; Certo et al., 2001; Chung et al., 2003; Daily et al., 2000; Dalton et al., 1999; Gugler, 2003; Hill and Snell, 1988, 1989; Wright and Kroll, 2002; Zahra, 1996) suggests that four are most relevant and also the most consistently used in the literature. Using Jensen and Meckling's (1976) framework of corporate governance as the balance between ownership and control, our model focuses on ownership concentration. This is related to the degree to which institutional and private stockholders can exert their preferences for risk taking. Finally, we assess board independence, which measures the degree to which chief executive officers (CEOs) and board members have discretion over risky investment decisions.[3]

It is important to note that more than 30 years of empirical research in corporate governance has produced a very long list of governance variables that we could include in our empirical model. However, our goal is to test the theoretical generalizability of the relationship between governance and innovation. Therefore, we only selected those representative constructs that consistently appeared in the studies we reviewed. We realize that in making this decision, we traded off predictive power for theoretical generalizability.

Ownership Concentration

Agency theory recognizes the different risk preferences between shareholders and managers (Jensen, 1993). This is because executives' net present value of future income streams is concentrated within the firm, making their risk preference curve more concave (Figure 6.1), whereas investors' net present value of future income is diversified over several cash flow streams, rendering the risk preference curve less concave (Fama and Jensen, 1983; Jensen and Meckling, 1976). As Figure 6.1 illustrates, investors would prefer riskier investments with higher mean-variance expected cash flows than executives since the former's hurdle rates for undertaking such investments are lower.

Given the difference in risk averseness, what are the circumstances under which managers are free to exert their preferences? Boeker (1992) and

Figure 6.1   Investors' and managers' risk/return tradeoffs

Boeker and Goodstein (1993) pointed to the impact of significant block ownership – institutional and private owners – on the ability of CEOs to act freely. According to the US Securities and Exchange Commission (SEC) rules and corporate tradition, block owners with 5 percent or more of a firm's outstanding common shares are given the legal right to make shareholder proposals during annual shareholder meetings. Proposals can be used to initiate change in the boardroom. Hence, as ownership concentration increases, the ability for investors to exert their preferences on the board increases, restricting the ability of management to act freely.

Some authors have suggested that because institutional owners are well-informed investors their presence is positively related to innovation (Baysinger et al., 1991; Hill and Hansen, 1991). Others argue that institutional owners are driven by bottom-line considerations (Graves, 1988), which suggests that they might be negatively predisposed to long-term R&D spending. First, we acknowledge that institutional investors are not a homogeneous group. Different types of institutional investors have different investment time horizons (Kochhar and David, 1996) so that pension funds (for example, CalPers), controlling 62 percent of the total holdings of all institutional investment funds (Monks and Minow, 2001), with 25-year investment horizons may be less averse to risk than mutual funds whose managers have quarterly performance targets.

Regardless of the relative differences in risk aversion among shareholder groups, agency theory suggests that investors are more able to diversify firm-related risks (that is, innovation projects) and therefore may have a more concave risk function than managers because it is more costly for managers to diversify firm-related risks. Hence, it is more likely that institutional investors, relative to managers, prefer riskier innovation projects with the promise of higher returns (Jensen and Meckling, 1976):

Hypothesis 1: A higher proportion of institutional ownership relative to total ownership will be positively related to innovation.

Following previous studies, we treat institutional owners and individual block shareholders separately. Private block shareholders who hold at least 5 percent or more of a firm's outstanding common shares have a platform to make their voices heard by the board of directors (for example, they can make shareholder proposals). Like institutional investors, private block shareholders can also diversify their investment portfolios and so would have a lower internal rate of return requirements than managers for any particular investment. Similar to institutions, private block shareholders suffer from stock immobility since it is fairly problematic to trade very large blocks of shares without simultaneously affecting the stock price. However, unlike institutional shareholders, who act as paid agents for investors, and are thus partially insulated from poor investment decisions, private block shareholders act for themselves. Private block shareholders bear the full costs of poor investment outcomes and are therefore more likely to act quickly against managers that they regard as behaving against their interests before having to vote with their feet. Finally, such investors, perhaps through direct representation on the board of directors, are positioned to encourage commitment to long-term innovation (Baysinger et al., 1991; Hill and Hansen, 1991). Thus, the governance-innovation linkage may be even tighter for individual block shareholders.

Hypothesis 2: A higher proportion of 5 percent block ownership relative to total ownership will be positively related to innovation.

Board Independence

Agency theory is primarily a theory of value appropriation – the struggle for the control of cash flow between managers and investors. Thus, any form of control that vests power with one party will favor value appropriation to that party. The standard agency theoretic view about the role of the chair and CEO suggests that CEO duality can erode the independence of a board (Daily and Dalton, 1997; Finkelstein and D'Aveni, 1994). Board-level decisions rely on information provided by top management, much of which can be tacit. Hence, an individual who holds both positions of CEO and chairman controls the information flows to the board and thus influences the decisions made by the board (Jensen and Meckling, 1976). On the other hand, Pennings (1992) and Van de Ven and Drazin (1985) posit that CEO duality attenuates the flexibility and responsiveness in decision-making that can come from the unity of command (see also Boyd, 1995; Daily and Dalton, 1997; Finkelstein and D'Aveni, 1994). To be consistent with the theoretical stance we adopted in Hypotheses 1 and 2, we argue that CEO duality attenuates the independence of the board of directors and therefore acts to advance the interests of management, and possibly at the expense of the shareholders:

Hypothesis 3: CEO duality will be negatively related to innovation in industries where innovation is a primary source of value creation.

According to normative agency theory, outside board members are regarded as custodians of shareholder value (Jensen, 1993). Indeed, the separation of ownership and control can only be properly governed when there is a corresponding separation of decision control and decision management (Fama and Jensen, 1983). The weight of the theoretical research also suggests a bias for outsider control because board structure, which reflects the relative power of the directors to exert their influence, is heavily influenced by the composition of its members (Boyd, 1995; Daily and Dalton, 1997). Outside directors are more likely to protect the interests of shareholders' preferences for high-risk strategies because their personal wealth, unlike insider directors (directors who are also employees of the firm), is not tied to the outcomes of those decisions. Therefore, they are more likely to act independent of self-interest. Indeed, consistent with this perspective, recent revisions of the New York Stock Exchange (NYSE) listing rules, SEC regulations and the Sarbanes-Oxley Act have either encouraged or mandated the formation of boards in which outside directors have majority control.

Hypothesis 4: A higher inside to outside ratio of board members will be negatively related to innovation in industries where innovation is a primary source of value creation.

In summary, our theoretical model is illustrated in Figure 6.2. Agency theory suggests that when shareholders have more power relative to management, via concentrated ownership holdings, efficient innovation

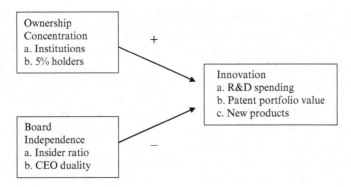

Figure 6.2   The theoretical model

projects that yield positive outcomes are more likely to occur. Agency theory also suggests that independent boards, wherein directors who are less beholden to management (that is, outside directors) hold sway, efficient innovation projects that yield positive outcomes are also more likely to occur.

METHODS

Sample

To test the hypotheses outlined above, we sought a sample of pharmaceutical firms as these firms provide an unambiguous test of the governance-innovation linkage (list of companies available from the authors). Indeed, executives and board members of pharmaceutical firms face irreversible long-term investment decisions in R&D. Decision-making in the pharmaceutical industry particularly is challenging because of the uncertainty regarding R&D projects. Although there are approximately 200 publicly traded pharmaceutical firms in the USA (SIC 2834), mergers, acquisitions and divestitures narrowed our sample to 86 companies that have (a) remained autonomous for five consecutive years from 1995 to 1999 and (b) reported complete financial, R&D investment and governance data for the period. We confined the time period to this range to avoid confounds resulting from the Internet stock boom and bust and the explosion of business methods patent applications that flooded the United States Patent and Trademark Office (USPTO) during that time and may have impacted the approval process for utility patents, which is the subject of our study.

To create the dataset, we collected and verified our data from four different sources. First, we used 10-K reports obtained from the SEC Global Access database for accounting and financial data. Second, we collected each firm's utility patent portfolio data, excluding design and reissued patents, from the USPTO. Then, we obtained each firm's newly approved products from the Center for Drug Evaluation and Research database. Finally, we gathered ownership and board structure data from the Standard and Poor's (S&P) *Register of Corporations, Directors and Executives*. To ensure reliability, each data source was cross-checked with at least one other source. For example, profitability and sales data from the SEC 10-K reports were cross-checked with the S&P Register. We did not find inconsistencies in the dataset that would systematically bias the results.

Measures

Ownership structure

The ownership structure of a firm determines the dispersion of the firm's equity holdings and indicates the degree to which investors have influence over the board. We measured this in two ways. First, we determined if the firm was subject to the influence of block shareholders who controlled at least 5 percent of total outstanding shares of the corporation. Once these private block shareholders were found, we measured the degree to which these block owners held sway over the board of directors by calculating the percentage of common shares they controlled relative to total outstanding common shares.

Our second measure of ownership structure is the degree to which a firm's equity is controlled by institutions. We ensured that the two measures were orthogonal by not double counting private and institutional block shareholders. The subsequent low correlation (Table 6.1) between the two measures assured us that we performed the counting procedure correctly. We used the same method to measure the concentration in institutional shareholdings as we did with private block shareholders. That is, we took the ratio of common shares held by institutions against total outstanding common shares.

CEO duality

CEO duality occurs when a firm's CEO is also the chairperson of the board of directors. CEO duality data were gathered from the S&P's *Register of Corporations, Directors and Executives*. The construct was operationalized as a dichotomous variable where a CEO who is on record as chair of the board is coded as 1, and otherwise coded as 0 (Boyd, 1995; Conyon and Peck, 1998; Daily and Dalton, 1994).

Inside/outside ratio
We used the most conservative measure of independence articulated in the literature (Daily et al., 1995) and defined an outside director as one who has not had an employment affiliation with the firm for at least five years, does not draw a salary or have a commercial relationship with the firm (except for director's fees) and is not related to a member of the management team.[4] Other board members who do not meet this qualification are coded as insiders. The data were gathered from S&P's *Register of Corporations, Directors and Executives*.

Innovation
We used three temporally sequenced measures to capture the artifacts of a pharmaceutical firm's innovation process: R&D spending; intellectual property (IP) value; and new products. Many authors have used R&D spending as an indicator of innovation (for example, Balkin et al., 2000; Baysinger et al., 1991; Hill and Snell, 1988). Hence, we follow this literature and operationalized our first measure of innovation as the annual R&D spending of each pharmaceutical firm. We logged the measure in order to account for extreme skewness in the distribution of the variable.

We go beyond this initial measure of innovation because we know that R&D spending is an input and does not fully capture the complexity of the innovation process (cf. Zahra, 1996). For instance, high R&D spending may indicate conservative decision-making, in which a firm bets resources on a large portfolio of 'safe' products, rather than aim for technological breakthroughs. Stated differently, because the financial community closely monitors R&D spending figures in innovation-driven industries, managers can maintain a high R&D spending rate but hedge by focusing on well-traveled, though potentially lower yielding, technological corridors. Thus, one needs to capture the productivity of a firm's R&D spending.

Because the primary way in which new products or biochemical entities retain their initial value is through patent protection, we measured the annual number of patents multiplied by the citations per patent. This is a measure of the value of a firm's IP portfolio. Patenting is a rigorous process in which a firm must prove it is first in conceptualizing the product or technology. Therefore, the ability to obtain patents is a measure of the firm's innovative prowess and its organizational capabilities. Early studies relied on patent counts to operationalize this measure but we now have data on patent citations. Highly cited patents indicate that a firm may be seeking to identify the owner of a technology in order to apply the technology to a commercial opportunity. The technology-seeking firm could buy the patent, license it or form a partnership with the owner by exchanging resources such as with a cross-licensing agreement (Markman et al., 2004).

All of these possibilities indicate that patent citations signal potential commercial activity. Past studies have shown direct and positive links between a patent's economic value and its citation rate (Fleming, 2001; Harhoff et al., 1999).

We obtained the data on each firm's utility patent portfolio from the USPTO. Normally, with patent citations, we would use a Heckman selection procedure to account for the zero values that typify the distribution of this type of data. However, because our sample is confined to the pharmaceutical industry, in which every firm engages in patenting as a core activity, and because we calculated the value of the patent portfolio by multiplying patent counts with citations (hence, the data is transformed to a continuous variable), there was no need to use the Heckman method.

Thus far we have argued that R&D spending and creating valuable patent portfolios are important steps in the innovation process. However, in order to create economic wealth on a sustained basis, firms must bring discoveries to market, and the primary way to do this is through the innovation and commercialization process. In the pharmaceutical industry, the most direct indicator of a firm's value creation potential is its ability to develop new products. Examples include drugs, drug delivery systems, medical applications, measurement devices, agricultural products and food supplements. Data on each firm's new products came from the Center for Drug Evaluation and Research.

Control variables

Because size and prior financial performance can significantly dictate the amount of discretionary resources a pharmaceutical firm can devote to the innovation cycle (from R&D spending to product commercialization), we sought to rule out firm-specific fixed effects due to financial slack. We also included prior financial performance data to rule out the endogeneity hypothesis that a positive relationship between institutional investors and innovation can simply indicate that such institutional investors are good stock pickers. Thus, following past research, we collected data on annual sales and return on assets (ROA), which are the control variables for firm size and firm performance, respectively (Baysinger et al., 1991; Sanders and Carpenter, 1998). Since accounting performance is highly correlated with market performance, we did not include a stock performance variable. Also, we did not do this because the data for this industry are very noisy and temporally unstable, often subject to rumors of drug trial outcomes, patent infringement lawsuits and the like. For example, it is not uncommon for a firm stock price to gain or lose 10 percent of its stock value on the basis of a regulatory ruling, which can later be reversed on appeal (Debaise, 2002).

Estimation

In this study, we report the results for the one-year lag between each component of the innovation process (R&D expenditure in 1997, patents in 1998 and new products in 1999) and the independent variables (1996). As with time series data, absent a theoretical constraint, the choice of the lag between independent and dependent variables reflects a compromise between the risk of data noise with longer lags and model under-specification with shorter lags. Basically, the core issue is the tradeoff between statistical power and theoretical robustness (that is, minimizing type I versus type II errors). To resolve this issue, we examined a number of theoretical and statistical tradeoffs.

We are aware that some innovation cycles might take longer than five years as they include clinical trials for drugs. On the other hand, there is a common misconception that innovation in the pharmaceutical industry involves only prescription drugs. In fact, drug conveyance mechanisms, measurement tools and medical devices form a large portion of the innovation outputs in this industry, and these take significantly shorter time periods from lab bench to store shelf. Indeed, the decline in R&D productivity among pharmaceutical firms has prompted many to divert more R&D dollars into new drug delivery systems as ways to increase the efficacy, and thus market appeal, of existing drugs (Hensley, 2002). Additionally, the time limit on patent protection means that pharmaceutical companies routinely begin product development before final patent approval in order to be first-to-market so they are positioned to extract maximum rents. Finally, because the critical path for innovation in pharmaceuticals involves parallel development processes with significant overlaps in R&D spending, patents and product commercialization, shorter lags can still capture the hypothesized causal effects.

Statistically, given the choice of under- or over-specifying the size effects for the impact of governance on innovation, preference for a conservative test of our hypotheses leads us to err on the side of under-specification. This would imply shorter lags that may not capture the full effects of the innovation cycle, but would at least provide a stricter test of the hypothesis.

In sum, when deciding on the appropriate lag between the independent and dependent variables, we considered the mix in type-of-innovation, the desire for parsimony and the risk of data noise with longer lags. As a practical matter, we also tested the models with longer lags (two and four years) and found no improvement (actually we found degradation) in the fit of the data to the model. Indeed, lags longer than two years resulted in lower variance explained because of increasing data noise with the longer time periods. Therefore, in the interest of parsimony, we report the results for a one-year lag effect model (that is, R&D, 1997; patents, 1998; and new products, 1999). While imperfect, these measures offer a theoretical improvement over previous research that use only cross-sectional data or rely only on R&D and/or patent counts as dependent variables.

In terms of the data analysis, it is standard practice to employ negative binomial regression for patent count data, because of the Poisson distribution characterized by this type of data. However, because we transformed the dependent variable by multiplying count with citation rates, the distribution of the variable is no longer of the Poisson form. Hence, we employed panel regression techniques. In addition to distribution considerations, we also had to account for the possible endogeneity in our model.

There are two ways to deal with the endogeneity inherent in such models. The first is to use a simultaneous 2-stage least squares technique to check for recursive effects. This is usually done when only cross-sectional data are available. A theoretically and empirically more robust method is to lag the model such that the direction of causation, which is temporally defined, moves only in a single direction and to do this using standard panel regression techniques. Because we had access to time series data, we chose the latter approach, which is a more powerful approach since it deals with endogeneity both empirically as well as statistically.

Our analysis accounts for firm-specific heterogeneity (we deal with industry-specific heterogeneity by restricting our sample to one industry) that is constant over time, arising, for example, from differences in firm-specific innovation practices. Unobserved firm-specific heterogeneity is eliminated by subtracting the lagged value of the control variable, ROA. Second, endogeneity issues that arise when explanatory variables are correlated with an error term are easily addressed. Endogeneity could arise in two ways in our model. If the dependent variable were a function of the error term, and the lagged dependent variable were in turn a function of the dependent variable, the lagged dependent variable would be correlated with the error term. Ownership, which represents a discretionary choice, is determined in part by a firm's prior performance and other unobservable factors, such as the firm's idiosyncratic innovation practices and is therefore potentially correlated with the error term. Prior research has emphasized the importance of modeling endogeneity by using instrumental variables for ownership structure to control for possible reverse causality (Chung et al., 2003).[5] We used three fixed effects hierarchical regressions to examine the relationship between the set of four governance measures and the innovation cycle, while controlling for firm size and prior firm performance.

Prior to analyses, all variables were examined for accuracy of data entry, missing values and distributions. Following Tabachnick and Fidell (1996), single missing values were replaced with median scores, while those cases with missing values on more than 5 percent of the variables were deleted. To satisfy the linearity assumption in our models, we attenuated the inherent skewness and kurtosis in the R&D spending and firm size variables through a logarithmic transformation. We centered the values of the explanatory variables by subtracting the means, to reduce potential multicollinearity in our tests of the interaction effects (Aiken and West, 1991). We examined variance inflation factors (VIF) to check for multicollinearity and found the values to be less than 2, well below the cut-off value of 10 that indicates excessive multicollinearity (Greene, 2003).

Our first equation regresses the governance variables (1996) – duality, inside to outside board members ratio, private shareholders and public shareholders – on R&D (1997). Our second equation regresses the same four governance variables (1996) and R&D (1997) on IP value (1998). Our last and most inclusive equation regresses the governance variables (1996), R&D (1997) and IP value (1998) against the number of new products (1999).

RESULTS

Table 6.1 presents the means, standard deviations and correlations among the study's variables. The means for institutional and private stockholders, CEO duality and ratio of inside to outside board members are consistent with past research (Zahra, 1996). As shown in Table 6.1, CEO duality was present in 41 percent of the pharmaceutical firms in our sample. Similarly, the average ratio of inside to outside board members was 0.44, reflecting a trend toward more outside board representation. Finally, private block shareholders controlled, on average, 6 540 000 shares (slightly over 6 percent of total outstanding shares), whereas institutional shareholders controlled 18 074 000 shares (18 percent of total outstanding shares). The average annual sales and R&D expenditures were $1.1 billion and $121 million, respectively (the correlation matrix reports the mean of the log transformations of sales and R&D). Consistent with industry estimates (Hensley, 2002) the average number of new products for each pharmaceutical firm was 1.65.

Table 6.2 displays the standardized regression coefficients, overall R^2, change in R^2, F and adjusted R^2 statistics. Because the independent variables were statistically related to each other, we needed to know if heteroskedacity would be a problem and thus calculated an overall VIF for each of our regression models. The VIF did not exceed 4 and so we concluded that the model did not suffer too severely from multicollinearity.

Table 6.1 Correlations and descriptive statistics

	Mean	SD	1	2	3	4	5	6	7	8
1. ROA	−0.32	28.35								
2. Sales (ln)[a]	10.72	2.54	−0.50**							
3. Private S/H[b]	6541	0.38	−0.04	0.19*						
4. Inst. S/H[b]	18074	3205	−0.03	0.30**	0.02					
5. Duality	0.41	1.25	0.04	0.20**	0.18*	0.22*				
6. Inside/Outside	0.44	0.67	−0.07	−0.05	0.00	0.26**	0.25**			
7. R&D (ln)[c]	9.77	297	−0.06	0.49**	0.41**	0.22*	0.17*	0.76**		
8. IP value	695	1107	0.00	0.28**	0.30**	0.14	0.20*	0.49**	0.74**	
9. New products	1.65	4.73	0.21	0.51**	0.37**	−0.03	0.01	0.69**	0.44**	0.59**

Notes:
* $p < 0.05$ (2-tailed); ** $p < 0.01$ (2-tailed).
a. Mean sales is $1.1 billion.
b. Means of private and institutional shareholder variables are reported in thousands of shares.
c. Mean R&D is $121 million.

171

Academic entrepreneurship

Table 6.2   Results of fixed effects regression[a]

Variables	R&D		IP value		New products	
Steps:	1	2	1	2	1	2
ROA_{t-1}	−0.24**	−0.11	−0.15	0.01	−0.08	0.02
Sales (ln)	0.85**	0.44**	0.43**	−0.05	0.32*	0.08
Private S/H		0.17*		0.28**		−0.05
Inst. S/H		0.33**		0.78**		0.49**
Duality		0.19*		−0.04		0.13
Inside/Outside		0.10		−0.02		0.18*
Log R&D			0.24*	−0.04	0.01	−0.12
IP value					0.44**	0.28*
Overall R^2	0.52	0.58	0.29	0.55	0.39	0.49
D Overall R^2		0.06**		0.26**		0.10**
F		20.52***		15.99***		11.14***
Adj. R^2		0.56***		0.49***		0.39***

Notes:
* $p < 0.05$; ** $p < 0.01$; *** $p < 0.001$.
a.   Variance Inflation Factors (VIF) < 4.0.

The adjusted R^2 in each step in all three regressions were statistically significant, and while they corrected for the effects of multicollinearity the conclusions from the empirical findings were the same.

Everything else being equal, we found that ROA was significantly and negatively related to R&D ($r = -0.24$, $p < 0.01$). We speculate that this may be an artifact of the long lags between R&D expenditures and products in the industry, coupled with high fixed cost of entry. However, as expected, size was a positive and significant predictor of pharmaceutical firms' investment in R&D ($R^2 = 0.52$). Controlling for sales and ROA (that is, size and performance), the second step in the first equation regressed the governance variables on R&D. Adding the block of four governance variables explained an additional 6 percent of variance, with three of the governance variables as significant predictors of R&D spending ($F = 20.52$, $p < 0.001$). As predicted, the regression coefficients of institutional shareholders and private shareholders were significant and positive while the finding for CEO duality ran contrary to the hypothesized direction. Only the inside/outside ratio variable was not significant.

The second equation regressed the same control variables (size and performance), along with R&D and the four governance variables on IP value (patents × citations). As seen in Table 6.2, sales was again a positive and significant predictor of patent value, R&D was positive and significant (r = 0.24, p < 0.05), while ROA was not significant ($R^2 = 0.29$). Including the block of four governance variables explained an additional 26 percent of the variance (F = 15.99, p < 0.001). As predicted, the regression coefficients for institutional shareholders and private shareholders were significant and positive. However, neither CEO duality nor inside/outside ratio variables were significant predictors of IP value.

Finally, the complete model regressed size, performance, R&D and patents ($R^2 = 0.39$), followed by the four governance variables on new products ($R^2 = 0.49$, F = 11.14). Sales and patents were significant and positive predictors of new products in step one, suggesting that the greater a firm's sales and patents, the larger its portfolio of new products. The four governance variables explained an additional 10 percent of the variance. The regression coefficients for inside/outside ratio and institutional shareholders were significant and positive, but neither CEO duality nor private shareholders were significant predictors of new products.

In sum, institutional shareholders (Hypothesis 2) was significantly related to all three measures of innovation (R&D, IP value and new products); private block shareholders (Hypothesis 1) was significantly related to two innovation measures; CEO duality (Hypothesis 3) and inside to outside board ratio (Hypothesis 4) were significantly positively related to one measure of innovation, respectively. Thus, the findings provide strong support for Hypotheses 1 and 2, and reject Hypotheses 3 and 4.

With respect to the relative impact of the variables in the models we note that the effect of institutional shareholding appears to be consistently larger than that of the other variables and operates across all three phases of the innovation cycle. We also notice that private (block) shareholders, some of which may represent venture capitalists or private placements, drop out of significance at the new product stage. We speculate that, unlike large institutional investors, they may lack liquidity and therefore seek earlier exit in the innovation cycle.

Interestingly, we notice that duality, though having a much smaller effect than shareholdings, eventually drops out of significance from the later stages of the innovation cycle. Although we explained that this may show the importance of having internal knowledge to make risky investments (Hypothesis 3), it may also indicate the potential for an escalation of commitment on the part of the CEO/chair, leading to over-investments in R&D. However, to the extent that we found a positive correlation between R&D and IP value and new products, we believe that the over-investment conjecture is weak.

Why did duality drop out from the subsequent stages? We speculate that this may be due to the possibility that once decisions on technological investments are made, a firm enters a 'corridor' such that the influence of individual managers becomes muted. In short, byproducts of the R&D decision are a natural outcome unless the project is terminated. At the same time that duality drops out of significance, we also note that the effect of shareholder concentration increases in size. Hence, our data empirically demonstrate the link between value appropriation (shareholder concentration) and value creation (innovation).

Finally, we note that the influence of inside board members is only meaningful at the last stage of the innovation cycle (new products). The effect of size is small compared to institutional shareholdings but to the extent that commercialization represents another major, albeit less risky relative to the initial decision to invest in R&D, investment for the firm, the knowledge of the insiders may be important in this regard. Interestingly, it appears that duality and inside directors have similar relative impacts on innovation, although they occur at different stages of the cycle.

DISCUSSIONS AND CONCLUSIONS

The results of this study reinforce the view that among pharmaceutical firms, governance can matter to innovation. Although the corporate governance literature has generally been concerned with questions of value appropriation, this study suggests that governance can also play a role in value creation, to the extent that the governance structures designed to protect the residual value for the residual claimant also have implications for the way a firm can create value. These findings while broadly consistent with previous research (Baysinger et al., 1991; Boeker, 1992; Daily et al., 2000; Dalton et al., 1999; Zahra, 1996) also yield some interesting results.

First, contrary to our predictions, we note the positive relationship between CEO duality and innovation, which is generally considered a high-risk investment strategy. These findings suggest that a positive agency theoretic, rather than normative agency theoretic explanation may be better at understanding board structure and innovation. Specifically, a positive agency theory explanation suggests that boards of directors in which the chair is also the CEO are less likely to suffer from an information asymmetry problem and therefore, everything else being equal, are more able to accurately assess the risk/return prospects of an R&D project. Hence, if first mover advantages mean that second place is a permanent lock-out from a future revenue stream, boards with better information flows are able to make positive value decisions more quickly and accurately.

In technology-intensive industries, such as pharmaceuticals, where expedient decision-making on big bets is necessary to achieve first-to-market status, a unitary command structure can work to the firm's competitive advantage. Clarity in the leadership structure is particularly vital in large complex firms where sub-cultures and sub-groups can create inefficiencies in decision-making. A unitary leadership structure sends an unambiguous message to management, employees, board members and the investment community (Daily et al., 1995; Wallace et al., 1990). A dual leadership structure, on the other hand, can create multiple or even conflicting authority relationships, lack of strategic focus and divided loyalties (Galbraith, 2001; Wallace et al., 1990). Since the unification of organizational leadership and control are essential to effective strategy formulation and implementation CEO duality will have positive implications for risky strategic decisions. In short, whether the CEO duality has net positive or negative effects is probably content dependent and therefore better explained in positive agency theory terminology.

Second, the finding that insider-controlled boards result in positive innovation outcomes can also be interpreted in the light of positive agency theory. The same logic suggests that inside board members may contribute positively to innovation in highly turbulent and complex environments (Daily and Dalton, 1997; Finkelstein and D'Aveni, 1994). Although outside board members are generally regarded as custodians of shareholder value (Jensen, 1993), there is recognition that inside board members are usually more knowledgeable about a firm's internal resources, strategic assets and technological capabilities. Indeed, because insiders are also members of the top management team, they are positioned to evaluate the firm's value creation strategies (Conger et al., 2001). In the pharmaceutical industry, the involvement of knowledgeable directors is particularly critical since the wrong bet can set a firm back many years in the race to the marketplace. Finally, the reputation of inside board members is closely linked to their company's success, which creates a natural incentive for them to maximize the value creation potential of the firm.

Our study is subject to a number of important limitations that constrain our ability to generalize. First, although we attempt to deal with the potential for fixed effects biases, through industry selection and firm-level control variables, we cannot ignore the potential that the biotechnology firms are different from the pharmaceutical firms in our sample. We used a Kolomogorov-Smirnov test to check for systematic differences in the distributions of the variables in the sub-samples and did not find differences. However, because we are using a constrained set of variables (there are many governance variables such as management ownership or director ownership of equity that we did not include), we cannot be sure that the sample is truly homogeneous with respect to the type of firms. In addition, we used a one-year lag between each stage of the innovation cycle.

This was a pragmatic decision since the longer the lags we tested with the data, the more noise we encountered. Yet, because of this we have to be very careful about the claims we can make regarding the empirical findings. For example, we are hesitant to speculate on the economic significance of the results, since the constrained model means that the size of the effects will likely change with the addition of omitted variables. In any case, our empirical test was designed to verify the direction and significance of the relationships we hypothesized, and not to offer a predictive model of innovation in the pharmaceutical industry. Hence, we are comfortable with the conservative nature of our tests and our reticence to make too much of the economic implications of our findings.

Second, the formulation of the value of a firm's intellectual property is unique to this study. This can be a problem or a contribution. Based on the absorptive capacity argument, a firm with an established pipeline of research projects, and hence a large patent portfolio is more likely to be valuable when compared to a firm with a small patent portfolio. But it is still possible for a large patent portfolio to have very little economic value – the contrast in the market value of biotechnology firms with relatively small patent portfolios and large pharmaceutical firms with very large portfolios is an example of this.

The problem we encounter is that estimating an *a priori* financial value to a patent portfolio is technically difficult as there isn't a 'Black and Scholes' algorithm for doing this since estimating the cash flows of a patent is fraught with uncertainty. However, we do know that patents that are highly cited are more basic, more important to a line of research (much like the seminal published papers in a field). We also know that patent holders can claim a share of the profits from commercial products based on their patents. Therefore, it stands to reason that large portfolios with more heavily cited patents are more valuable than small portfolios with un-cited patents, which led us to compute the value index in the manner we did.

As far as we could tell from the patenting and innovation literature, there is no precedence for such an index, although our reasoning suggests the measure has some face validity. It is certainly superior to simple counts of patents (the traditional way such measures are computed). It allowed us to avoid the use of different estimation techniques for each of our dependent variables since a patent count measured would have called for a negative binomial or Poisson estimation model, a different estimation model from the other dependent variables. In any case, to properly validate the construct will require an entirely different study, the subject of future work. In the meanwhile, we believe we have started a conversation in the right direction.

Having stated our caveats, our study suggests that one cannot fully discuss the role of corporate governance in innovation without considering value appropriation and value creation together. Institutional and large private investors in protecting their investments from managerial expropriation by aligning management interests in making the appropriate innovation decisions are simultaneously engaging in the process of value creation. More generally, our findings suggest that the two branches of agency theory can be employed flexibly and can be fruitfully used to explain strategic decisions, not just decisions related to shareholder issues, faced by the firm.

Specifically, a normative prescription in agency theory is for decision control and decision monitoring to be separated (Jensen and Meckling, 1976). Generally, this means that the board of directors should not be involved in strategy setting (decision initiation) and operational decisions (decision implementation), since this would compromise the board's objectivity in assessing management (decision ratification and assessment). Our findings, however, suggest that in the pharmaceutical industry, where high-risk decisions have to be made under substantial uncertainty, unitary command structures and strategically involved boards provide additional explanatory power for the governance-innovation link.

We are not suggesting that our findings refute agency theory, which has been linked to a negative bias against CEO duality and inside board members. Our data does not permit this strong claim. We are suggesting that agency models can be productively contextualized in order to fully account for the specific economic structure of an industry. When the problem is about protecting the residual through the restraint of CEO power with checks and balances in the boardroom, the appropriate context in which this can be applied is the majority of technologically stable industries, in which value creation involves routine decision-making. In innovation-intensive industries, where considerable risky bets are critical to value creation, an explicit consideration for the link between value appropriation and value creation, as we have tried to do here, provides an elaboration that can increase the explanatory power of standard agency theory models.

Our findings suggest that while concentrated ownership can be a check on managerial discretion, the institutional investors in our study also accept the importance of unitary command structures and knowledgeable boards when taking necessary bets on unproven technological investments. Note that Table 6.1 reports statistically significant positive correlations between ownership concentration and CEO duality and higher inside/outside ratios. Perhaps such investors view R&D investments, quality patent portfolios and the successful commercialization of new products as strategic options that add to the firm's capacity to create long-term value. Investors are therefore willing to bet on management by handing over more discretion in the processes related to commercializing R&D investments. In sum, we suggest that future researchers take a less pessimistic view of agency theory when generalizing that it is always better to have an arms-length relationship between the board of directors and management (Boyd, 1995; Ocasio, 1994).

Our study suggests that the governance-innovation link may be more nuanced than previously thought. For example, firms with more resources are more likely to invest in R&D but this does not mean that they will be more successful at patenting or generating new products. Instead, the abundance of resources, coupled with a lack of oversight, may contribute to inefficient R&D. Our data does not seem to indicate that this is the case (the relationship between R&D spending, patenting quality and new products are positive). However, it is premature to make conclusive statements about the appropriate levels of R&D expenditure. Instead, our study encourages more work in this direction and once the relationships between corporate governance and innovation are fully articulated and corroborated by empirical evidence, future efforts at normative theories on governance structure will be more fruitful.

In closing, we suggested at the beginning of this study that governance structure matters on the issue of value creation through innovation. By elaborating the standard agency theory framework we showed the importance of sensitizing governance models to the industrial context and the dependent variables under study. Future research could take a multi-theory approach to model building. Finally, for theory to advance the generalizability and robustness of our findings need to be established. For example, it has been suggested that different types of investors react differently to strategic investments in risky innovation projects (Zahra, 1996). This implies that future studies examining the commitment of investors to innovation should first classify investors in terms of their investment staying power (Kochhar and David, 1996) or activism tendency (Roe, 1996). Understanding the investment horizon and motivations of investors might result in a richer appreciation of a firm's propensity to innovate.

NOTES

1. Title 3, Section 302.
2. For example, boards have the right to recommend the sale of the firm.
3. The literature sometimes lists CEO compensation and board monitoring as dependent variables in the ownership and structure paradigm. In our research model, they would be treated as mediators since the ultimate dependent variables are dimensions of innovation.

However, to keep our model parsimonious, we choose to keep them as latent variables. Their inclusion would increase the explanatory power of the model but not change the overall direction of the arguments.
4. Strictest test of independence in any corporate governance code; adopted 1 August 2002 by the NYSE as an amendment to its listing rules (http://www.nyse.com/pdfs/corp_gov_pro_b.pdf). This test is also part of the Sarbanes-Oxley Act of 2002, Title 4 (http://files.findlaw.com/news.findlaw.com/hdocs/docs/gwbush/sarbanesoxley072302.pdf) (accessed 12 June 2015).
5. The Hausman test rejected the null hypothesis, which confirmed our choice of a fixed effects model over the random effects regression model.

REFERENCES

Aiken, L.S. and West, S.G. (1991). *Multiple Regression: Testing and Interpreting Interactions*. Newbury Park, CA: Sage Publications, p. 35.

Aldrich, H.E., Bolton, M.K., Baker, T. and Sasaki, T. (1998). Information exchange and governance structures in US and Japanese R&D consortia: institutional and organizational influences. *IEEE Transactions on Engineering Management*, **45**, 263–75.

Balkin, D.B., Markman, G.D. and Gomez-Mejia, L.R. (2000). Is CEO pay in high technology firms related to innovation? *Academy of Management Journal*, **43**, 1118–29.

Baysinger, B., Kosnik, R.D. and Turk, T.A. (1991). Effects of board ownership structure on corporate R&D strategy. *Academy of Management Journal*, **34**, 205–14.

Berle, A.A. and Means, G.C. (1932). *The Modern Corporation and Private Property*. New York: Macmillan.

Boeker, W. (1992). Power and managerial dismissal: scapegoating at the top. *Administrative Science Quarterly*, **37**, 400–21.

Boeker, W. and Goodstein, J. (1993). Performance and successor choice: the moderating influence of governance and ownership. *Academy of Management Journal*, **36**, 172–86.

Boyd, B.K. (1995). CEO duality and firm performance: a contingency model. *Strategic Management Journal*, **16**, 301–12.

Casper, S. and Matraves, C. (2003). Institutional frameworks and innovation in the German and UK pharmaceutical industry. *Research Policy*, **32**, 1865–79.

Certo, S.T., Covin, J.G., Daily, C.M. and Dalton, D.R. (2001). Wealth and the effects of founder management among IPO-stage new ventures. *Strategic Management Journal*, **22**, 641–58.

Chung, K.H., Wright, P. and Kedia, B. (2003). Corporate governance and market valuation of capital and R&D investments. *Review of Financial Economics*, **12**, 161–72.

Conger, J.A., Lawler, E.E. and Finegold, D.L. (2001). *Corporate Boards: New Strategies for Adding Value at the Top*. San Francisco, CA: Jossey-Bass.

Conyon, M.J. and Peck, S. I. (1998). Board control, remuneration committees, and top management compensation. *Academy of Management Journal*, **41**, 146–57.

Daily, C.M. and Dalton, D.R. (1992). The relationship between governance structure and corporate performance in entrepreneurial firms. *Journal of Business Venturing*, **7**(5), 375–86.

Daily, C.M. and Dalton, D.R. (1994). Bankruptcy and corporate governance: the impact of board composition and structure. *Academy of Management Journal*, **37**, 1603–17.

Daily, C.M. and Dalton, D.R. (1997). CEO and board chair roles held jointly or separately: much ado about nothing? *Academy of Management Executive*, **11**(3), 11–20.

Daily, C.M., Johnson, J.L. and Dalton, D.R. (1995). The many ways to board composition: if you have seen one, you certainly have not seen them all. Paper presented at the Academy of Management Annual Meeting, Vancouver, BC, Canada, 6–9 August 1995.

Daily, C.M., Certo, S.T. and Dalton, D.R. (2000). International experience in the executive suite: the path to prosperity? *Strategic Management Journal*, **21**, 515–23.

Dalton, D.R., Daily, C.M., Johnson, J.L. and Ellstrand, A.E. (1999). Number of directors and financial performance: a meta-analysis. *Academy of Management Journal*, **42**, 674–86.

Debaise, C. (2002). AstraZeneca has victory in ruling on drug patent. *Wall Street Journal*, 14 October, B4.

Eisenhardt, K.M. (1989). Agency theory: an assessment and review. *Academy of Management Review*, **14**(1), 57–75.

Fama, E. and Jensen, M.C. (1983). Separation of ownership and control. *Journal of Law and Economics*, **26**, 301–25.

Finkelstein, S. and D'Aveni, R.A. (1994). CEO duality as a doubled-edged sword: how boards of directors balance entrenchment avoidance and unity of command. *Academy of Management Journal*, **37**, 1079–108.

Fleming, L. (2001). Recombinant uncertainty in technological search. *Management Science*, **47**(1), 117–32.

Galbraith, J.R. (2001). *Designing Organizations: An Executive Guide to Strategy, Structure, and Process Revised*. San Francisco, CA: Jossey-Bass.

Graves, S.B. (1988). Institutional ownership and corporate R&D in the computer industry. *Academy of Management Journal*, **31**, 417–27.

Greene, W.H. (2003). *Econometric Analysis*, 5th edn. Upper River, NJ: Prentice Hall.

Gugler, K. (2003). Corporate governance, dividend payout policy, and the interrelation between dividends, R&D, and capital investment. *Journal of Banking & Finance*, **27**, 1297–1321.

Harhoff, D., Narin, F., Scherer, F.M. and Vopel, K. (1999). Citation frequency and the value of patented inventions. *Review of Economics and Statistics*, **81**(3), 511–15.

Hensley, S. (2002). Death of Pfizer's 'Youth Pill' illustrates drug makers' woes. *Wall Street Journal*, 2 May, p. 1.

Hill, C.W.L. and Hansen, G.S. (1991). A longitudinal study of the cause and consequences of changes in diversification in the U.S. pharmaceutical industry 1977–1986. *Strategic Management Journal*, **12**, 187–99.

Hill, C.W.L. and Phan, P.H. (1991). CEO tenure as a determinant of CEO pay. *Academy of Management Journal*, **34**(3), 707–17.

Hill, C.W.L. and Snell, S. (1988). External control, corporate strategy, and firm performance in research intensive industries. *Strategic Management Journal*, **9**, 577–90.

Hill, C.W.L. and Snell, S. (1989). Effects of ownership structure and control on corporate productivity. *Academy of Management Journal*, **32**, 25–46.

Jensen, M.C. (1993). The modern industrial revolution, exit, and the failure of internal control systems. *Journal of Finance*, **48**(3), 831–80.

Jensen, M.C. and Meckling, W. (1976). Theory of the firm: managerial behavior, agency costs and ownership structure. *Journal of Financial Economics*, **3**, 305–60.

Kochhar, R. and David, P. (1996). Institutional investors and firm innovation: a test of competing hypotheses. *Strategic Management Journal*, **17**, 73–84.

Lacetera, N. (2001). Corporate governance and the governance of innovation: the case of the pharmaceutical industry. *Journal of Management and Governance*, **5**(1), 29–59.

Markman, G.D., Balkin, D.B. and Schjoedt, L. (2001). Governing the innovation process in entrepreneurial firms. *Journal of High Technology Management Research*, **12**, 273–93.

Markman, G.D., Espina, M.I. and Phan, P.H. (2004). Patents as surrogates for inimitable and non-substitutable resources. *Journal of Management*, **30**(4), 529–44.

Miyajima, H., Arikawa, Y. and Kato, A. (2002). Corporate governance, relational banking and R&D: evidence from Japanese large firms in the 1980s and 1990s. *International Journal of Technology Management*, **23**, 769–87.

Mizruchi, M.S. (1983). Who controls whom? An examination of the relation between management and boards of directors in large American corporations. *Academy of Management Review*, **8**, 426–35.

Monks, A.G. and Minow, N. (2001). *Corporate Governance*, 2nd edn. Malden, MA: Blackwell Publishers.

Ocasio, W. (1994). Political dynamics and the circulation of power: CEO succession in U.S. industrial corporations, 1960–1990. *Administrative Science Quarterly*, **39**, 285–312.

Pennings, J.M. (1992). Structural contingency theory: a reappraisal. In B.M. Staw and L.L. Cummings (eds), *Research in Organizational Behavior*, Vol. 14. Greenwich, CT: JAI Press, pp. 267–309.

Roe, M.J. (1996). *Strong Managers, Weak Owners*. Princeton, NJ: Princeton University Press.

Ruef, M. and Scott, R.W. (1998). A multidimensional model of organizational legitimacy: hospital survival in changing institutional environments. *Administrative Science Quarterly*, **43**, 877–904.

Sanders, W.G. and Carpenter, M.A. (1998). Internationalization and firm governance: the roles of CEO compensation, top team compensation, and board structure. *Academy of Management Journal*, **41**, 158–78.

Tabachnick, B. and Fidell, L. (1996). *Using Multivariate Statistics*, 3rd edn. New York: Harper Collins College Publishers.

Tushman, M.L. and Rosenkopf, L. (1992). Organizational determinants of technological change: toward a sociology of technological evolution. In L.L. Cummings and B.M. Staw (eds), *Research in Organizational Behavior*, Vol. 14. Greenwich, CT: JAI Press, pp. 311–47.

Van de Ven, A.H. and Drazin, R. (1985). The concept of fit in contingency theory. In L.L. Cummings and B.M. Staw (eds), *Research in Organizational Behavior*, Vol. 7. Greenwich, CT: JAI Press, pp. 333–65.

Van de Ven, A.H., Polley, D.E., Garud, R. and Venkataraman, S. (1999). *The Innovation Journey*. New York: Oxford University Press.

Wallace, N.D., Worrell, D.C. and Cheng, L. (1990). Key executive succession and stockholder wealth: the influence of successor's origin, position and age. *Journal of Management*, **16**, 647–64.

Wright, P. and Kroll, M. (2002). Executive discretion and corporate performance as determinants of CEO compensation, contingent on external monitoring activities. *Journal of Management and Governance,* **6**, 189–214.

Zahra, S.A. (1996). Governance, ownership, and corporate entrepreneurship: the moderating impact of industry technological opportunities. *Academy of Management Journal*, **39**, 1713–35.

PART III

Institutional causes and policy consequences
of technology entrepreneurship

7. The institutional inertias that constrain technology-driven economic development

G. Reza Djavanshir

INTRODUCTION

Developing and transitioning countries (DTCs) spend billions of dollars to acquire, use and diffuse different technologies in order to improve their entrepreneurship and development processes and to create new entrepreneurial opportunities for their people. While they are typically successful in acquiring and importing their targeted technology from other countries, they often fail to take full advantage of their technology transfer in ways that create productive entrepreneurial activities and allow them to compete in today's global economy. In other words, they fail to create the kind of competitive advantages that Singapore, South Korea, Japan and many other nations have accomplished over the past half century.

In any economy, technological activities can create entrepreneurial opportunities and act as development tools. Verheul et al. (2002) make the case that there is a two-way relationship between technological advancements and entrepreneurial activities. In other words, technological activities create demand for entrepreneurship and vice versa. Thus, business leaders and policy makers should think about technology transfer and development as levers for their economic and entrepreneurship development efforts.

Entrepreneurship policy is more systemic than simple policy initiatives; it embraces a broad range of institutions, agencies and actors (Audretsch, 2003). Moreover, technology transfer is a complex non-linear process requiring well-planned policies and congruence among the institutions that support it (Malerba and Nelson, 2012b). This means that in order for a country to realize the effective transfer and development of technology, it must ensure that its institutions function well. Thus, we also need to consider the important role that institutional elements play in making a country's technology-driven entrepreneurship and economic development efforts more effective. These institutional elements include the rule of law; effective and consistent enforcement of laws, policies and property rights; the creation of incentives for entrepreneurial activities; the cost and time associated with obtaining business licenses; the ability to access undistorted information; and transparent operation of government and financial organizations.

In addition to the institutions mentioned above, we also need to consider the critical role that normative and cultural-cognitive institutional elements play in achieving effective technology-driven entrepreneurship and economic development. Critical factors in normative and cultural-cognitive institutions include people's propensity toward respecting the rule of law, equal rights for and equal treatment of women and minorities, the prevalence of tribal and discriminatory norms and the extent to which a culture fosters people's ability to learn and adapt to the dynamics of changing environments. These normative and cultural-cognitive factors are critical because they directly impact a nation's ability to imitate, learn quickly and synthesize its local knowledge, talents and skill sets with technology in order to create a unique amalgam of core capabilities that make it competitive in a global economy.

Today, DTCs recognize the importance of innovation and technology transfer as catalysts for their entrepreneurship and economic development strategies. Many of these countries have even built their own national innovation and entrepreneurship systems. These systems, along with regional clusters and other necessary elements, are similar to the structure that Freeman (2002), Edquist (1997) and others have recommended as best practice. Furthermore, a number of developing countries (for example, Saudi Arabia) are trying to follow the successful technology transfer models that leading research universities in the USA and Europe have used. Evidence of this approach can be observed in the country's decision to open technology transfer offices in their leading engineering schools. This approach is similar to what exists in the developed economies studied by Siegel et al. (2003). Additionally, based on their governments' policies on university-industry collaboration and technology transfer, some of the leading universities in DTCs have adopted official mission statements regarding the critical role of technology transfer, which has been suggested by Markman et al. (2005).

Despite all of this focus, there are some missing links in developing countries' technology transfer, development and entrepreneurial efforts. One such major link is the persistence of anachronistic or inefficient formal and informal institutions, which act as inertias and negatively impact their efforts.

Douglas North (1990) has identified the impact that institutions have on a country's economic development. North makes an important distinction between formal and informal institutions. Formal institutions are the visible rules of the game. These include legal institutions such as the rule of law and intellectual property rights, but they also include educational institutions that contribute to research and development (R&D). Formal institutions can be changed and enforced quickly to adapt to an evolving environment.

In contrast, informal institutions can be thought of as the invisible rules of the game. These include cultural values, norms, legitimate (acceptable) behaviors and codes of conduct. In other words, informal institutions define 'the general habits of action and thoughts' (Veblen, 1915) in a society. These norms and other cultural institutions also determine the level of trust in a country, which impacts the sense of cooperation among its individual members (Fukuyama, 2004). Moreover, normative and cultural elements impact the creation of the kind of meaningful interactions between individuals that can result in entrepreneurial activities (Audretsch and Aldridge, 2012).

In light of the large impact of formal and informal institutions, it is clear that in order to succeed in their technology-driven economic and entrepreneurship development efforts, DTCs need functioning formal and informal institutions (Aidis and Estrin, 2014). It is also important that informal institutional elements should evolve to complement formal institutions. If informal and formal institutions clash, non-compliant behaviors proliferate, and this can cause inertias in the country's development efforts. The result of these inertias is failed economic and technology-driven entrepreneurship development strategies and policies. As North (1997) and Aidis and Estrin (2014) have noted, changing the formal rules and policies can create the desired outcomes only when the informal norms and codes of conduct complement the changes in rules and policies, and only when the enforcement of these rules and policies is effective and consistent.

This chapter attempts to elaborate on the institutional inertias that work to prevent DTCs from benefiting from technology-driven developments in entrepreneurship. It discusses how both formal and informal institutional forces maintain their influence on the complex processes of technology development, technology transfer and entrepreneurship development.

The following section lays out the theoretical framework used in this chapter. It discusses institutional inertias in DTCs and briefly outlines the importance of institutions in enabling countries to benefit from their efforts toward technology transfer and economic development. This section also discusses the relevant institutional elements for technology-driven economic development strategies in DTCs. It describes the elements that these nations need in order to build effective capabilities and benefit from their technology transfer efforts.

The third section outlines some policy recommendations and the final section provides some recommendations for possible future studies.

THEORY

The level of technological activity and the corresponding entrepreneurial activities in a country are embedded in its economic, socio-cultural and legal environment. The development and transfer of technology is a complex, non-linear process, which requires institutional changes in developing countries (Cohen, 2004; Freeman, 1994, 2002, 2010). As such, institutional theory can provide an appropriate framework for addressing the national contexts that shape entrepreneurial activity (Baughn et al., 2006). Institutional theory focuses on the role of legal systems as well as the cultural and normative elements that surround organizations and individuals (North, 1990; Scott, 2008).

As we have seen, the quality of a country's regulative, normative and cultural-cognitive institutions play a key role in its efforts toward promoting technology development, technology transfer and entrepreneurship. The presence and effective enforcement of a nation's laws, intellectual property and contract rights are integral in the country's technology-driven entrepreneurship development strategy. Additionally, in DTCs, these formal institutions are directly impacted by the country's normative and cultural elements.

The key cultural and normative elements that impact developing countries' technology-driven entrepreneurship development include attitudes toward equality for women and minorities, attitudes toward entrepreneurship and foreign investment and general respect for the law and for contracts. An individual's preferences are manifested in their cultural values, and attitudes are shaped during their childhood. These preferences, which also include attitudes toward risk-taking, are determined by an individual's cultural background (Audretsch et al., 2007; Audretsch et al., 2014).

Scott (2008) enumerates the regulative, normative and cultural-cognitive elements of institutions. While the regulative pillar is formal and encoded in laws and policies, the normative pillar includes the uncodified attitudes in society (Welter et al., 2004). When such normative expectations and attitudes are broadly diffused, they tend to 'take on a rule-like status in social thought and action' (Covaleski and Dirsmith, 1988, p. 562; see also Baughn et al., 2006). As Scott (2008) notes, institutions provide stability, order and predictability to social behavior. The different institutional elements provide different forms of stability. While the underlying 'logic' of the regulative pillar is instrumental conformity to rules and laws, the logic of the normative pillar is the 'appropriateness' of any decision or behavior (Baughn et al., 2006; Scott, 1995, p. 35).

Thus, this chapter follows the approaches employed by North (1990), Nelson (2002, 2012), Aidis and Estrin (2014), Freeman (1986, 1994, 2010), Baumol (1990) and Bell and Pavitt (1993), and builds on a theoretical framework primarily based on the theories of institutions articulated by Scott (2008), DiMaggio and Powell (1991), Zucker (1991) and Abramovitz (1986). During the last 25 years, institutional theory has emerged as a powerful approach in explaining the impact of institutions on the behavior of individuals and on organizational decision making. As Liang et al. (2007) noted, institutional forces cannot impact the behavior of a nation without impacting the behavior of human actors within the nation's organizations and firms. The rationale for applying institutional theory in this chapter is that it explains the forces and inertias that impact the behaviors of individuals in economic systems.

Formal Institutional Inertias

In this chapter, formal institutional forces include laws, regulations and policies set by the government. They also include government agencies that enforce the law.

The rule of law, with an effective and consistent enforcement mechanism, is necessary to protect contracts, property rights and investments. In some DTCs, inconsistent and ineffective enforcement of laws, regulations, public policies and contracts can be the result of either the financial interests of the enforcement agents or can be caused by the dominance of primary relationships (family or tribal) over secondary relationships (formal or business). Both cases can lead agents in the public and private sectors to engage in opportunistic behavior and make decisions that are sub-optimal in terms of the nation's development efforts. This also results in an agency problem when the government agency's interests coincide with the interest of the individual who is engaged in opportunistic and illegal activities (North, 1990, p. 54).

Agency theory emphasizes the difficulty and cost for principals to accurately monitor the behavior of agents. Therefore, agency theory tries to align the interests of the agent with that of the principal by designing contracts between the principal and agent based on incentives and sanctions. The purpose of this is to minimize the impact of the agent's opportunistic behavior and of the asymmetric information that he or she provides to the principal (Milgrom and Roberts, 1992).

According to North (1990, p. 64), monitoring and enforcing the contract between the principal and agent is the responsibility of the government. However, he also warns (North, 1990, p. 54) of the possible problem that arises when the government agency's interests (he refers to the agency's 'utility function') coincide with the interest of the agent and result in biased outcomes. Thus, the personal interests of decision makers in both public and private sectors may result in the misallocation of public and private resources. Moreover, the same personal interests may result in poorly constructed infrastructure as well as opportunistic decisions when negotiating and structuring contracts and in selecting appropriate technology to support the country's technological, entrepreneurship and economic development.

Opportunistic behavior is a chronic problem in some DTCs that results in ineffective and inconsistent enforcement of laws, regulations, public policies and contracts. Audretsch et al. (2014) suggest that, to the extent that there are problems with enforcing contracts, there are negative implications regarding the ability of the government and other organizations to capture the benefits of their technology transfer efforts. In DTCs specifically, these problems slow down technology-driven economic development efforts; in particular, they increase transaction costs and reduce the incentives for entrepreneurial activities and investments. Specific outcomes of ineffective formal institutions are briefly outlined in the following paragraphs.

Lack of effective education and training systems
In an economy, education and training are the heart of building capabilities for scientific discovery, innovation and technological development. In order to train educated, competent and employable graduates, a country needs high-quality education and training systems surrounded by efficient cultural and normative institutional elements. In fact, the quality of a country's system of education is often highly impacted by its normative and cultural institutions.

Porter (1998) makes the point that countries and the companies operating within them cannot compete on sophisticated products and services without well-educated employees and well-informed customers. Formal education and training along with membership in professional networks, professional publications and trade associations are effective mechanisms to develop such employees and customers – those who have the 'know-how', the 'know-why' and other necessary cultural-cognitive elements. These institutions not only train competent scientists, technologists and managers, but also help to define accepted norms and behaviors that become institutionalized among members of the group and manifest themselves in their 'life-styles,' preferences, attitudes, discourse and codes of conduct (Williamson, 1979).

Due to the ineffective educational policies and anachronistic norms and cultural elements that exist in some DTCs, the quality and content of their educational systems do not meet the demands of today's technology-driven entrepreneurial economies. As a result of this deficiency, their graduates are usually not well positioned to engage in productive scientific discoveries and technological activities. In other words, these countries' education systems, combined with their normative and cultural institutional elements, are not fully capable of providing their people with the skill sets that they need to compete in today's global economy.

In addition to formal education systems, dominant norms and cultural-cognitive elements play an enormous role in a country's technology development, technology transfer and entrepreneurial activities. Audretsch et al. (2007) emphasize the importance of an individual's preferences on his or her decision to become an entrepreneur. These preferences, which are expressed through values and attitudes developed and articulated during one's upbringing (Audretsch et al., 2007), include one's attitudes toward taking risks, one's aspirations to become a business owner and one's desire to learn and excel. However, individuals' preferences are, to a large extent, determined by their family backgrounds and surrounding normative and cultural institutional elements. As such, it takes a long time to change or modify people's dominant preferences, attitudes and values. However, governments can influence and shape individual preferences by fostering an entrepreneurial culture (Audretsch et al., 2007). They can achieve this in part by introducing entrepreneurial values, attitudes, 'know-hows' and 'know-whys' into their education system. Governments can also shape individuals' preferences and attitudes by promoting entrepreneurship in the mass media, professional publications, professional conferences, training workshops and through social networks.

Entrepreneurs in all countries, but especially in DTCs, face risk and uncertainty. When facing a situation of risk and uncertainty, people tend to mimic the behavior of other people facing a similar situation (Liang et al., 2007). When a DTC has unclear technological and entrepreneurial policies, or when its technological and entrepreneurial policies are misunderstood, entrepreneurs may mimic the behaviors of others in the society whom they perceive as having been successful. Mimicking, therefore, is often associated with joining the successful crowd (Staw and Epstein, 2000). If the crowd prefers technology startup businesses to other professional alternatives, others may be encouraged to follow this path.

The process of institutionalizing new norms and cultural elements (for example, attitudes toward entrepreneurship or risk-taking) is a long and complex process. It starts with understanding the benefits of the new norms and culture. The next step is unlearning the old norms and cultural elements and learning the new ones. Finally, through a long process of repetition and internalization, the new norms and cultural elements become institutionalized (DiMaggio and Powell, 1991; Scott, 2008).

In this way, globalization presents a major threat to native norms and cultures. Lundvall et al. (2002) suggest that as the economies open up and interactions between different nations become more frequent, societies restructure themselves accordingly. Thus, local norms and native cultures are readily 'unlearned' and forgotten. That is, they are replaced by globally accepted culture and norms through the process of institutionalization.

A country's education systems, mass media and professional associations, along with the process of globalization, are critical to the process of institutionalizing new norms and culture in a nation, and improving the capabilities needed to engage in technology-driven entrepreneurship.

Lack of effective technical and social capabilities
Capability building complements formal education. It focuses on creating technical, managerial and social capabilities that developing countries need in order to achieve their desired goals of technology transfer and entrepreneurship. Thus, building technical capability that meets international standards should be the main objective of any technology transfer and development process (Cohen, 2004; Millman, 1990). In addition to effective education systems, things like workshops, seminars, vocational training, professional networks and publications can build capabilities that technological and entrepreneurial efforts depend on. In the following sub-sections of this chapter, we attempt to outline the specific capabilities that developing countries need to focus on in order to succeed in their technological and entrepreneurial efforts.

Capability to evaluate, develop and transfer the right technologies
Assessing the value of any technology is critical. This is because DTCs have limited resources, and therefore need to ensure that they acquire and transfer technologies that meet their local needs. In addition, acquiring and transferring the right technology not only makes the process of absorbing, adapting and diffusing it easier, but can also be effectively aligned with the internal and external dynamics of the country's entrepreneurship and socio-economic development processes. Thus, the targeted technology should be evaluated based on its ability to improve the country's productivity, innovations, entrepreneurship and socio-economic development.

Social capability to make institutional changes

This is a critical factor, because in order for developing countries to make technological changes, they must also have the necessary capabilities to make the required institutional change (Abramovitz, 1986). In a seminal article about 'Catching up, forging ahead, and falling behind,' Abramovitz (1986) argues that historically, the countries that succeeded in achieving their industrial, technological and economic development goals were the ones that created 'social capability to make institutional and technical changes.' He posits that 'technological backwardness' and a low level of productivity and economic development are not usually mere accidental misfortunes; rather they have 'tenacious societal characteristics.' In other words, institutional failures in countries account for a substantial part of their failure to achieve high levels of technological and economic development that have been achieved by other successful and advanced countries during the course of history (Abramovitz, 1986).

The process of building social capabilities is complex and non-linear. Social capabilities include not only the capability to make institutional changes, but also technical capabilities. A study by Dahlman et al. (1987) shows that the successes of countries' efforts toward technology transfer and development have been due, in large part, to their governments' consistent policies on technology, education, and making social changes. This means that in order to be successful, DTCs need to formulate policies to build both required technical and social capabilities. These capabilities together will enable them to make the necessary technological and institutional changes that they need in order to create core competencies and establish competitive advantage in the global economy.

Diminishing incentives and misuse of talent

One of the major objectives of technology transfer and development is to create opportunities for new entrepreneurial ventures (Audretsch et al., 2007; Audretsch et al., 2014). Indeed, the importance of incentives in entrepreneurial opportunities is a well-understood concept. Baumol (1990) notes the critical roles that formal and informal institutions play in creating the incentive structure in a given country. Formal and informal institutions impact incentive structures that, in turn, influence the dynamics of technology development, technology transfer and entrepreneurial activities. However, in some DTCs, due to their weak formal and informal institutions, the incentive structure makes it more lucrative for an individual to engage in unsanctioned opportunistic behaviors than in productive technological and entrepreneurial activities. That is, individuals in a country's talent pool may be driven to get involved in unproductive behaviors that serve their immediate interests (North, 1990), instead of putting their talents, skills and capabilities into productive, technology-driven entrepreneurial efforts. This is a major problem in some developing countries with inefficient formal and informal institutions, to the extent that it diminishes the incentives for engaging in productive business activities. Thus, it results in the misallocation of talent and creates adverse effects for a country's technology and entrepreneurship development efforts.

Lack of accurate information
The ability to access undistorted and accurate information is the *sine qua-non* of not only scientific, technological and business activities, but also of making decisions about allocating resources, structuring contracts, and reducing risk and uncertainty, among other areas. Access to undistorted information is therefore crucial for discovering and capitalizing on entrepreneurial opportunities (Audretsch et al., 2014).

In DTCs, the ability to access accurate information is a systemic problem that stems from weak institutions. Inaccurate information can create weak banking and financial credit systems in developing countries, resulting in improper lending by public and private banking and credit institutions. For Audretsch et al. (2007), accurate information is critical to credit markets; when information is highly asymmetrical, credit rationing can emerge. In their seminal work, Audretsch et al. (2007) argue that, because the cost of obtaining accurate information depends upon the size of the firm, new and small firms become more exposed to asymmetric information and therefore to credit rationing. Thus, the lack of accurate information can become an entry barrier to young and small ventures in a country. Moreover, Auerswald (2007) makes the case that information problems can cause not only costly and incomplete contracts, they can also be a source for market failures in technology entrepreneurship. Thus, in developing countries, firms with access to accurate information are better positioned to adopt and transfer appropriate technology and to reduce the risks of inaccurate decisions, incomplete contracts and market failures.

Therefore, policy makers in developing countries should formulate consistent policies with effective enforcement mechanisms that place high penalties on sources of inaccurate and distorted information. They should also work to create a public information repository or bank. These measures can serve to minimize the level of inaccuracy and asymmetry in their country's information, and enable people to access undistorted information.

Obtaining business licenses with minimum cost and within minimum time
Young and small companies make up the majority of the firms in DTCs. Some of the major challenges that new startup entrepreneurs face in these countries relate to obtaining business licenses, registering patents

and obtaining intellectual property rights with minimum cost and within minimum time. This is a major problem in many developing countries because it effectively creates a barrier to entry for startup technology businesses. Therefore, public policy makers should formulate policies with effective enforcement mechanisms that minimize the required time and monetary cost of registering patents, registering intellectual property and starting new businesses.

Informal Institutional Inertias – Normative and Cultural-cognitive Elements

Normative and cultural-cognitive institutional contexts define the norms, beliefs, culture and default values that are deeply encoded in a society. These institutional contexts play a critical role in determining how people behave, interact, trust and relate with each other, and how they learn and use their knowledge and capabilities (Lundvall et al., 2002). Institutional norms define the legitimate or socially accepted behaviors and routines (repeated patterns of behaviors that are taken for granted).

Cultural-cognitive institutions define the behavioral maps or scripts for an individual. Employing Hofstede's (1991) metaphor, they are the 'software of the mind' (see also Scott, 2008). Cultural elements also define the shared image of life, unquestioned assumptions or default values of an individual's activities (Gharajedaghi, 2007). Scott (2008, p. 127) notes that individuals organize their material world based on their mental categories. This means that cultural-cognitive elements create an internalized microcosm of the world in an individual's mind, which serves as the information-process agent and determines an individual's preferences and attitudes, and how they organize, interpret, encode, prioritize, evaluate and respond to events (Markus and Zajonc, 1985).

Additionally, norms and cultural-cognitive elements are mutually reinforcing, and they create social obligations for an individual (March and Olsen, 1984). These elements not only impact an individual's goals, routines and organizational activities, but also influence the processes of strategy formulation, planning and implementation (DiMaggio and Powell, 1991; Scott, 2008). The following paragraphs outline some impacts of informal institutions in developing countries.

Social networks
Informal institutions such as social networks between technologists, businesses and individuals can enable technology entrepreneurs to access resources, information, labor and talent pools, and can enhance the entrepreneur's opportunity recognition capability (Aidis and Estrin, 2014;

Hills et al., 1997). Thus, in any country, the existence of effective informal institutions is critical to the survival of their innovation, technology development, technology transfer and entrepreneurial activities. However, due to ineffective formal institutions in some developing countries, social networks and connections can sometimes create mechanisms to circumvent the rule of law. That is, some individuals in DTCs may attempt to ignore the law by taking advantage of their close connections and ties with influential people. Thus, in the absence of effective and consistent enforcement of laws, personal connections can penetrate all branches of government, creating favoritism and corruption.

Tribal cultural values and norms

In many developing countries, normative and cultural elements are heavily influenced by the 'tribal' or group identities. The group's rights, choices and identity replace those of the individual. Close cultural bonds between the group members define their legitimacy, and members seek to achieve recognition from group-mates or tribe leaders who monopolize political and economic power (Fukuyama, 2004). Clan and tribe leaders define the map of 'reality' in loyal members' minds and provide scripts for their 'legitimate' (accepted) behaviors. This script or map for group members' behaviors becomes the set of institutionalized norms and cultural-cognitive elements of the group. These behaviors act as their own reinforcing mechanisms. This can result in xenophobia (Fukuyama, 2004) where resistance to any new idea, any suggestion from an 'outsider' or any foreign investment is interpreted as a threat to their local norms and cultural identities. These beliefs run contrary to the country's development goals, since foreign investments can be a key factor for a successful development strategy.

Furthermore, a tribal worldview (*weltanschauung*) strongly opposes any innovative culture and spontaneous behavior. Tribal networks also create a culture of inspection and punishments, in which obedience and following the rules of a tribe's clan become a routine habit (Aidis and Estrin, 2014). Thus, the tribe suppresses risk-taking and independent actions among the loyal members.

Bypassing the law

In any market economy, the respect for the law, contracts and property rights are considered critical to conducting business. Specifically, for technology-driven entrepreneurship, protection of intellectual property rights and honoring contracts are the key elements that secure investments. Moreover, R&D activities and technology transfer processes may depend on obtaining financial credit, raising capital and bearing high risks. All of these activities require transactional trusts – protecting contracts and intellectual property rights with effective and consistent enforcement (Aidis and Estrin, 2014).

However, in some developing countries, there is a weak propensity toward respecting the rule of law, honoring contracts and protecting intellectual property. Thus, some individuals among the private and public citizens may try to bypass the law and contracts by taking advantage of their ties to government officials or through bribery, extortion and other illegal activities. Thus, these norms and attitudes can create major problems for developing countries' technology transfer and entrepreneurship development processes. For example, violation of intellectual property and copyrights, software piracy and breach of contracts diminish the incentives for individuals to engage in technological and entrepreneurial activities.

Policy makers in these countries should formulate laws and policies that establish the rule of law and respect for contracts and property rights, and ensure that they are strictly and consistently enforced. Further, their media and education systems should actively promote norms and attitudes related to respecting the law, contracts and property rights.

Direct and indirect discrimination against women

In many DTCs, women represent a major untapped professional talent pool, where women's level of involvement in technology transfer and technology-driven entrepreneurship processes is significantly lower than in developed countries. In DTCs, either a large percentage of women are often not employed at all or they are not involved in technological and entrepreneurial activities. This may stem from the DTCs' normative and cultural values that directly or indirectly discriminate against women. Thus, one of the major challenges in some such countries is the incorporation of women into entrepreneurial activities.

Countries should address the issue of equal treatment and equal rights for women, not only from a human rights point of view, but also because countries that discriminate against women deprive themselves of the talents, knowledge, skills and efforts of a large part of their population. Moreover, discrimination against women creates a major inertia in the ability of business and government organizations to involve women in their entrepreneurship and economic development processes (Aidis et al., 2007).

Aidis et al. (2007) suggest that, if a nation's population is to contribute to its entrepreneurship and development efforts, it is important that women, along with men, fully participate in the country's development efforts. Moreover, Welter et al. (2004) argue that women-owned businesses are important to the transition process of developing countries for several reasons. First, they tend to employ and engage other women in their country more frequently, which reduces the impact of discrimination against women in the labor force. Second, women entrepreneurs can become role models for later generations. Third, by encouraging women to engage in entrepreneurial activities, a country could see more successful transition and development processes emerging through increased innovation capabilities and entrepreneurship development.

However, according to Welter et al. (2004), in many developing countries, this kind of discrimination against women is manifested in different forms. For example, even when gender equality is legally or constitutionally endorsed in a given DTC, there may exist differences in role allocations or implicit discrimination against women. This may stem from traditional attitudes of society that forbid women to carry out certain activities (Welter et al., 2004). Differing 'appropriate' jobs or normative expectations for men and women may be manifested in work preference, as children are taught which career choices are deemed appropriate for their gender (Baughn et al., 2006; Harriman, 1985; Hisrich, 1986). Thus, as Baughn et al. (2006) note, these traditional norms and cultural values have led to gender-segregated labor forces, involving both horizontal (in which women are clustered in different occupations from their male counterparts) and vertical (in which women are more frequently found at lower levels of occupations) labor market segregation. Gender inequality creates forces that may decrease the level of female participation in entrepreneurship (and technology transfer and development) efforts; thus diminishing the effectiveness of the country's efforts to catch up with the developed economies (Baughn et al., 2006).

Baughn et al. (2006) examine national characteristics related to attitudes toward women and the relative rates of women to men engaged in entrepreneurship in different countries. They suggest that anti-discrimination laws and government policies play critical roles in eliminating gender discrimination. However, although changes in regulative institutions and policies can be implemented in a short period of time, norms and cultural values take much longer to be changed. Therefore, in these countries, policy makers should take greater steps toward accelerating the pace of eliminating gender discrimination and increasing the rate at which women engage in all activities of the country's development processes. Moreover, in DTCs, the education and training systems should strongly and actively oppose all kinds of discrimination. The media in these countries can also play a critical role in eliminating the discriminatory norms, attitudes and cultural values.

Trust and social capital

In any country, successful businesses are those that have established trust and a sense of cooperation with their customers, suppliers, distributors, creditors and even with their competitors. Trust plays a critical role in creating a sense of cooperation and social capital among individuals in a social network. Trust and social capital increase the efficiency, effectiveness and productivity of any technological partnership between the engaged parties. Audretsch and Aldridge (2012) define social capital as cooperative interactions and social networking among individuals, and they suggest that social capital enhances entrepreneurship development activities. Further, cooperative interactions facilitate coordination among individuals and organizations, creating mutual benefits in an efficient way. Thus, trust and social capital make a developing country more conducive to investment and create an efficient process of technology-driven entrepreneurship and development.

Podolny (2009) suggests that individuals usually trust each other if they share the same values and if they make sure that their expectations are met. There are many elements that erode trust and cooperation. These include corruption, lack of fairness, lack of transparency, inconsistent behaviors and disparity between the credibility of a message and the credibility of its messenger. In many developing countries, a lack of trust and social capital can be inevitable problems, mostly due to ineffective and inconsistent enforcement of laws, contracts, intellectual property rights, corruptions, tribal norms, lack of transparency and fairness.

Fukuyama (1995) argues that to build an efficient economy, developing countries not only need to integrate technological advancements into their economies, they also need to build nationwide trust networks. However, the strength of any nationwide trust network depends on the strength of the country's regulative institutions along with their norms and cultural values. Thus, these three institutional elements are critical to technological and entrepreneurial development processes. Nevertheless, some developing countries experience high levels of interaction, trust and cooperation within tribal sub-networks, and low levels outside tribal networks or within the entire nation. The lower level of nationwide trust and cooperation can be detrimental to DTCs because it can result in lower public support for the country's technological and entrepreneurial development processes and increase transaction costs. Moreover, lower levels of trust and cooperation in these countries can result in lower respect for laws and government policies. In this regard, trust becomes a critical factor to reduce the transaction costs by providing a necessary means to enforce policies, laws and business contracts.

POLICY RECOMMENDATIONS

DTCs face unique challenges in technology development, technology transfer and technology-driven entrepreneurial activities. These challenges include a lack of awareness about the benefits of technology transfer and entrepreneurial activities; lack of business opportunities and incentives to start new ventures; scarcity of resources; lack of access to credit, loans and financing; need for capability building and technical and administrative assistance; and lack of access to undistorted information, counseling and training. These challenges partly stem from formal and informal institutions in these countries. Thus, DTCs should engage in reforming and improving the institutions and critical infrastructures that they need in order to create a robust, technology-driven entrepreneurial economy. Specifically, policy makers in developing countries should create mechanisms that ensure the effective enforcement of laws, contracts and intellectual property rights. Without these mechanisms in place, potential technologists and entrepreneurs may not be properly incentivized to engage in innovative, technological and entrepreneurial activities. Moreover, governments should formulate policies to resolve the problems that can cause market failures in their countries. Chief among these problems are the lack of access to undistorted information and the high monetary and time costs that a business must incur to obtain a license. These can create barriers to entry that stand in the way of these countries' technology-driven entrepreneurship development processes.

Technology development is often the driving force for entrepreneurship and vice versa (Verheul et al., 2002; Wennekers and Thurik, 1999). In developing countries, technology development and technology transfer create opportunities for technology-driven entrepreneurship development, which can result in more technology development and technology transfer. Thus, there is a circular causal loop between technological and entrepreneurial development. This means that entrepreneurial activities can create the necessary condition for technology development and transfer activities in a country. Therefore, policies aimed at promoting entrepreneurship can relate directly to technological development and technology transfer activities. Moreover, Audretsch et al. (2012) suggest that technology-driven economic development relates directly to fostering entrepreneurship in DTCs. They view entrepreneurial activities as an effective vehicle to transform scientific and technological knowledge into entrepreneurship development in a way that fosters economic growth. The more entrepreneurial activities in developing countries, the more rapid, technology-based economic developments. In today's competitive global economy, Audretsch et al. (2014) argue that policy makers, managers of firms and academic institutions should work together to create mechanisms to expand the effectiveness of technology transfer in their country. Thus, from a policy perspective, DTCs may look at their technology transfer and economic development activities from the perspective of entrepreneurship development. That is, policy makers in developing countries should focus on integrating their policies regarding technology transfer and innovation with their policies regarding entrepreneurship. Moreover, DTCs can structure incentives in order to create networks of technological collaboration at the national, regional and global levels (Audretsch et al., 2012). In academic entrepreneurship based on technology transfer, the number and quality of networks fostering industrial collaboration are key (Siegel et al., 2003). In this environment, entrepreneurs can collaborate on issues resulting in increased R&D, knowledge spillover, technology development and transfer, education and training. Working together, businesses and governments can evaluate which technologies fit their national and regional conditions and provide the best response to their needs. Additionally, policy makers in different developing countries should have a comprehensive systemic view of technology development, technology transfer and technology-driven entrepreneurial ventures. The alternative 'siloed' view of these critical activities ignores the systemic interactions among many critical actors like banks, policy makers, universities, individuals and institutions (Acs et al., 2014). Similarly, Audretsch et al. (2007) suggest a comprehensive or a systemic view of any entrepreneurship policy that includes individuals, organizations, countries, industries and geographic locations.

In two seminal articles, Verheul et al. (2002) and Audretsch et al. (2007) suggest policy frameworks for entrepreneurship development. These authors explain the level of entrepreneurship in a country by making distinctions between its demand and supply side policies (Audretsch et al., 2007; Verheul et al., 1999).

The demand side of entrepreneurship focuses on policies impacting technology development, market size, competition, regulatory and industrial structure, availability of resources and financing policies that create opportunities for entrepreneurship. In many DTCs, due to scarcity of venture capital and financial credit, government subsidies play a key role in R&D, technology development and entrepreneurial activities.

The supply side represents policies impacting the country's demographics, socio-cultural factors, capabilities, abilities and entrepreneurial attitudes. Thus, it includes the country's education system, training workshops, consulting and other necessary services that foster technology-driven entrepreneurship development. In other words, the supply side focuses on developing and implementing policies that encourage, empower and enable individuals to take advantage of the opportunities created by technology development (Audretsch et al., 2007; Verheul et al., 1999). Thus, in DTCs, governments can work in cooperation with universities and private companies to offer education, workshops and training on issues such as:

1. Development of entrepreneurship and entrepreneurial awareness.
2. Processes and key elements of technology development and technology transfer, as well as ways to capture the values and opportunities created by technological activities.
3. Global supply chain and inventory management.
4. Negotiations techniques.
5. Business and strategic planning.
6. Project management and risk-reward analysis.
7. Cultural training aimed at eliminating discrimination against women, minorities and foreigners.
8. Cultural training focused on eliminating tribalism.

CONCLUSIONS

This chapter has attempted to outline the impacts of different institutional inertias on DTCs' complex strategies for technology-driven economic development. The chapter has discussed the systemic barriers in developing countries' formal and informal institutions and how they can impede their efforts to benefits from technology transfer and entrepreneurship developments. The chapter specifically focused on discussing the weaknesses in developing countries' regulative, normative and cultural-cognitive institutions that act as inertias in those countries' technology transfer, development and entrepreneurial strategies, which can prevent a country's technology-driven economic development processes from achieving its desired strategic goals.

Finally, the chapter provides some policy recommendations on how to improve DTCs' institutional weaknesses and what policies they may need to formulate and implement in order to benefit from their efforts in technology transfer and entrepreneurship developments.

For further study, we recommend investigating which mechanisms are effective in extracting undistorted and reliable data from DTCs, and whether data analytics might be a way of accomplishing this. Moreover, future research may study and analyse what other mechanisms may exist that countries can employ to effect changes in their normative and cultural-cognitive institutional inertias.

REFERENCES

Abramovitz, M.A. (1986). Catching up, forging ahead, and falling behind. *Journal of Economic History*, **46**, 385–406.

Acs, Z.J., L. Szerb and E. Autio (eds) (2014). *Global Entrepreneurship and Development Index*. Washington, DC: CreateSpace Independent Publishing Platform, The Global Entrepreneurship and Development Institute.

Aidis, R. and S. Estrin (2014). Institutions, incentive, and entrepreneurship. In Z.J. Acs, L. Szerb and E. Autio (eds), *Global Entrepreneurship and Development Index*. Washington, DC: CreateSpace Independent Publishing Platform, The Global Entrepreneurship and Development Institute, pp. 27–37.

Aidis, R., F. Welter, D. Smallbone and N. Isakova (2007). Female entrepreneurship in transition economies: the case of Lithuania and Ukraine. *Feminist Economics*, **13**(2), 157–83.

Audretsch, D.B. (2003). Entrepreneurship policy and the strategic management of places. In David M. Hart (ed.), *The Emergence of Entrepreneurship Policy*. Cambridge: Cambridge University Press, pp. 20–38.

Audretsch, D.B. and D. Aldridge (2012). Transnational social capital and scientists entrepreneurship. In D.B. Audretsch (ed.), *Public Policy in the Entrepreneurial Society*. Cheltenham, UK and Northampton, MA, USA: Edward Elgar, pp. 193–200.

Audretsch, D.B., I. Grilo and A.R. Thurik (2007). Explaining entrepreneurship and the role of policy: a framework. In D.B. Audretsch, I. Grilo and A.R. Thurik (eds), *Handbook of Research on Entrepreneurship Policy*. Cheltenham, UK and Northampton, MA, USA: Edward Elgar, pp. 1–18.

Audretsch, D.B., E.E. Lehmann and M. Wright (2014). Technology transfer in a global economy. *Journal of Technology of Technology Transfer*, **39**, 301–12.

Auerswald, P.E. (2007). The simple economics of entrepreneurship: market failure reconsidered. In D.B. Audretsch, I. Grilo and A.R. Thurik (eds), *Handbook of Research on Entrepreneurship Policy*. Cheltenham, UK and Northampton, MA, USA: Edward Elgar, pp. 18–35.

Ausubel, J.H. (1991). Diffusion of technologies and social behavior. In N. Nakicenovic and A. Grubler (eds), *Rat Race Dynamics and Crazy Companies: The Diffusion of Technologies and Social Behavior*. Berlin: Springer-Verlag, pp. 1–7.

Baughn, C., B.-L. Chua, B-L. and K.E. Kent (2006). The normative context for women's participation in entrepreneurship: a multicountry study. *Entrepreneurship Theory and Practice*, September, **30**(5), 687–708.

Baumol, W. (1990). Entrepreneurship: productive, unproductive and destructive. *Journal of Political Economy*, **98**, 893–921.

Bell, M. and K.L.R. Pavitt (1993). Industrial and corporate change. *Oxford Journal*, **2**(2), 157–210.

Cohen, G. (2004). *Technology Transfer: Strategic Management in Developing Countries*. New Delhi and London: Sage.

Covaleski, M.A. and M.W. Dirsmith (1988). An institutional perspective on the rise, social transformation, and fall of a university budget category. *Administrative Science Quarterly*, **33**, 562–87.

Dahlman, C.J., B. Ross-Larson and L.E. Westphal (1987). Managing technological development: lessons from the newly industrializing countries. *World Development*, **15**(6), 1373–88.

DiMaggio, P.J. and W.W. Powell (1991). The iron cage revisited: institutional isomorphism and collective rationality in organizational fields. In W.W. Powell and P.J. DiMaggio (eds), *The New Institutionalism in Organizational Analysis*. Chicago, IL: University of Chicago Press, pp. 63–82.

Edquist, C. (1997). Systems of innovations approaches – their emergence characteristics. In C. Equist (ed.), *Systems of Innovation, Technologies, Institutions and Organizations*. London: Printer, pp. 1–29.

Freeman, C. (1986). The diffusion of innovations – microelectronic technology. In R. Roy and D. Wield (eds), *Product Design and Technological Innovation*. London: Open University Press, pp. 193–200.

Freeman, C. (1994). The economics of technical change: a critical survey article. *Cambridge Journal of Economics*, **18**(5), 463–514.

Freeman, C. (2002). Continental, national and sub-national innovation systems – complementarity and economic growth. *Research Policy*, **31**, 191–211.

Freeman, C. (2010). Formal scientific and technological institutions in the National System of Innovation. In *National Systems of Innovation: Toward a Theory of Innovation and Interactive Learning*. UK: Anthem Press, pp. 173–88.

Fukuyama, F. (1995). *Trust: The Social Virtue and Creation of Prosperity*. New York: Free Press Paperbacks.

Fukuyama, F. (2004). *State Building Governance and World Order in the 21st Century*. Ithaca, NY: Cornell University Press.

Gharajedaghi, J. (2007). *Systems Thinking, Managing Chaos and Complexity: A Platform for Designing Business Architecture*, 2nd edn. Amsterdam: B.H. Elsevier.

Harriman, A. (1985). *Women/Men/Management*. New York: Praeger.

Hills, G., G. Lumpkin and R. Singh (1997). Opportunity recognition: perceptions and behaviors of entrepreneurs. In P. Reynolds, E. Autio, C.G. Brush et al. (eds), *Frontiers of Entrepreneurships Research*. Wellesley, MA: Babson College, pp. 203–218.

Hisrich, R. (1986). The woman entrepreneur: characteristics, skills, problems, and prescriptions for success. In D. Sexton and R. Smilor (eds), *The Art and Science of Entrepreneurship*. Cambridge, MA: Ballinger Publishing, pp. 61–84.

Hofstede, G. (1991). *Culture and Organizations: Software of the Mind*. New York: McGraw Hill.

Liang, H., N. Saraf, Q. Hu and Y. Xue (2007). Assimilation of enterprise systems: the effect of institutional pressures and mediating role of top management. *MIS Quarterly*, **31**(1), 59–87.

Lundvall, B.-K., B.E. Johnson, S. Andersen and B. Dalum (2002). National systems of production, innovation and competence building. *Research Policy*, **31**, 213–31.

Malerba, F. and R.R. Nelson (eds) (2012a). *Economic Development as a Learning Process: Variation across Sectoral Systems*. Cheltenham, UK and Northampton, MA, USA: Edward Elgar.

Malerba, F. and R.R. Nelson (2012b). Introduction. In F. Malerba and R.R. Nelson (eds), *Economic Development as a Learning Process*. Cheltenham, UK and Northampton, MA, USA: Edward Elgar, pp. 1–20.

March, J.G. and J.P. Olsen (1984). The new institutionalism: organizational factors in political life. *American Political Science Review*, **78**, 734–49.

Markman, G., P. Phan, D. Balkin and P. Giannodis (2005). Entrepreneurship and university-based technology transfer. *Journal of Business Venturing*, **20**(2), 241–63.

Markus, H. and R.B. Zajonc (1985). The cognitive perspective in social psychology. In G. Lindzey and E. Aronson (eds), *Handbook of Social Psychology*, Vol. 1, 3rd edn. New York: Random House, pp. 137–230.

Milgrom, R. and J. Roberts (1992). *Economics, Organization and Management.* Englewood Cliffs, NJ: Prentice Hall.

Millman, A.F. (1990). Technology strategy and inward transfer of foreign technology in the UK machine tool industry. Doctorial dissertation, University of Warwick, UK.

Nelson, R.R. and K. Nelson (2002). Technology, institutions, and innovation systems. *Research Policy*, **31**, 265–72.

North, D.C. (1990). *Institutions, Institutional Changes and Economic Performance.* Cambridge: Cambridge University Press.

North, D.C. (1997). The contribution of the new institutional economics to an understanding of the transitional problem. Wider Annual Lectures, United Nations University World Institute for Development Economics Research, Helsinki, Finland.

Podolny, J.M. (2009). The buck stops (and starts) at business school. *Harvard Business Review*, **87**(6), 62–7.

Porter, M.E. (1998). Clusters and the new economics of competition. *Harvard Business Review*, **76**(6), 77–90.

Scott, W.R. (1995). *Institutions and Organizations.* Thousand Oaks, CA: Sage.

Scott, W.R. (2008). *Institutions and Organizations*, 3rd edn. Thousand Oaks, CA: Sage.

Siegel, D.S., D. Waldman and A.N. Link (2003). Assessing the impact of organizational practices on the relative productivity of university technology transfer offices: an exploratory study. *Research Policy*, **32**(1), 27–48.

Staw, B.M. and L.D. Epstein (2000). What bandwagons bring – effects of popular management techniques on corporate performance, reputation and CEO pay. *Administrative Science Quarterly*, **45**(3), 523–56.

The Global Competitiveness Report. (2013). 2013–2014 full data report. In K. Schwab (ed.), World Economic Forum. Geneva: World Economic Forum.

Veblen, T. (1915). *The Imperial Germany and Industrial Revolution.* New York: Macmillan.

Verheul, I., S. Wennekers, D.B. Audretsch and A.R. Thurik (2002). An eclectic theory of entrepreneurship: policies, institutions, and culture. In D.B. Audretsch, A.R. Thurik, I. Verheul and A.R.M. Wennekers (eds), *Entrepreneurship: Determinants and Policy in a European-US Comparison.* Boston, MA and Dordrecht: Kluwer Academic Publications, pp. 11–81.

Welter, F., D. Smallbone, N. Isakova, E. Aculai and N. Schakirova (2004). Women entrepreneurs in Ukraine, Republic of Moldova and Uzbekistan: results of a comparative study. In UNECE (ed.), *Access to Financing and ICT: Women Entrepreneurs in the ECE Region.* Geneva: United Nations, pp. 39–52.

Wennekers, A.R.M. and A.R. Thurik (1999). Linking entrepreneurship and economic growth. *Small Business Economics*, **13**(1), 27–55.

Williamson, O.E. (1979). *Markets and Hierarchies: Analysis and Antitrust Implications.* New York: Free Press.

Zucker, L.G. (1991). Postscript: microfoundations of institutional thought. In W.W. Powell and P.J. DiMaggio (eds), *The New Institutionalism in Organizational Analysis.* Chicago, IL: University of Chicago Press, pp. 83–107.

8. The economic impact of public universities in the United Kingdom

Maribel Guerrero, David Urbano and James A. Cunningham

INTRODUCTION

In the entrepreneurial economy, the dominant production factor is knowledge capital as the source of competitive advantage, which is complemented by entrepreneurship capital, representing the capacity to engage in and generate entrepreneurial activity (Audretsch, 2007). Thus, an entrepreneurial society generates scenarios in which its members can identify and exploit economic opportunities and knowledge to promote new entrepreneurial phenomena that have not been previously visualized (Mueller, 2007; Shane, 2004). An increased importance of the university, in terms of its impact on the economy, is observed within the entrepreneurial economy (Audretsch, 2012). As a consequence, the economic impact of universities has gained the attention of academics, governments and policymakers around the world.

Given the complexity of university functions, previous studies have evidenced the economic impact of university teaching, research or entrepreneurial activities by adopting different theoretical approaches and methodologies (Drucker and Goldstein, 2007). Traditionally, in the 1980s, the analysis focused on the impact via the labour force supported on the foundations of a managed economy, and research was conducted using descriptive input-output analysis at the university level (Elliott et al., 1988). In the 1990s, the methodology of choice to measure the economic impact of university research activities was input-output analysis (Goldstein, 1990; Jaffe, 1989). Later, in the 2000s, more sophisticated methodologies were employed (that is, productivity, total factor productive analysis, return of investments analysis, quartile regression analysis and so on) to explore the direct impact of specific research activities or the indirect impact of knowledge spillover (Audretsch et al., 2008; Bessette, 2003; Martin, 1998; Roessner et al., 2013; Siegel et al., 2003). However, the natural role of universities in economic development is less well understood than is often presumed (Bramwell and Wolfe, 2008).

Our main objective is to contribute to a better understanding of the regional economic impact of public universities' activities (teaching, research and entrepreneurial). With this objective, our conceptual framework fundamentally adopts the endogenous growth theory with the understanding that the main forces of economic growth – in particular, investment in human capital, knowledge and entrepreneurship – are endogenous (Audretsch and Keilbach, 2004a, 2004b). Methodologically, this exploratory study tests the proposed model of the economic impact of entrepreneurial universities with a two-stage least square regression weighted by regions (2SLS) using the data of 147 United Kingdom (UK) public universities located in 74 of the 139 NUTS-3 regions of the country. The chapter is organized as follows. The following section introduces the theoretical background regarding the regional benefits of public universities; the research hypotheses are also proposed. The third section describes the methodology (data, variables and statistical techniques used). The fourth section outlines the results and discussion. The final section provides the concluding remarks, study limitations and the future research lines.

THEORETICAL BACKGROUND

It has long been observed that entrepreneurial activity varies across geographic space, and the economic benefits of universities could also vary according to their localization (Audretsch and Lehmann, 2005). According to the microeconomic foundation of endogenous economic theory (Lucas, 1988; Romer, 1986), investments in knowledge and human capital generate economic growth. In this respect, Audretsch (2012, p. 7) argues that the role of universities is broader than only generating and transferring knowledge; a university contributes and provides leadership for the creation of entrepreneurial thinking, actions, organizations and what he refers to in his previous studies as 'entrepreneurship capital'. Under this scenario, universities become more entrepreneurial in order to compete, and they become more productive and creative in establishing links between education and research (Kirby et al., 2011).

In general, an entrepreneurial university is an organizational adaptation to environmental changes (Clark, 1998), managerial and governance distinctiveness (Subotzky, 1999), new activities oriented to the development of entrepreneurial culture at all levels and the contribution to economic development with the creation of new ventures (Chrisman et al., 1995) or commercialization of research (Jacob et al., 2003). As a consequence, entrepreneurial universities have emerged as central actors playing an active role in promoting teaching, innovation, knowledge transfer and entrepreneurship (Guerrero et al., 2015; Urbano and Guerrero, 2013). Moreover, an entrepreneurial university can provide new alternatives to the university community, which typically identifies entrepreneurial opportunities. In this line, beyond generating commercial knowledge (patents, licences and agreements) and qualified research scientists (graduate students), universities produce other impacts, such as the generation of and attraction to new ventures, jobs, talent and collaborations with local, regional and international agents (Guerrero and Urbano, 2012). Moreover, entrepreneurial universities within regions have an important role in regional economic development and in realizing this contribution have adopted different processes and approaches (Guerrero et al., 2014).

Following this perspective, the outcomes of universities could be transformed on the determinant of economic development and later could positively impact the economy/society of a specific region (Audretsch, 2012; Audretsch and Keilbach, 2004a; Coleman, 1988; Lucas, 1988; Romer, 1986; Solow, 1956). In particular, based on the Cobb-Douglas production function,

$$Yi = \alpha K i^{B1} L i^{1 - B1} R i^{B2} E i^{B3}$$

Y represents economic output, L represents labour, K represents the factor of physical capital, R represents knowledge capital and E represents entrepreneurship capital. The subscript i refers to UK regions. Under this perspective, it is possible to link the measure of regional economic performance through the traditional factors of capital, labour and knowledge, as well as the new factor of entrepreneurship capital to the outcomes of each university activity.

Human capital, considered a factor of production by Lucas (1988), refers to the stock of competencies, knowledge, abilities and skills gained through education and training (Becker, 1993). In this line, the universal function of universities has been teaching activities. Then, universities educate and train students, who have assumed public and private responsibilities after graduation when they become job seekers or job creators (Van Vught, 1999). Therefore, entrepreneurial universities could contribute to economic impacts through the generation, attraction and retention of job seekers and entrepreneurs (Simha, 2005). Concerning knowledge capital, Solow (1956) and Romer (1986) identified such knowledge as a separate input in production with increasing marginal productivity (that is, copyrights, patents, licences and trademarks). In this sense, universities contribute to the knowledge generation, attraction and retention of prestigious researchers (Bramwell and Wolfe, 2008), who, in turn, facilitate the innovation process and the transference of knowledge through patents, licences and spin-offs (Colombo et al., 2010). Therefore, the economic impact of entrepreneurial universities could be associated with the generation and transference of knowledge (Roessner et al., 2013).

Linking to entrepreneurship capital, Audretsch and Keilbach (2004a) introduced into the production function the role of entrepreneurship in the contribution to economic growth; more concretely, entrepreneurship capital serving as a conduit for knowledge spillovers, increasing competition and injecting diversity. As a consequence, these impacts could produce several demographic, economic, infrastructure, cultural, mobility, educational and society challenges that later would be reflected in productivity, competitive advantages, regional capacities, networks, identity and innovation (Mueller, 2007; Mustar and Wright, 2010). It is one of the most critical missions of universities oriented to generate initiatives that promote competition and diversity. There are several conduits; for example, the creation or attraction of new enterprises resulting from the activities developed by the university community (Urbano and Guerrero, 2013).

Finally, in order to achieve all these activities, universities need diversified sources of financial resources (Clark, 1998). For example, teaching activities are guaranteed by incomes from government, campus services or student fees; large-scale science projects are co-sponsored by industry, government or others (Klofsten and Jones-Evans, 2000); and entrepreneurial initiatives are supported by venture capital, loans, subsidies or grants obtained through university channels (Wright et al., 2007). In this respect, Powers and McDougall (2005) determined a positive and statistically significant relationship between annual expenditure and university activities. In summary, Table 8.1 shows the proposed model of this exploratory chapter.

Table 8.1   Economic benefit of universities

Outcomes of universities' activities	Consequences
Teaching Activities Outcomes: Human capital (employment generated by jobseekers or potential entrepreneurs)	Economic impact in each region
Research Activities Outcomes: Knowledge capital (knowledge generation and transference through patents, licences and contracts with the local industries and economic agents)	
Entrepreneurial Activities Outcomes: Entrepreneurship capital (number of start-ups/spin-offs created by the university community)	

METHODOLOGY

Data and Variables

We collected secondary data from several higher education official databases in the United Kingdom.[1] The sample was integrated for 147 public universities in the United Kingdom located in 74 of the 139 NUTS-3[2] regions of the country in 2005. The dependent variable is (Ln_GVA *per* $capita_{t+2}$) that measures the value of goods and services produced in an area of an economy linked as a measurement to the gross domestic product (GDP), identified at the NUTS-3 level for the region within which each analysed university is located. Therefore, this proxy allows us to explore the economic effect of each entrepreneurial university's activities in the county/region it is located in, using a two-year time lag (Roessner et al., 2013). This lagged relationship also reflects causality between an entrepreneurial university's activities in one period and its economic impacts in subsequent periods (Audretsch and Keilbach, 2004a). Regarding the independent variables, they are linked to each university's outcome as follows.

The teaching university's outcome measured through the $Ln\_$ $Employment_{t_0}$ or the natural logarithm of the employment indicator per student and per university in the year of analysis (Bessette, 2003; Mueller, 2007).

The research university's outcome measured through the $Ln\_Research$ $contracts_{t_0}$ or the natural logarithm of the total value of research contracts per staff and the $Ln\_Intellectual\ property_{t_0}$ or the natural logarithm of the income from all intellectual property agreements per staff (Mueller, 2007; Siegel et al., 2003).

The university's outcome measured through the $Ln\_Spin\text{-}offs\ from\ graduated\ ownership_{t_0}$ or the natural logarithm of the number of active spin-offs owned by graduates/alumni to the country's population (Chrisman et al., 1995; Mueller, 2007).

Our main control variable was $Ln\_Expenses_{t_0}$ or the natural logarithm of the total expenditure of all university activities per student. This variable encompasses the salaries of university staff and the operating expenses associated with the outcomes for a particular year (Mueller, 2007; O'Shea et al., 2007). Finally, we included Ln_GVA *per* $capita_{t_{-1}}$ that represents the budgets a year ahead based on the funds they expect to receive. It helps us to control the inverse relationship between entrepreneurial universities' activities and economic impact (Audretsch and Keilbach, 2004b). Table 8.2 shows correlations among the proxies of university's outcomes with the regional economic benefits. This table shows that the measure of

Table 8.2 Correlations matrix

Variables	Mean	S.D.	1	2	3	4	5	6	7	8
1 Ln_GVA per capita$_{t+2}$	9.595	1.136	1							
2 Ln_Employment$_0$	−0.429	1.254	0.556***	1						
3 Ln_Research contracts$_0$	1.986	2.163	0.35***	0.3***	1					
4 Ln_Intellectual property$_{t_0}$	−0.038	1.642	0.395***	0.291***	0.339***	1				
5 Ln_Spin-offs from graduated ownership$_{t_0}$	−1.197	1.746	0.36***	0.299***	0.02	0.182**	1			
6 Ln_Expenses$_{t_0}$ (from step1)	1.790	1.315	0.34***	0.109	0.117	0.326***	0.265***	1		
7 University age	131.340	120.620	0.003	−0.051	−0.088	0.199**	0.222**	0.258***	1	
8 Region	6.480	3.413	−0.492***	−0.469***	−0.291***	−0.177**	−0.269***	−0.221**	0.052	1

Note: Level of statistical significance: *** $p \leq 0.001$, ** $p \leq 0.01$, * $p \leq 0.05$.

teaching is strongly correlated with economic development, while the correlation between research and entrepreneurship measures is much weaker. On the other hand, the general measure of university expenses is also weakly correlated.

Estimations

At the beginning of this exploratory study we tried to test the proposed model of the economic impact of universities with a geographically weighted regression (GWR). However, we had some difficulties with the number of observations to show geographically the impact of each university. For this reason, we decided to start with an initial analysis using a two-stage least square regression (2SLS) weighted by regions. In the first stage, we capture the reverse relationship via $Ln\_Expensest_0$ that is strongly linked to the development of each university and influenced by the university budget $Ln\_GVA\ per\ capitat_{-1}$. In other words, the generation of opportunities within the university emanate from the investments in its activities. The estimation of this relationship was included in the second model that tested the effect of each university outcome but weighted by region (as an alternative mechanism to introduce the spatial dispersion of the regions within the regression).

RESULTS AND DISCUSSION

Traditionally, economic impact studies are used to justify expenditures on higher education. However, this impact contributes to the short- and long-term benefits of economic activities. According to the literature about universities, these contributions are associated with their main activities (teaching, research and entrepreneurial). Table 8.3 shows the regression results of Model 1 and Model 2 estimated using 2SLS. Specifically, Table 8.3 shows that the higher standardized coefficients are associated with teaching activities and research activities. Similar to previous studies regarding teaching activities, this evidence is not surprising because this activity has been the universal function of every university and the most direct impact is associated with the creation of local jobs (Van Vught, 1999). Concerning research activities, our measures are linked to the generation, transfer and commercialization of knowledge. In line with past studies (Bessette, 2003; Mueller, 2007; Simha, 2005), the results confirm the relevance of investments in internal factors with more emphasis on social and human resources. Therefore, indirectly, the universities of these regions could have the capacity to attract students and academics. Finally,

Table 8.3   *Estimating a university's outcomes and economic benefits*

Step 2[a]	Dependent variable: Ln_GVA per $capita_{t+2}$			
	B (S.E.)	Beta	t	Sig.
$Ln\_Employment_{t0}$	0.175 (0.72)	0.190	2.45	**
$Ln\_Research\ contractst_0$	0.063 (0.04)	0.126	1.56	
$Ln\_Intellectual\ propertyt_0$	0.131 (0.04)	0.235	2.98	**
$Ln\_Spin\text{-}offs\ from\ graduated$ $ownershipt_0$	0.098 (0.04)	0.184	2.46	*
$Ln\_Expenses t_0$ *(from step1)*	0.063 (0.23)	0.214	2.71	**
University age	−0.001 (0.001)	−0.106	−1.36	
Constant	9.024 (0.23)		39.52	***
Pseudo R^2	0.247			

Step 1[b]	Dependent variable: $Ln\_Expenses t_0$			
	B (S.E.)	Beta	t	Sig.
Ln_GVA per $capitat_{-1}$	2.535 (0.58)	2.936	4.36	***
Constant	5.057 (1.07)		4.71	***
Pseudo R^2	0.340			
Number of observations	147			

Notes:
Level of statistical significance: *** $p \leq 0.001$, ** $p \leq 0.01$, * $p \leq 0.05$.
a.   Weighted by the region where the university is located.
b.   Mechanism to control the reverse relationship between the dependents variables of both regressions.

the results for entrepreneurial activities present the lower coefficients. This is not surprising given the phenomenon of entrepreneurial universities has become a strong presence in the past decade (Guerrero and Urbano, 2012).

In particular, the main economic impacts of UK public universities are associated with the outcomes of human capital. However, this does not mean that these universities do not contribute via research (knowledge capital) and entrepreneurial activities (entrepreneurship capital). This observation is supported by previous studies, for example, Simha (2005) found that research universities play a key role in the Boston region's economic health and welfare. These organizations contribute in terms of jobs, annual talent pool of graduates, exploitation of patents and licensed technology and so on. Other explanations about the level of entrepreneurship capital would be linked to the negative relationship between Total Entrepreneurial Activity (TEA) and GDP in high-income countries as in our sample (Reynolds et al., 2005). Further explanation could also be associated with the period of analysis.

CONCLUSIONS

The main contributions of this exploratory study are two-fold. First, we propose a theoretical framework to understand the economic benefits of each university's core activity (teaching, research and entrepreneurship) on the entrepreneurial society. Second, we explore a new way to test this phenomenon and overcome the shortcomings of other techniques, such as input-output analysis (that is, the economic impacts of universities extend well beyond the types that can be accounted for in this analysis).

Nevertheless, this study is not exempt from limitations that open new windows of opportunity for further research: (1) to improve the proxies used to measure the university's outcomes and also include other control variables related to economic development; (2) to explore these relationships using data at a university level of analysis, despite the difficulty in finding homogeneous data from secondary sources; and (3) to use a longitudinal data (panel data) analysis and other techniques to explore in depth the influence on each specific region (geographically weighted regression). It would also be interesting to analyse other indirect impacts such as social contributions in terms of reputation in the region, sustainability (Pastor et al., 2012), the concentration of the labour force, political leadership, environmental quality (Simha, 2005), as well as other moral hazards inherent in the processes associated with who conducts university impact studies (incentives), including the policymakers (legislations and perspectives such as planning Europe 2020[3]).

Implications of the study are both conceptual and practical. From the theoretical perspective, this research advances the development of an integrative model for the analysis of entrepreneurial universities. From a practice perspective, the study could be useful for the design of university and governmental policies fostering entrepreneurism within these higher education organizations, particularly during the economic crisis as most regions with the European Union have been impacted by this crisis. University management teams need to recognize their core role at this time in not only building but also enforcing the university environment that nurtures entrepreneurial potential (incentives, new learning tools, role models) and stimulates skills, competencies and tools useful in the creation of entrepreneurial mindsets to drive innovation (not only inside universities but also within the existent firms) and develop entrepreneurial organizations. This can in turn support firms that are seeking to grow, internationalize and are investing in research and development. It also supports the attraction of new human capital to lead and contribute to publicly funded research programmes in regional public universities.

More research is needed to examine the economic impact of regional universities. Using entrepreneurial university theoretical and empirical studies provides opportunities to examine the variations and real connectivity regional universities have to regional development and to regional innovation systems. Such research can provide a body of work that allows for further examination of the nuanced processes, practices, governance and strategies pursued by regional universities in becoming more entrepreneurial within regional innovation systems.

NOTES

1. The Higher Education Funding Council for England (HEFEC) and the Centre for International Competitiveness.
2. Based on the European Nomenclature of Territorial Units (NUTS), the United Kingdom is divided into 12 major economic regions (NUTS-1), 37 basic regions for the application of regional policies (NUTS-2) and 139 small regions (NUTS-3). For further information, see http://epp.eurostat.ec.europa.eu/portal/page/portal/nuts_nomenclature/introduction (accessed October 16, 2015).
3. The Entrepreneurship 2020 Action Plan is the Commission's answer to challenges brought by the economic crisis. It aims to ease the creation of new businesses and to create a much more supportive environment for existing entrepreneurs to thrive and grow. The Entrepreneurship 2020 Action Plan identifies three areas for immediate intervention: (1) entrepreneurial education and training to support growth and business creation; (2) removing existing administrative barriers and supporting entrepreneurs in crucial phases of the business lifecycle; (3) reigniting the culture of entrepreneurship in Europe and nurturing the new generation of entrepreneurs. The Action Plan and its key actions will be followed up by the Commission through the competitiveness and industrial policy and the Small Business Act governance mechanisms. See http://ec.europa.eu/growth/smes/promoting-entrepreneurship/action-plan/index_en.htm (accessed October 16, 2015).

REFERENCES

Audretsch, D. (2007). *The Entrepreneurial Society*. New York: Oxford University Press.

Audretsch, D. (2012). From the entrepreneurial university to the university for the entrepreneurial society. *Journal of Technology Transfer* **39**(3), 313–21.

Audretsch, D. and Keilbach, M. (2004a). Does entrepreneurship capital matter? *Entrepreneurship Theory and Practice* **28**, 1697–705.

Audretsch, D. and Keilbach, M. (2004b). Resolving the knowledge paradox: knowledge-spillover entrepreneurship and economic growth. *Regional Studies* **37**(8), 949–59.

Audretsch, D. and Lehmann, E. (2005). Does the knowledge spillover theory of entrepreneurship hold for regions? *Regional Studies* **34**, 1191–202.

Audretsch, D., Bönte, W. and Keilbach, M. (2008). Entrepreneurship capital and its impact on knowledge diffusion and economic performance. *Journal of Business Venturing* **23**, 687–98.

Becker, G. (1993). *Human Capital: A Theoretical and Empirical Analysis with Special Reference to Education*. Chicago, IL: University of Chicago Press.

Bessette, R.W. (2003). Measuring the economic impact of university-based research. *Journal of Technology Transfer* **28**(3–4), 355–61.

Bramwell, A. and Wolfe, D.A. (2008). Universities and regional economic development: the entrepreneurial University of Waterloo. *Research Policy* **37**(8), 1175–87.

Chrisman, J.J., Hynes, T. and Fraser, S. (1995). Faculty entrepreneurship and economic development: the case of the University of Calgary. *Journal of Business Venturing* **10**(4), 267–81.

Clark, B.R. (1998). *Creating Entrepreneurial Universities*. Oxford: Elsevier Science.

Coleman, J.S. (1988). Social capital in the creation of human capital. *American Journal of Sociology* **94**, 95–120.

Colombo, M., D'Adda, D. and Piva, E. (2010). The contribution of university research to the growth of academic start-ups: an empirical analysis. *Journal of Technology Transfer*, **35**(1), 113–40.

Drucker, J. and Goldstein, H. (2007). Assessing the regional economic development impacts of universities: a review of current approaches. *International Regional Science Review* **30**(1), 20–46.

Elliott, D.S., Levin, P.S.L. and Meisel, J.B. (1988). Measuring the economic impact of institutions of higher education. *Research in Higher Education* **28**(1), 17–33.

Goldstein, H.A. (1990). Estimating the regional economic impact of universities: an application of input-output analysis. *Planning for Higher Education* **18**(1), 51–64.

Guerrero, M. and Urbano, D. (2012). The development of an entrepreneurial university. *Journal of Technology Transfer* **37**(1), 43–74.

Guerrero, M., Urbano, D., Cunningham, J. and Organ, D. (2014). Entrepreneurial universities in two European regions: a case study comparision of their conditioning factors, outcomes and outputs. *Journal of Technology Transfer* **39**(3), 415–34.

Guerrero, M., Cunningham, J.A. and Urbano, D. (2015). Economic impact of entrepreneurial universities' activities: an exploratory study of the United Kingdom. *Research Policy* **44**(3), 748–64.

Jacob, M., Lundqvist, M. and Hellsmark, H. (2003). Entrepreneurial transformations in the Swedish university system: the case of Chalmers University of Technology. *Research Policy* **32**(9), 1555–69.

Jaffe, A.B. (1989). Real effects of academic research. *American Economic Review* **79**(5), 957–70.

Kirby, D.A., Guerrero, M. and Urbano, D. (2011). The theoretical and empirical side of entrepreneurial universities: an institutional approach. *Canadian Journal of Administrative Sciences* **28**, 302–16.

Klofsten, M. and Jones-Evans, D. (2000). Comparing academic entrepreneurship in Europe: the case of Sweden and Ireland. *Small Business Economics* **14**(4), 299–310.

Lucas, R. Jr. (1988). On the mechanics of economic development. *Journal of Monetary Economics* **22**(1), 3–42.

Martin, F. (1998). The economic impact of Canadian university R&D. *Research Policy* **27**(7), 677–87.

Mueller, P. (2007). Exploiting entrepreneurial opportunities: the impact of entrepreneurship on growth. *Small Business Economy* **28**, 355–62.

Mustar, P. and Wright, M. (2010). Convergence or path dependency in policies to foster the creation of university spin-off firms? A comparison of France and the United Kingdom. *Journal of Technology Transfer* **35**(1), 42–65.

O'Shea, R.P., Allen, T.J., Morse, K.P., O'Gorman, C. and Roche, F. (2007). Delineating the anatomy of an entrepreneurial university: the Massachusetts Institute of Technology experience. *R&D Management* **37**(1), 1–16.

Pastor, J., Pérez, F. and Fernández, J. (2012). Measuring the local economic impact of universities: an approach that considers uncertainty. *Higher Education* **65**(5), 539–64.

Powers, J. and McDougall, P.P. (2005). University start-up formation and technological licensing with firms that go public: a resource-based view of academic entrepreneurship. *Journal of Business Venturing* **20**, 291–311.

Roessner, D., Bond, J., Okubo, S. and Planting, M. (2013). The economic impact of licensed commercialized inventions originating in university research. *Research Policy* **42**(1), 23–34.

Romer, P. (1986). Increasing returns and long-run growth. *Journal of Political Economy* **94**(5), 1002–37.

Shane, S. (2004). *Academic Entrepreneurship: University Spinoffs and Wealth Creation*. Cheltenham, UK and Northampton, MA, USA: Edward Elgar.

Siegel, D.S., Waldman, D. and Link, A. (2003). Assessing the impact of organizational practices on the relative productivity of university technology transfer offices: an exploratory study. *Research Policy* **32**(1), 27–48.

Simha, O. (2005). The economic impact of eight research universities on the Boston region. *Tertiary Education and Management* **11**, 269–78.

Solow, R. (1956). A contribution to the economic growth theory. *Quarterly Journal of Economics* **70**(1), 65–94.

Subotzky, G. (1999). Alternatives to the entrepreneurial university: new modes of knowledge production in community service programs. *Higher Education* **38**(4), 401–40.

Urbano, D. and Guerrero, M. (2013). Entrepreneurial universities: socio-economic impacts of academic entrepreneurship in a European region. *Economic Development Quarterly* **27**(1), 41–56.

Van Vught, F. (1999). Innovative universities. *Tertiary Education and Management* **5**(4), 347–54.

Wright, M., Clarysse, B., Mustar, P. and Lockett, A. (2007). *Academic Entrepreneurship in Europe*. Cheltenham, UK and Northampton, MA, USA: Edward Elgar.

9. A comparative study of ecosystem development in regenerative medicine

Adam J. Bock and David Johnson

INTRODUCTION

Many technology-based entrepreneurial ecosystems bridge academic institutions, industry and government. As universities have been spotlighted as potential engines for high-value economic development, these ecosystems have received significantly more research and policy attention (Etzkowitz, 2003). Entrepreneurial ecosystems are complex, often poorly defined clusters of economic activity whose participants are linked variously by field, technology, geographic proximity or parent institution. It is not surprising that the innovation and commercialization outcomes of these systems are contingent on a variety of factors, including entrepreneurial behavior, cultural norms and the context of the originating university (Walshok et al., 2012; Zahra and Wright, 2011).

Universities drive regional economic outcomes via basic research, teaching, knowledge transfer, policy developments, economic initiatives and other activities (Breznitz and Feldman, 2012). Although the regional economic benefits of university technology transfer are not consistent (Miner et al., 2001), universities clearly contribute to the formation of industry and innovation clusters (Porter, 1998). One important university activity that contributes to cluster development is the generation of *de novo* ventures.

Venture development at the university-industry (UI) boundary is difficult and uncertain. Entrepreneurs, often academics with limited business training or experience, must acquire scarce resources, capabilities and partners (Alvarez and Barney, 2005). The experiences of academic entrepreneurs are highly idiosyncratic, and the outcomes of any given university spinout is difficult to predict from either endogenous or exogenous factors (Festel, 2013; Wright et al., 2012a; Yosuf and Jain, 2010). At the same time, characteristic and structural patterns suggest that the underlying venturing processes are similar across ecosystems (George and Bock, 2008).

The regenerative medicine (RM) industry provides a useful setting to study entrepreneurial behavior and ecosystem development at the UI boundary. The RM field presents unusually high levels of uncertainty associated with complex and unresolved regulatory and intellectual property (IP) frameworks (Ledford, 2008). This limits entrepreneurial planning, hinders the identification of key capabilities and prevents *ex ante* validation of stem cell-based business models (George and Bock, 2012; Heirman and Clarysse, 2004). In this context, RM ventures must simultaneously explore unfamiliar territory and acquire the knowledge resources to navigate that territory.

In robust clusters, new ventures acquire and create knowledge through spillovers and human capital (Saxenian, 1994; Zucker et al., 1998). Human capital, such as prior venture experience of the entrepreneur, can enable greater network ties and more diverse social networks (Mosey and Wright, 2007). Across ecosystems, specific resource assembly challenges and entrepreneurial behavior differ (Clarysse et al., 2011). In the RM space, valuable knowledge, capabilities and IP are extremely sophisticated, scarce and tightly contested. We use the backdrop of the complex and uncertain RM field to explore micro-level dynamics of entrepreneurial ecosystems in the context of knowledge acquisition. First, we investigate entrepreneurial attributions across apparently similar RM ecosystems. Second, we consider how entrepreneurial ecosystems develop differently, with specific emphasis on imprinting effects of the parent institution.

We report on a cross-national study of RM venturing in Edinburgh (Scotland, United Kingdom) and Madison (Wisconsin, United States) to explore entrepreneurial behavior and ecosystem development. Our findings emphasize how entrepreneurial coping strategies may be partly driven by university culture. The data shows apparently similar ecosystems at different stages and points toward the dynamic and evolving nature of entrepreneurial ecosystems. Based on the situational context presented in the data, we propose a model of entrepreneurial ecosystem development.

This chapter proceeds as follows. In the following section, we review prior research on entrepreneurial ecosystems at the UI boundary, with particular reference to RM ecosystems. We report the methods in the third section. Findings are presented in the fourth section, highlighting ecosystem and informant role differences. In the fifth section we discuss these differences. We conclude with limitations and directions for future research.

ENTREPRENEURIAL ECOSYSTEMS

Broadly speaking, business clusters embody the co-evolution of firms around particular innovations, technologies or markets. The industrial-organizational literature specifically defines a cluster as 'a geographically proximate group of interconnected companies and associated institutions' (Porter, 2000, p. 16). These firms interact cooperatively and competitively to generate new products, meet market needs and stimulate further innovations (Moore, 1993). Clustered ventures benefit from reduced transaction costs, specialized pools of labor and improved access to resources and knowledge, particularly through collaborating and competing with other cluster members (Bell et al., 2009).

An entrepreneurial ecosystem is a specialized type of organizational-industrial cluster, which develops over time within a specific geographic region and is replenished or expanded by new ventures (Cohen, 2006). Ecosystem participants are connected by venture formation and growth activities, potentially spanning otherwise disparate technology fields and capability sets. The ecosystem generates incentives for entrepreneurial activity, linking potentially surplus resources to extant ecosystem participants and opportunity-oriented individuals outside the system (Spilling, 1996). Participants in an entrepreneurial ecosystem may or may not be closely connected. Spinouts from the same university laboratory may share fundamental technology capabilities and human capital. For example, Cellular Dynamics International, Inc. and Stem Cell Products, Inc. were both spun out of the University of Wisconsin-Madison based on stem cell innovations associated with research by Professor James Thomson. These firms even shared physical facilities and certain executive managers.[1] Other ecosystem participants may be connected only by formative links to the parent university or by relationships to other specialized businesses in the ecosystem, such as IP law firms.

Networks are especially important to the development and performance of these ecosystems. Network content, connections and structures affect resource assembly practices and outcomes (Hoang and Antoncic, 2003). This is especially relevant for access to resources and the creation and exchange of knowledge (Aldrich and Martinez, 2001; Ardichvili et al., 2002). As entrepreneurial ecosystems commonly span otherwise disparate industrial sectors, social networks play an important role in venture formation and development (Birley, 1985; Jack, 2010). These social networks are influenced by differences in human capital (Mosey and Wright, 2007). Entrepreneurs must invest in operating and managing networks for venture formation and growth (Nijkamp, 2003). Such networks enable entrepreneurs and ventures to interact (directly and indirectly) with economic and social organizations and institutions. These interactions are mediated by cultural norms within the wider ecosystem (Johannisson et al., 2002).

When social networks facilitate knowledge acquisition, ventures are often better placed to exploit knowledge for competitive advantage (Yli-Renko et al., 2001). Under uncertainty, particularly in emerging or nascent markets, ventures are likely to benefit from a diverse network and the ability to form ties with a wide range of networked partners (De Vaan, 2014; Meyskens and Carsrud, 2013). When uncertainty is high, network openness improves ecosystem performance by accepting new participants, supporting diversity and facilitating tie-formation to other ecosystems. Networks enable the spillover of knowledge, which further promotes clustering between ventures in similar industries (Audretsch and Feldman, 1996; Hayter, 2013).

There is clear evidence of the importance of context and institutional forces in ecosystem formation and development. Considering ecosystem development from a range of contextual frameworks, such as technological, institutional, social and spatial contexts, is important to gain a richer understanding of ecosystems (Autio et al., 2014). Networks thus play a critical role in the outcomes of individual ventures and the overall ecosystem (Eisingerich et al., 2010). Yet, research has not generally been directed at the impact of the central institution (university) on the participants in the ecosystem and their entrepreneurial decision-making.

University-centric Ecosystems

Research universities often anchor entrepreneurial ecosystems in knowledge-intensive fields. Since many technology-intensive firms have potential high-growth profiles, special emphasis is commonly placed on the role of university spinouts in regional economic growth (Etzkowitz, 2003). Although the actual economic impact of university-based entrepreneurship is overshadowed by media focus on outlier successes, universities and technology transfer offices (TTOs) are commonly identified as important engines of economic growth (Bock, 2012; Miner et al., 2001).

The dynamics of entrepreneurial ecosystems at the UI boundary are poorly understood. On the one hand, universities may foster entrepreneurial activity and subsequent interaction between ecosystem participants (Swamidass, 2013). Many universities and civic-minded entities support subject-specific research, translational resources and practices, access to seed funding and venture capital (VC), investments in human capital and even subsidized professional services. Yet, geographic, economic, socio-demographic and other factors beyond the control of the university or any ecosystem participant are also relevant. Policy differences across ecosystems result in variations in spinout activity and performance (Goldfarb and Henrekson, 2003; Mustar and Wright, 2010). Innovation and economic outcomes may derive from initial configurations and path dependencies, limiting the influence of policymakers (Zacharakis et al., 2003).

In particular, venture formation at the UI boundary has received a great deal of attention (cf. Djokovic and Souitaris, 2008; O'Shea et al., 2004). Venturing activity is informed and influenced by institutional norms and culture. The motivation for technology transfer, and the choice of transfer instrument, are driven by ecosystem norms and university-based incentive structures (Decter et al., 2007; Henrekson and Rosenberg, 2001).

Venturing at the UI boundary is challenging. Academic entrepreneurs usually lack resources and commercialization expertise. Spinouts face significant uncertainties related to proving technologies, market needs and value creation potential (Doganova and Eyquem-Renault, 2009; Lehoux et al., 2014; Vohora et al., 2004). Resource access and configurations are highly dependent on exogenous factors outside the entrepreneur's control (Clarysse et al., 2011). New ventures generated at the UI boundary may require entirely new business models specific to the innovation (Pries and Guild, 2011).

Knowledge Spillover and Creation

Universities play an important role in knowledge creation within ecosystems. The spillover of knowledge from universities is important for innovation and ultimately ecosystem development and economic growth (Acs et al., 1994; Audretsch and Feldman, 1996). New knowledge generated within the university can spill over to the surrounding ecosystem, which is facilitated by the entrepreneurial culture at the focal university (Audretsch, 2014). External ecosystem actors are able to exploit and benefit from this spillover of knowledge (Agarwal et al., 2010), which is often tacit in nature (Agarwal and Shah, 2014). When there are greater levels of university-based knowledge spillovers, there are likely to be higher levels of new venture startups located around the university (Audretsch and Lehmann, 2005). The highly sophisticated technological requirements of RM venturing indicate that new RM ventures are most likely to locate themselves around the university in order to capitalize on localized university knowledge spillovers (Acosta et al., 2011; Audretsch et al., 2005). By being in close proximity to the university, RM ventures may benefit from smoother transmission of tacit knowledge (Kolympiris and Kalaitzandonakes, 2013). Spatially, university ventures spun out to university-linked science parks; in contrast those spun out within the wider ecosystem may be better placed to overcome resource scarcity and uncertainty (Lofsten and Lindelof, 2003).

The generation of new knowledge in ecosystems, and the subsequent spillover of this knowledge, drives entrepreneurial opportunities (Audretsch and Belitski, 2013). Exploiting these opportunities requires absorptive capacity to understand, recognize and commercialize this knowledge (Qian and Acs, 2013). Entrepreneurs must find ways to distinguish partnerships that create exploitable knowledge, rather than expropriate otherwise protected knowledge assets (Hernandez et al., 2015; Katila et al., 2008).

Regenerative Medicine Ecosystems: Venturing under Irreducible Uncertainty

RM venturing is a complex and resource-intensive process. Individual and institutional tensions are driven by conflicting motivations at the UI boundary, as well as business model uncertainty in the marketplace (Ledford, 2008). RM spinouts are generally capital-intensive yet capability-poor. They face field-specific challenges in manufacturing scale-up, distribution logistics and exit uncertainty. RM ventures must operate with little or no slack in their resource pool, limiting product-market and business model exploration and testing (Bock et al., 2012; George, 2005). This capabilities gap between university RM innovation and RM entrepreneurial activity requires new ventures to partner for critical industry knowledge and deep capabilities, in order to explore RM opportunities (George et al., 2008).

The development of a RM ecosystem ultimately depends heavily on the actions of individual entrepreneurs (Feldman, 2014; Wright et al., 2012b). The decision to become an inventing entrepreneur in the RM field may be controversial, difficult and uncertain (George and Bock, 2008). Academic scientists participating in commercialization activities will be required to modify their role identity (Jain et al., 2009). Shifting from a scientific orientation to a more market-driven approach creates tensions for the individual, university and the venture. The deeply embedded culture within academic institutions preferentially focuses on research and publications at the expense of patent and commercialization activities and is, therefore, at odds with an entrepreneurial approach (Decter et al., 2007).

Despite the noted research on entrepreneurial ecosystems, numerous questions require further attention. Broadly speaking, the full effects of university-based translational and commercial activity on local ecosystems and regional economies remains uncertain (Audretsch et al., 2013; Audretsch et al., 2014; Wright, 2013). More specifically, we know relatively little about the emergence of these ecosystems or the institutional characteristics that influence their development (Autio et al., 2014; Thomas and Autio, 2014). The impact of university policy, practice and culture on micro-level entrepreneurial cognition and behavior also requires more attention (Jennings et al., 2013). Specifically, there is a need for a deeper understanding of how different contexts affect entrepreneurial coping, especially under uncertainty (Autio et al., 2014). From a field perspective, venturing in RM has not been rigorously studied. It presents an edge case, highly specific to university-centric entrepreneurial ecosystems, in which uncertainty limits the value of strategic planning. Venturing activity in the RM field offers clues to the emergence and dynamics of entrepreneurial ecosystems.

METHODS

As we were primarily focused on the sensemaking and behavior of eco-system participants, we utilized a qualitative approach to data collection (Locke, 2001). We interviewed ecosystem participants, relying on the long interview as our data collection method (McCracken, 1988). To explore entrepreneurial processes and ecosystem elements in RM venturing, we initiated a study of activity in two distinct but similar areas. We discuss the ecosystems studied and the procedures for analysis.

Entrepreneurial Ecosystems under Investigation

We investigated RM venturing centered on the University of Edinburgh (Edinburgh, Scotland, United Kingdom) and the University of Wisconsin-Madison (Madison, Wisconsin, United States). These ecosystems present useful and surprisingly similar contexts to explore the development of a RM ecosystem at the UI boundary.

The University of Edinburgh and the University of Wisconsin-Madison are large research institutions with long-standing RM programs. RM research at the University of Edinburgh has been popularized by media attention to Dolly the sheep. Research led by Professor Sir Ian Wilmut led to the first cloned mammal from an adult somatic stem cell. The University of Edinburgh houses the Scottish Centre for Regenerative Medicine (SCRM). This world-leading research center employs more than 230 research scientists and clinicians, and was specifically commissioned to translate stem cell research to the clinic and industry. In addition, the Scottish government has a key focus on RM translation and the development of a viable RM ecosystem.

The University of Wisconsin-Madison also has an established history of RM research, with Professor James Thomson deriving the first primate and human embryonic stem cell lines and the first human-induced pluripotent stem cell lines. The Stem Cell and Regenerative Medicine Center at the University of Wisconsin-Madison is focused on being a world leader in stem cell and RM research and translation. The Wisconsin Alumni Research Foundation (WARF), the TTO for the University of Wisconsin-Madison, is generally recognized as holding the world's most foundational patent portfolio covering stem cell technology (Bergman and Graff, 2007).

Comparative information between the institutions and relative economic context is provided in Table 9.1 to demonstrate the surface similarities of the venturing context. The areas present strong similarities across a variety of measures. Both represent large research institutions in Tier 2 metropolitan areas. Additional similarities include the university size, socio-geographical context and relative dearth of local VC. Both ecosystems remain relatively small, providing a conducive context for investigation. The pairing is preferable to comparisons against more established and significantly larger RM ecosystems, such as San Diego (metro population 3.1 million), Boston (metro population 4.5 million), London (metro population 15 million) and Seoul (metro population 25.6 million). The similarities between the two ecosystems under investigation allowed for a more controlled exploration of variation in entrepreneurial cognition and behavior. While no two metropolitan or regional ecosystems will present enough similarity to warrant fully controlled investigation of target variables, the Scotland-Wisconsin parallel was (perhaps unusually) sufficiently similar to justify comparison over many other possible ecosystem choices.

Long Interview

Target informants were purposefully selected (Morse et al., 2002) according to their involvement in RM commercialization. To capture full aspects of the phenomena being examined, we interviewed several categories of informants from Edinburgh and Madison. Categories included RM entrepreneurs and firms (n = 10), academic scientists (n = 4) and RM/life science support entities (n = 16). RM/life science support entities were defined as organizations that supported RM venturing processes. They included TTOs, agencies that supported life science innovation and governmental bodies concerned with economic development in the life sciences.

We conducted interviews in Edinburgh between November 2012 and September 2013. Interviews in Madison were conducted between March and May 2014. We adopted a narrative interview approach in which informants were asked to describe their participation in the commercialization of RM innovation. Such an approach is especially useful

Table 9.1   Institution and regional economic data

	University of Edinburgh, Edinburgh, Scotland	University of Wisconsin-Madison, Madison, Wisconsin
University student population	30 579	43 275
Annual research budget	$458 million	$1 billion
Metropolitan population	Edinburgh: 495 360	Madison: 240 323
City status	Capital of Scotland	Capital of Wisconsin
State/Region population	Scotland: 5 295 000	Wisconsin: 5 726 000
GDP for region	Scotland: $216 billion	Wisconsin: $261 billion
Significant local industries	Finance, insurance, health, education, agriculture, tourism, whiskey	Insurance, health, education, agriculture, tourism, machinery
VC in region	< 5	< 5
School/College of Medicine research and academic faculty no.	2594	4447
University research income	$506 million	N/A
University research expenditures	N/A	$1.2 billion
Medical research expenditures	Estimated $175 million	$333 million
TTO activity (funding, patents)	TTO founded in 1969 423 patents filed 2007–12. $5.6 million license/ royalty income in 2011	TTO founded in 1928 2300 patents granted $57.7 million license royalty income in 2011
License/spinouts	Currently maintains 160+ commercial license agreements 171 spinout/startups since 1969	Currently maintains 380+ commercial license agreements 280+ spinout/startups since founding
RM patents granted between 2009–11	9	15
RM publicity	Dolly the sheep	Jamie Thomson, WARF

Note: All data for 2012–13 unless otherwise noted.

Sources: University of Wisconsin-Madison and subsidiary school/college websites; University of Edinburgh and subsidiary school/college websites and Annual Report; Scottish and Wisconsin government websites (including UK Intellectual Property Office); and Milwaukee *Journal Sentinel.*

for theory generation within entrepreneurship studies (Fletcher, 2007; Larty and Hamilton, 2011). Beyond this initial narrative request, informants were not provided with any further direction. When appropriate, the interviewer requested additional information about specific topics of interest. Consistent with long interview practices (McCracken, 1988), the interviewer encouraged the informant to discuss whatever topics, personal stories and opinions seemed relevant. Allowing informants to freely discuss areas of interest to them helps alleviate possible socially desirability bias (Podsakoff et al., 2003).

To limit participant bias and prejudicial preparation of information or materials, informants were not provided with detailed information about the interview in advance. Interviews ranged from 14 minutes to 85 minutes in duration. Additional field notes were generated during and immediately after the interviews to support data analysis. All interviews were recorded and transcribed. We provide information on the interview informants in Table 9.2.

Procedures

Our analysis of the narrative interviews was guided by grounded theory building (Strauss and Corbin, 1990). The Edinburgh interviews were open-coded to generate first-order codes. This was guided by findings from an initial pilot survey. Following the open coding, we developed theoretical categories and dimensions through inductive and deductive reasoning. To ensure theoretical sensitivity and a deep understanding of the relationships between categories, we constantly shifted between the data, coding and constructs during our analysis (Charmaz, 2006; Glaser, 1965). Transcripts were reviewed at the semantic level, seeking out the meaning of phrases, sentences and short passages. All coding was performed using NVivo software.

The Madison data was coded using the same data structure. The researchers were sensitive to the possibility of entirely new codings in the Madison data. Although some new constructs were observed in the Madison data, we chose to emphasize consistent, comparative analysis for three reasons. First, the prevalence of novel constructs in the Madison data was low. Second, re-coding the Edinburgh data with the novel constructs would not have been possible in a tabula rasa framework. Third, the Madison dataset was slightly smaller than the Edinburgh dataset, with a slightly different ratio of informant roles. For the sake of parsimony, we focused on the extant data structure, though we strove to remain open to novel or unexpected phenomena.

Table 9.2   Study informant and organization information

Informant no.	Category	Informant role	Organization type
1	SE	Executive	Provides support to the RM community. Government-backed initiative.
2	E/RMF	Founder	Main operations are in tools/diagnostics. Also offers services to other organizations and actively developing in the cell therapy space.
3	E/RMF	Manager	Involved in providing stem cell technical support and services to other organizations.
4	E/RMF	Founder	Primarily involved in providing stem cell training and consultancy to other organizations.
5	AS	Manager	University academic scientist (Principal Investigator).
6	SE	Manager	Governmental organization to encourage economic growth in Edinburgh.
7	SE	Executive	Supports academic innovation and commercialization.
8	SE	Manager	Supports technology transfer and innovation.
9	AS	Executive	University academic scientist (Principal Investigator).
10	E/RMF	Founder	Operates in RM products and services.
11	SE	Manager	Generates economic growth for Scotland through supporting a life science community.
12	SE	Manager	Supports a healthcare community and enables innovation.
13	E/RMF	Founder	Operates in the RM tools and diagnostics space.
14	E/RMF	Founder	Biotechnology and stem cell services organization.
15	SE	Executive	Establishing a cell therapy industry and community.
16	E/RMF	Executive	Products and services organization with operations in stem cell space.
17	SE	Manager	Supports innovation and economic development in Scotland.
18	SE	Manager	Supports economic growth in Edinburgh and Scotland.
19	SE	Manager	Supports technology transfer and company formation.
20	E/RMF	Founder	Operates in the RM tools space with therapeutic potential.

Informants 1–18 are grouped under **Edinburgh**; informants 19–20 are grouped under **Madison**.

Table 9.2 (continued)

Informant no.	Category	Informant role	Organization type
21	E/RMF	Founder	Operates in the RM tools space with therapeutic potential.
22	SE	Manager	Supports regional economic growth.
23	SE	Executive	Supports scientific and technological innovation.
24	SE	Executive	Supports new venture creation and growth.
25	E/RMF	Founder	Operates in the tools and diagnostics space. Also developing stem cell therapeutics.
26	SE	Manager	Supports technology transfer and innovation.
27	AS	Executive	University academic scientist (Principal Investigator).
28	AS	Manager	University academic scientist (Principal Investigator).
29	SE	Executive	Supports technology transfer and innovation.
30	SE	Senior Manager	Supports company investments.

(Rows 21–30 are grouped under the label "Madison".)

Note: E/RMF – entrepreneur and regenerative medicine firm; AS – academic scientist; SE – support entity.

FINDINGS

In this section, we report the findings from the data coding. We explore the theoretical dimensions revealed by the data and consider how these differ within and across ecosystems. We provide examples from the interview transcripts to illustrate the results of the coding analysis and emphasize key findings.

The multi-level data structure based on the interview coding is presented in Table 9.3 to highlight the relative prevalence of codes in each dataset (Walsh and Bartunek, 2011). The first column in the table shows the prevalence (percentage) of codes for (a) all informants; (b) informants in the Edinburgh ecosystem (ED) and (c) informants in the Madison ecosystem (MSN).

Ecosystem and Informant Role Comparisons

Comparisons across ecosystems and informant role highlight several differences. These are presented in Table 9.4. The data presented compares

Table 9.3 Data structure

Prevalence in study sample (%)*			First-order codes	Theoretical categories	Theoretical dimensions
TOTAL	ED	MSN			
57	61	50	Risk	Types of uncertainty	Perceived environmental uncertainty (PEU)
77	67	92	Funding issues		
30	44	8	Manufacturing, scale-up and distribution uncertainty		
47	44	50	Regulatory uncertainty		
30	28	33	Scientific uncertainty		
27	28	25	Ethics		
13	17	8	Reimbursement uncertainty		
33	28	42	Academic conflicts	Inventing entrepreneurs	University entrepreneurial culture
40	28	58	Academic motivations		
23	22	25	Academic metrics		
30	17	50	TTO business models and processes	TTO business models and processes	
73	89	50	Collaborations with industry	Collaborative partners	Coping strategies
63	72	50	Collaborations with academia		
30	44	8	Collaborations with hospitals		
37	44	25	Collaborations with support entities		
33	44	17	Collaboration for sharing of resources	Collaborative outcomes	
20	28	8	Collaboration for process improvement		
13	11	17	Collaboration for funding purposes		
7	11	0	Collaboration costs		
3	6	0	Collaboration for legitimacy building		
47	56	33	Legitimacy building	Legitimacy building	

				Resource exchange mechanisms	Collaborative knowledge
60	56	67	Knowledge transfer		
63	61	67	Communication		
33	22	50	Learning		
23	28	17	Language differences		
60	61	58	RM and scientific communities	Networks	Venture development
73	89	50	Governmental funding	Funding sources	
47	44	50	Angel/VC funding		
23	28	17	'Big pharma' funding		
60	67	50	Spinout venture formation	Spinout venture formation	
47	33	33	Business models	Business models	
87	78	100	Resources	Existing resources	
17	28	0	Innovation		
27	28	25	Regional investment and growth	Economic development	Outcomes
67	83	42	Commercialization timeframes	Future scenarios	
10	11	8	Potential industry structure		

Note: * Does not account for multiple occurrences within a single interview.

Table 9.4   Ecosystem and informant role comparisons

	ED (%)	MSN (%)	Entrepreneurs/ RM firms (%)	Academic scientists (%)	Support entities (%)
PEU	18	15	19	19	14
University entrepreneurial culture	5	18	4	15	12
Coping strategies	21	14	20	19	18
Collaborative knowledge	13	19	9	13	21
Venture development	32	29	43	23	25
Outcomes	11	5	5	11	10
Total (%)	100	100	100	100	100

normalized code frequency to account for differences in interview length and informant speaking styles. We calculate values for each ecosystem (and informant role) by dividing the total number of references for each theoretical dimension by the total number of all references across all theoretical dimensions.

Differences across Ecosystems

The data shows much higher reference to *university entrepreneurial culture* in Madison than Edinburgh. Both ecosystems highlight the conflicts faced by academic scientists looking to commercialize their stem cell innovations, since commercialization activities are at odds with traditional academic culture:

> [A]cademics are judged by their papers and their grants . . . Spinouts take a lot of time and a huge amount of work . . . group leaders find that extremely difficult because that's time that they're not doing their academic work and ultimately they will be judged with the current metrics much more on their academic work than they will on their commercialization work. (Informant no. 9)

Other informants placed blame on the larger academic context:

> That's the way that our scientific environment is structured. We publish papers and get proposals funded without pushing toward the edges of the spectrum . . . we can't have impact. (Informant no. 28)

Informants from Madison highlight stronger motivation toward venture formation at the UI boundary. In Edinburgh there are perceptions that licensing, rather than spinout formation, is the preferred method of technology transfer:

> [U]niversities don't do spinout companies, I know it sounds a bit daft, but conceptually that's not . . . they tend to do licensing deals and spinouts are not something they want to get involved with. (Informant no. 7)

We also see a greater emphasis in Madison on the TTO policies that encourage commercialization and the resources available at the TTO to enable entrepreneurial activities. WARF has a long history of technology commercialization. It is one of the oldest and most successful TTOs in the world and has particular expertise with RM technologies, stemming from the early seminal research and discoveries by Dr James Thomson.

The business development capabilities of TTO personnel have been shown to influence venturing activity (Lockett and Wright, 2005). Academic scientists disclosing their innovations at the University of Wisconsin-Madison have access to a diverse team within the TTO. This includes licensing managers, IP managers, legal counsel and patent and market intelligence analysts. The University of Edinburgh has fewer resources allocated to this type of pre-commercialization activity.

Across ecosystems there are differences in *collaborative knowledge*, with greater emphasis on this in Madison. We see higher reference to knowledge transfer during RM venturing activities in Madison:

> So we'll be in constant communication with the inventors and communication with our outside patent counsel and work with them to build a strong patent portfolio that we can market. (Informant no. 30)

The flow of knowledge within networks results in specialized knowledge being created, transferred or recombined, which results in learning (Dyer and Nobeoka, 2000). Findings from Madison highlight greater perceptions of learning taking place during the venturing process. Some emphasized lessons related to their institutional role:

> What I've learned over time is that you have to be published in peer reviewed journals. (Informant no. 25)

Others emphasized learning specifically about venturing:

> There were just a lot of dynamics in the process that were tremendous learning experiences. (Informant no. 28)

Ecosystem comparisons illustrate a greater emphasis on *coping strategies* in Edinburgh compared to Madison. To overcome the high levels of perceived environmental uncertainty (PEU) (Milliken, 1987), the dataset highlights the implementation of coping strategies. These include collaboration and legitimacy building. Collaborations can provide access to critical resources. Legitimacy building is especially useful when uncertainty and controversy surround a novel technology. We see support entities in Edinburgh building legitimacy in order to promote their offerings to RM ventures:

> we've become active internationally as a mechanism of trying to demonstrate that the UK is an attractive place to do this sort of work in and then we'll partner with potential inward investors to either set up manufacturing, get clinical trials done, being the entry point into the European arena through the UK. (Informant no. 15)

Findings also highlight differences in the emphasis and preference for *outcomes* between ecosystems. Edinburgh placed a greater emphasis on outcomes in comparison to Madison. In particular, informants in Edinburgh discussed regional economic development and innovation expectations arising from RM venturing activity:

> ... make sure that the innovation coming out of Scotland is developed in Scotland, is manufactured in Scotland ... that we have the economic benefit and we have the wealth gain and the health gain ... it's to try and help developments stay in Scotland. (Informant no. 11)

Informants in Edinburgh particularly focus on the timeframes involved in RM venturing. Some noted the conflict with policy expectations:

> ... I think linked to the lack of understanding of the science, often the timescales for these end games are just not understood at all. (Informant no. 1)

Others noted the potential mismatch with investor expectations:

> [the] time horizons of a VC investment just don't fit the time horizons of a development of a therapeutic ... (Informant no. 10)

Differences between Informant Roles

Entrepreneurs and RM firms place a greater significance on *venture development* than academic scientists and support entities. RM venture development relies on the availability of resources and the RM business model. Findings show entrepreneurs and RM firms extensively discussing the availability of financial resources. Informants reported that funding is accessible for RM research and development. Some funding is clearly linked to venture development:

> We've found that for this early stage activity, the Technology Strategy Board [UK government funding board] has been critical, they are a very good source of funding . . . the amounts of money are suitable for these early stage activities. (Informant no. 16)

The perception of funding accessibility may directly drive venture formation:

> And there was money available for seed funding to get started. And so that's how we ended up starting the company. (Informant no. 25)

Again, the link to scale-up funding, however, is less clear:

> only large pharmaceutical companies can really afford to [bring a therapeutic to market] . . . it's a very expensive deal . . . we don't have that level and the amount of money required. (Informant no. 13)

New ventures at the UI boundary require sufficient human capital. This is seen as a key driver to the growth of high-technology startups (Colombo et al., 2010). The academic founder may not possess the appropriate skills and capabilities necessary for commercialization (Venkataraman et al., 1992). Academics are also likely to lack the commercial experience that investors seek (Franklin et al., 2001), which suggests that new ventures need access to management with proven commercialization experience. However, there was strong support between informants in Madison that attracting the appropriate management team was problematic:

> And so that is the challenge . . . finding talented people to get us off the ground who are willing to take a risk . . . we have moved people here before and that can be harder. If they have no Midwestern ties, it's very hard to recruit to here. (Informant no. 25)

Entrepreneurs and RM firms are clearly concerned with the assembly of resources in the venturing process. As a result, they place less emphasis on *university entrepreneurial culture* and *outcomes* than support entities and academic scientists. Since support entities play an important role in establishing networks for RM venturing, they place greater emphasis on *collaborative knowledge* than RM entrepreneurs and firms and academic scientists.

Table 9.5   Informant role across ecosystem comparisons

	Entrepreneurs/ RM firms		Academic scientists		Support entities	
	ED (%)	MSN (%)	ED (%)	MSN (%)	ED (%)	MSN (%)
PEU	21	14	19	20	15	13
University entrepreneurial culture	0	19	10	20	9	17
Coping strategies	21	18	23	16	21	12
Collaborative knowledge	7	16	10	16	20	22
Venture development	46	31	23	24	21	30
Outcomes	5	2	15	4	14	6
Total (%)	100	100	100	100	100	100

Differences between Informant Roles across Ecosystems

Comparisons of informant roles across the two ecosystems are shown in Table 9.5. Again, values are normalized and calculated as previously reported.

Findings highlight less reference to *PEU* by entrepreneurs and RM firms in Madison than Edinburgh. Whilst funding uncertainties are highlighted in both ecosystems, Edinburgh faces particular challenges in acquiring angel and VC funding:

> We're too small for VC's but we're too big for angels. (Informant no. 2)

Results show a greater reference to *university entrepreneurial culture* for entrepreneurs and RM firms in Madison. This may be explained by the discrepancy in informant roles across the datasets. Two entrepreneur informants in Madison had been academic scientists prior to starting the new venture. Academic scientists and support entities in Madison also make greater reference to university entrepreneurial culture in contrast to Edinburgh. Academic scientists in Madison appear to show stronger motivations toward venturing activity at the UI boundary.

We see less reference to *coping strategies* but more emphasis on *collaborative knowledge* across all informant roles in Madison than Edinburgh. In particular, findings emphasize the individual learning that has taken place:

> So, I'm kind of learning myself . . . My hope is that interacting with people like you and talking to other people that I learn something. (Informant no. 20)

Entrepreneurs and RM firms refer less to *venture development* in Madison than Edinburgh. In contrast, support entities and to some extent academic scientists in Madison place a greater emphasis on venture development. Across all informant roles in Madison, there is less discussion of *outcomes* in comparison to Edinburgh, particularly for academic scientists and support entities.

DISCUSSION

Our cross-national comparative study contributes to research on entrepreneurial behavior, technology transfer and ecosystem development. We discuss these to emphasize both the key findings from our study as well as opportunities for further research.

Entrepreneurial Coping Strategies and Institutional Culture

Entrepreneurial behavior is driven by a variety of factors (Aldrich and Martinez, 2001; Alvarez and Barney, 2005). Entrepreneurs translating innovations from the university to industry experience significant changes in the role identity profile that drives their beliefs and goals (George and Bock, 2008). The cultural context from which entrepreneurs emerge directly affects the cognitive framework and interpretation of information used to make decisions under uncertainty. The culture of the 'parent' institution thus directly shapes the individual traits that drive entrepreneurial behavior (Hofstede, 1980; Mueller and Thomas, 2001).

A significant amount of university technology transfer takes place in fields with high levels of technological sophistication and correspondingly high levels of uncertainty. This is especially so for innovations in RM. Faced with irreducible uncertainty, participants in RM entrepreneurial ecosystems must utilize coping strategies to continue to make decisions without viable risk-reward calculations. Entrepreneurial coping strategies are the behavioral patterns entrepreneurs employ to contextualize or make sense of non-resolvable venturing problems (Johnson and Bock, forthcoming).

Prior research shows that entrepreneurs utilize both problem-focused coping and emotion-focused coping responses (Carver et al., 1989; Lazarus and Folkman, 1984). Problem-focused coping is associated with internal locus of control and the entrepreneur's perception that further information gathering and analysis will resolve uncertainties or mitigate their impact. By contrast, emotion-focused coping is associated with external locus of control and the belief that some or all aspects of the situation are either out of the entrepreneur's control or at least not amenable to influence via the entrepreneur's efforts. This distinction is especially important in RM, where entrepreneurs often rely on collaboration and partnerships to access knowledge and develop key capabilities.

The cross-national comparison suggests that the profile of dominant coping strategies may vary across similar entrepreneurial ecosystems. Since coping strategies are driven by persistent beliefs and assumptions about the nature of the technology transfer process, the most likely driver of coping strategy profiles is the culture of the originating institution. Prior research has emphasized the critical role of context and originating culture to entrepreneurial behavior and sensemaking (for example, Autio et al., 2014; Jennings et al., 2013). Our findings reveal differences between the dominance of originating university entrepreneurial culture and the application of coping strategies. We propose:

Proposition 1: Entrepreneurial culture at the originating institution is associated with coping strategies in the entrepreneurial ecosystem.

The ecosystem around Edinburgh presents higher levels of PEU, lower institutional entrepreneurial culture and a higher reliance on coping strategies. Participants in this ecosystem appear to rely more on emotion-focused coping than participants in the Wisconsin ecosystem. This has important implications for theories of entrepreneurial behavior at the UI boundary, including the prevalence of residual effects of institutional culture on the broader ecosystem. We further specify this relationship:

Proposition 1a: The level of entrepreneurial culture at the originating institution is negatively associated with the prevalence of emotion-focused coping strategies in the entrepreneurial ecosystem.

Proposition 1b: The level of entrepreneurial culture at the originating institution is positively associated with the prevalence of problem-focused coping strategies in the entrepreneurial ecosystem.

Entrepreneurial Ecosystem Characteristics

Ecosystem development is a multi-dimensional and idiosyncratic process. The structure and content of a given ecosystem emerges from a series of non-path-deterministic events and exogenous circumstances. Our findings suggest disparate paths for the observed ecosystems.

Distinctions between micro-level sensemaking and behavior across the ecosystems are clearly shown in Figure 9.1. The ecosystem around the

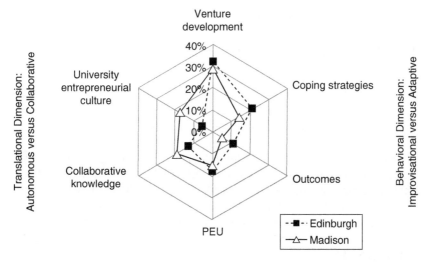

Figure 9.1   Comparison of micro-level factors across ecosystems

University of Wisconsin-Madison demonstrates a stronger entrepreneurial culture associated with the university as well as an emphasis on collaborative knowledge development in the venturing process. By contrast, the ecosystem around the University of Edinburgh presents a stronger emphasis on coping strategies and venturing outcomes. These reflect important differences in underlying dimensions of behavioral norms and translational approaches to technology commercialization and venture development.

RM venturing is disproportionately driven by individuals that are trained in academic institutions and that experience significant transitions when engaging in commercialization. While broad patterns for these transitions are consistent across institutions and ecosystems, the translational approach adopted by participants clearly varies across ecosystems. We therefore propose:

Proposition 2: The dominant translational approach of an entrepreneurial ecosystem is associated with the entrepreneurial culture of the originating institution and the utilization of collaborative knowledge development.

In the case of the RM ecosystem around the University of Wisconsin-Madison, the ecosystem combines a relatively strong entrepreneurial culture extant within the university with collaborative knowledge development. In other words, this ecosystem values a collaborative and opportunistic approach to translational activity. The ecosystem around the

University of Wisconsin-Madison presents much lower levels of coping strategies and outcome emphasis. This is indicative of an improvisational approach, with less emphasis on behavioral change in the service of achieving specific goals. We propose:

Proposition 2a: Improvisational entrepreneurial ecosystems are associated with higher levels of entrepreneurial culture in the originating institution and increased utilization of collaborative knowledge development.

By contrast, the ecosystem around the University of Edinburgh is lower on entrepreneurial university culture and collaborative knowledge development. Entrepreneurs and other ecosystem participants rely on a more autonomous and focused approach to translating technologies across the UI boundary. The ecosystem around the University of Edinburgh emphasizes coping strategies and venturing outcomes. This suggests an adaptive practice to addressing uncertainty.

Proposition 2b: Focused entrepreneurial ecosystems are associated with lower levels of entrepreneurial culture in the originating institution and decreased utilization of collaborative knowledge development.

The Development Paths of Entrepreneurial Ecosystems

Our study does not address performance outcomes at any level; we draw no conclusions at this time regarding whether specific translational or behavioral ecosystem profiles are correlated with the probability of success of entrepreneurs, TTOs or ecosystems. At the same time, prior research on venturing, learning, industry and cluster development suggest implications for profile differences as well as opportunities for future research.

Generally speaking, knowledge creation and collaborative learning are associated with more rapidly developing ventures and clusters (Porter, 1998). As learning is time-dependent, a translational preference for autonomous learning may unintentionally delay the development of dynamic capabilities that underpin firm and ecosystem development (Jantunen et al., 2012; Teece et al., 1997). Further, highly uncertain environments may necessitate trial-and-error learning in venture development (Loch et al., 2008; Sosna et al., 2010). Research on absorptive capacity also suggests that the sophisticated requirements of life science entrepreneurship make it unlikely that new ventures will possess adequate internal knowledge (Cohen and Levinthal, 1990; Zahra and George, 2002). The greater emphasis on knowledge exchange and entrepreneurial culture within the University of Wisconsin-Madison, linked to a more improvisational and collaborative ecosystem, may suggest long-term venture growth and success.

On the behavioral side, the ecosystem around Edinburgh presents an apparently more adaptive approach to RM venturing activity. While improvisation may be effective in some entrepreneurial contexts (Moorman and Miner, 1998), especially under uncertainty, firms must implement consistent structures, routines and predictive systems to manage risks and scale value creation activities (Baker and Nelson, 2005). Greater reliance on coping strategies may be explained by the perception of greater uncertainty within the ecosystem. Although specific coping strategies differ across individuals (Carver et al., 1989), coping responses can be effective in reducing, acknowledging and suppressing uncertainty (Lipshitz and Strauss, 1997).

A dynamic model of ecosystem development represents an important step forward in our understanding of technology transfer and translation of innovation (Autio et al., 2014; Thomas and Autio, 2014). Based on the comparison of characteristics, we propose a two-dimensional model of entrepreneurial ecosystem development. Although an ecosystem may be described by a variety of characteristics, these appear to have direct relevance to venturing activity at the UI boundary. Figure 9.2 shows the model, incorporating translational and behavioral dimensions of ecosystems.

To address the dynamics of ecosystem development, we presume that an entrepreneurial ecosystem centered on a university must be initiated with a relatively autonomous approach to translation and an improvisational approach to behavior. At the very earliest stages of university-based ecosystem formation in a sector that relies on long-term research, the innovations at the core of the nascent ecosystem originate within the university. While scientists and university or TTO administrators may be well attuned to market factors and industry dynamics, early activities will necessarily require researchers with potentially commercializable activities to operate independently. This is because there will be little to no comparable entrepreneurial culture or activity related to that type of innovation. The entrepreneurial culture at the university must be strong enough to manifest at the departmental level (Rasmussen et al., 2014). Since there will be little or no extant infrastructure to support translational activities for a specific innovation type, either within or outside the university, the inventing entrepreneur's behavior is likely to be primarily improvisational. Again, either the university or the regional technology cluster may provide a context for adaptive behavior through mentoring schemes, support entities and prior success stories. At the same time, when innovations are novel and uncertainty high, identifying proven behaviors and processes becomes more difficult. This is precisely the situation in RM.

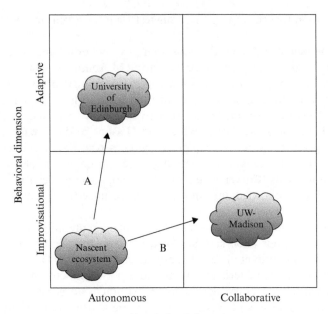

*Figure 9.2   Model of regenerative medicine venturing ecosystem
development*

The ecosystem around Madison has developed more collaborative translational approaches, while the ecosystem around Edinburgh has developed more adaptive behavioral norms. It is important to emphasize that this picture of ecosystem development does not reflect a purely linear process or a specific rate of development. On the other hand, the relative novelty of RM research and commercialization activity (see Table 9.1 for the relatively low number of RM patents compared to the overall portfolio of the TTOs) reinforces that these ecosystems are still relatively early-stage.

Despite significant surface-level similarities between the industrial-geographic regions around the universities, key differences should be noted. Collaborative effects in the Wisconsin ecosystem may benefit from WARF's extensive technology transfer history and the prior experience of numerous life science spinouts with exit events (for example, Nimblegen/Roche, Tomotherapy/Accuray, Lunar/GE, BoneCare/Genzyme and others) in the area. Although both areas have relatively limited VC resources (compared to other life science venturing hubs), numerous life science ventures in the Madison ecosystem have obtained mid- and late-stage investments from VC firms in California and the US East Coast.

Our model suggests that entrepreneurial ecosystem development at the UI boundary is a dynamic and path-independent process. The development of the ecosystem is both a driver and outcome of the nature and type of entrepreneurial coping strategies prevalent within the ecosystem. Coping responses are particularly important to *de novo* ventures, especially at startup, as they assist in resource and knowledge identification and access. Since cultural artifacts and ecosystem-specific factors affect coping responses, similar ecosystems may generate significantly different behaviors for knowledge and learning. It is not sufficient to characterize an ecosystem's configuration of resources and prior history to understand how the ecosystem is likely to develop further. The interplay of the central university's entrepreneurial culture and the dominant coping strategy profile of the ecosystem will be tightly linked to the ecosystem's locus of attention and collaborative knowledge emphasis.

Our findings have important theoretical and practical implications. We advance theories of UI technology transfer by presenting cross-national findings on the characteristics and dynamics of entrepreneurial ecosystem development under irreducible uncertainty. We further inform institutional entrepreneurship and technology transfer literature by developing specific propositions linking originating culture to resulting characteristics of the ecosystem.

We also extend research linking entrepreneurial cognition and sensemaking to ecosystem development (Wright et al., 2012b). Our findings highlight individual-level coping responses to institutional culture and high levels of uncertainty. We have shown coping strategies to be important for resource and knowledge acquisition and assembly. All of these factors are implicated in the process and outcome of new venture development at the UI boundary. These findings further emphasize the importance of the entrepreneur and entrepreneurial cognition in ecosystem development and competiveness. This is consistent with prior research (Feldman, 2014) but presents entirely new directions for further study of coping strategies and collaborative activities. In particular, our findings help identify the specific mechanisms that drive entrepreneurial decision-making in fields of high uncertainty, emphasizing that university policy and culture play a critical role in ecosystem outcomes (Audretsch et al., 2013; Audretsch et al., 2014; Wright, 2013).

LIMITATIONS AND RESEARCH DIRECTIONS

Certain limitations in this research must be kept in mind in the interpretation of the study. First, the datasets are relatively small and may not effectively capture the situational perspective of the entire ecosystems. Second, open coding has specific limitations, including the potential for biasing effects of prior researcher knowledge. Third, the datasets were coded asynchronously. It is possible that synchronous coding of the datasets in a randomized order might have generated a slightly different data structure. Since our data is not longitudinal or time-synchronized, we cannot address potential differential rates of ecosystem development between ecosystems.

The inductive, theory-driven approach was suitable for the development of novel phenomena. At the same time, our findings should be tested empirically to identify the strength of relationships and impact in context. We have shown how cognition and behavior of ecosystem participants is important for ecosystem development with potentially long-term effects on firm and ecosystem competitiveness. We hope to see large-scale, quantitative research that tests for the cognitive and behavioral characteristics in entrepreneurial ecosystems, as well as ecosystem development processes.

Our findings report on entrepreneurial ecosystem development of two similar but distinct ecosystems. While Edinburgh and Madison present close similarity, the difference in TTO activity between these two ecosystems warrants further analysis, since this will be implicated in ecosystem development. Given that we could not control all target variables between ecosystems, additional research could extend to other similar ecosystems. It would also be interesting for future research to investigate more established ecosystems in other industries and RM ecosystems in larger and more well-resourced industrial-geographic or non-western regions, in order to reveal differences in ecosystem development.

CONCLUSION

This study presents a cross-national analysis of ecosystem development under irreducible uncertainty. We use qualitative analysis of interview data collected from distinct but similar entrepreneurial ecosystems in the RM field. The results suggest that university culture and PEU impact the characteristics and development path of entrepreneurial ecosystems. The findings point toward important new theories of entrepreneurial ecosystem development and micro-level entrepreneurial behavior at the UI boundary.

NOTE

1. The firms were, in fact, ultimately merged in 2008.

REFERENCES

Acosta, M., Coronado, D. and Flores, E. (2011). University spillovers and new business location in high-technology sectors: Spanish evidence. *Small Business Economics*, **36**, 365–76.

Acs, Z., Audretsch, D.B. and Feldman, M.P. (1994). R&D spillovers and recipient firm size. *Review of Economics and Statistics*, **76**(2), 336–40.

Agarwal, R. and Shah, S. (2014). Knowledge sources of entrepreneurship: firm formation by academic user and employee innovators. *Research Policy*, **43**, 1109–33.

Agarwal, R., Audretsch, D.B. and Sarkar, M.B. (2010). Knowledge spillovers and strategic entrepreneurship. *Strategic Entrepreneurship Journal*, **4**, 271–83.

Aldrich, H.E. and Martinez, M.A. (2001). Many are called but few are chosen: an evolutionary perspective for the study of entrepreneurship. *Entrepreneurship Theory and Practice*, **25**(4), 41–56.

Alvarez, S.A. and Barney, J.B. (2005). How do entrepreneurs organize firms under uncertainty? *Journal of Management*, **31**(5), 776–93.

Ardichvili, A., Cardozo, R.N., Tune, C. and Reinach, J. (2002). The role of angel investors in the assembly of non-financial resources of new ventures: conceptual framework and empirical evidence. *Journal of Enterprising Culture*, **10**(1), 39–65.

Audretsch, D.B. (2014). From the entrepreneurial university to the university for the entrepreneurial society. *Journal of Technology Transfer*, **39**, 313–21.

Audretsch, D.B. and Belitski, M. (2013). The missing pillar: the creativity theory of knowledge spillover entrepreneurship. *Small Business Economics*, **41**, 819–36.

Audretsch, D.B. and Feldman, M.P. (1996). R&D spillovers and the geography of innovation and production. *American Economic Review*, **86**(3), 630–40.

Audretsch, D.B. and Lehmann, E.E. (2005). Does the knowledge spillover theory of entrepreneurship hold for regions? *Research Policy*, **34**, 1191–202.

Audretsch, D.B., Lehmann, E.E. and Warning, S. (2005). University spillovers and new firm location. *Research Policy*, **34**(7), 1113–22.

Audretsch, D.B., Lehmann, E.E., Link, A.N. and Starnecker, A. (2013). *Technology Transfer in a Global Economy*. Heidelberg: Springer.

Audretsch, D.B., Lehmann, E.E. and Wright, M. (2014). Technology transfer in a global economy. *Journal of Technology Transfer*, **39**, 301–12.

Autio, E., Kenney, M., Mustar, P., Siegel, D. and Wright, M. (2014). Entrepreneurial innovation: the importance of context. *Research Policy*, **43**, 1097–108.

Baker, T. and Nelson, R.E. (2005). Creating something from nothing: resource construction through entrepreneurial bricolage. *Administrative Science Quarterly*, **50**(3), 329–66.

Bell, S.J., Tracey, P. and Heide, J.B. (2009). The organization of regional clusters. *Academy of Management Review*, **34**(4), 623–42.

Bergman, K. and Graff, G.D. (2007). The global stem cell patent landscape: implications for efficient technology transfer and commercial development. *Nature Biotechnology*, **25**(4), 419–24.

Birley, S. (1985). The role of networks in the entrepreneurial process. *Journal of Business Venturing*, **1**(1), 107–17.

Bock, A.J. (2012). Beyond the magic beanstalk: a study of life science ecosystem formation at the university-industry boundary. http://www.business-school.ed.ac.uk/__data/assets/pdf_file/0014/45140/120405-Bock-BeyondBeanstalk.pdf (accessed 9 March 2013).

Bock, A.J., Opsahl, T., George, G. and Gann, D.M. (2012). The effects of culture and structure on strategic flexibility during business model innovation. *Journal of Management Studies*, **49**(2), 279–305.

Breznitz, S.M. and Feldman, M.P. (2012). The engaged university. *Journal of Technology Transfer*, **37**, 139–57.

Carver, C.S., Scheier, M.F. and Weintraub, J.K. (1989). Assessing coping strategies: a theoretically based approach. *Journal of Personality and Social Psychology*, **56**(2), 267–83.

Charmaz, K. (2006). *Constructing Grounded Theory: A Practical Guide Through Qualitative Analysis*. London: Sage Publications.

Clarysse, B., Bruneel, J. and Wright, M. (2011). Explaining growth paths of young technology-based firms: structuring resource portfolios in different competitive environments. *Strategic Entrepreneurship Journal*, **5**, 137–57.

Cohen, B. (2006). Sustainable valley entrepreneurial ecosystems. *Business Strategy and the Environment*, **15**, 1–14.

Cohen, W.M. and Levinthal, D.A. (1990). Absorptive capacity: a new perspective on learning and innovation. *Administrative Science Quarterly*, **35**, 128–52.

Colombo, M., Mustar, P. and Wright, M. (2010). Dynamics of science-based entrepreneurship. *Journal of Technology Transfer*, **35**, 1–15.

De Vaan, M. (2014). Interfirm network in periods of technological turbulence and stability. *Research Policy*, **43**, 1666–80.

Decter, M., Bennett, D. and Leseure, M. (2007). University to business technology transfer – USA and UK comparisons. *Technovation*, **27**, 145–55.

Djokovic, D. and Souitaris, V. (2008). Spinouts from academic institutions: a literature review with suggestions for further research. *Journal of Technology Transfer*, **33**, 225–47.

Doganova, L. and Eyquem-Renault, M. (2009). What do business models do? Innovation devices in technology entrepreneurship. *Research Policy*, **38**, 1559–70.

Dyer, J.H. and Nobeoka, K. (2000). Creating and managing a high-performance knowledge sharing network: the Toyota case. *Strategic Management Journal*, **21**(3), 345–67.

Eisingerich, A.B., Bell, S. and Tracey, P. (2010). How can clusters sustain performance? The role of network strength, network openness and environmental uncertainty. *Research Policy*, **39**, 239–53.

Etzkowitz, H. (2003). Innovation in innovation: the triple helix of university industry-government relations. *Social Science Information*, **42**, 293–337.

Feldman, M.P. (2014). The character of innovative places: entrepreneurial strategy, economic development and prosperity. *Small Business Economics*, **43**, 9–20.

Festel, G. (2013). Academic spin-offs, corporate spin-outs and company internal start-ups as technology transfer approach. *Journal of Technology Transfer*, **38**, 454–70.

Fletcher, D. (2007). 'Toy Story': the narrative world of entrepreneurship and the creation of interpretive communities. *Journal of Business Venturing*, **22**, 649–72.

Franklin, S.J., Wright, M. and Lockett, A. (2001). Academic and surrogate entre-preneurs in university spin-out companies. *Journal of Technology Transfer*, **26**, 127–41.

George, G. (2005). Slack resources and the performance of privately held firms. *Academy of Management Journal*, **48**(4), 661–76.

George, G. and Bock, A.J. (2008). *Inventing Entrepreneurs: Technology Innovators and their Entrepreneurial Journey*. Upper Saddle River, NJ: Prentice-Hall Pearson.

George, G. and Bock, A.J. (2012). *Models of Opportunity*. Cambridge: Cambridge University Press.

George, G., Kotha, R. and Zheny, Y. (2008). Entry into insular domains: a longitu-dinal study of knowledge structuration and innovation in biotechnology firms. *Journal of Management Studies*, **45**(8), 1448–74.

Glaser, B.G. (1965). The constant comparative method of qualitative analysis. *Social Problems*, **12**(4), 436–45.

Goldfarb, B. and Henrekson, M. (2003). Bottom-up versus top-down policies towards the commercialization of university intellectual property. *Research Policy*, **32**(4), 639–58.

Hayter, C.S. (2013). Conceptualizing knowledge-based entrepreneurship networks: perspectives from the literature. *Journal of Business Economics*, **41**, 899–911.

Heirman, A. and Clarysse, B. (2004). How and why do research-based start-ups differ at founding? A resources-based configurational perspective. *Journal of Technology Transfer*, **29**, 247–68.

Henrekson, M. and Rosenberg, N. (2001). Designing efficient institutions for science-based entrepreneurship: lessons from the US and Sweden. *Journal of Technology Transfer*, **26**(3), 207–31.

Hernandez, E., Sanders, G. and Tuschke, A. (2015). Network defense: pruning, grafting, and closing to prevent leakage of strategic knowledge to rivals. *Academy of Management Journal*, **58**(4), 1233–60.

Hoang, H. and Antoncic, B. (2003). Network-based research in entrepreneurship: a critical review. *Journal of Business Venturing*, **18**, 165–87.

Hofstede, G. (1980). *Culture's Consequences: International Differences in Work Related Values*. Beverley Hills, CA: Sage Publications.

Jack, S.L. (2010). Approaches to studying networks: implications and outcomes. *Journal of Business Venturing*, **25**, 120–37.

Jain, S., George, G. and Maltarich, M. (2009). Academics or entrepreneurs? Investigating role identity modification of university scientists involved in commercialization activity. *Research Policy*, **38**, 922–35.

Jantunen, A., Ellonen, H.K. and Johansson, A. (2012). Beyond appearances – do dynamic capabilities of innovative firms actually differ? *European Management Journal*, **30**, 141–55.

Jennings, P.D., Greenwood, R., Lounsbury, M.D. and Suddaby, R. (2013). Institutions, entrepreneurs, and communities: a special issue. *Journal of Business Venturing*, **28**, 1–9.

Johannisson, B., Ramirez-Pasillas, M. and Karlsson, G. (2002). The institutional embeddedness of local inter-firm networks: a leverage for business creation. *Entrepreneurship and Regional Development*, **14**(4), 297–315.

Johnson, D. and Bock, A.J. (forthcoming). Coping with uncertainty: entrepre-neurial sensemaking in regenerative medicine. *Journal of Technology Transfer*.

Katila, R., Rosenberger, J.D. and Eisenhardt, K.M. (2008). Swimming with sharks: technology ventures, defense mechanisms and corporate relationships. *Administrative Science Quarterly*, **53**, 295–332.

Kolympiris, C. and Kalaitzandonakes, N. (2013). Geographic scope of proximity effects among small life science firms. *Small Business Economics*, **40**, 1059–86.

Larty, J. and Hamilton, E. (2011). Structural approaches to narrative analysis in entrepreneurship research: exemplars from two researchers. *International Small Business Journal*, **29**(3), 220–37.

Lazarus, R. and Folkman, S. (1984). *Stress, Appraisal and Coping*. New York: Springer.

Ledford, H. (2008). In search of a viable business model. *Nature Reports Stem Cells*, 30 October. http://www.nature.com/stemcells/2008/0810/081030/full/stem cells.2008.138.html (accessed 17 September 2013).

Lehoux, P., Daudelin, G., Williams-Jones, B., Denis, J.L. and Longo, C. (2014). How do business model and health technology design influence each other? Insights from a longitudinal case study of three academic spin-offs. *Research Policy*, **43**(6), 1025–38.

Lipshitz, R. and Strauss, O. (1997). Coping with uncertainty: a naturalistic decision-making. *Organizational Behaviour and Human Decision Processes*, **69**(2), 149–63.

Loch, C.H., Solt, M.E. and Bailey, E.M. (2008). Diagnosing unforeseeable uncertainty in a new venture. *Journal of Product Innovation Management*, **25**(1), 28–46.

Locke, K. (2001). *Grounded Theory in Management Research*. London: Sage Publications.

Lockett, A. and Wright, M. (2005). Resources, capabilities, risk capital and the creation of university spin-out companies. *Research Policy*, **34**(7), 1043–57.

Lofsten, H. and Lindelof, P. (2003). Determinants for an entrepreneurial milieu: science parks and business policy in growing firms. *Technovation*, **23**, 51–64.

McCracken, G. (1988). *The Long Interview*. Qualitative Research Series 13. London: Sage Publications.

Meyskens, M. and Carsrud, A.L. (2013). Nascent green-technology ventures: a study assessing the role of partnership diversity in firm success. *Small Business Economics*, **40**, 739–59.

Milliken, F.J. (1987). Three types of perceived uncertainty about the environment: state, effect, and response uncertainty. *Academy of Management*, **12**(1), 133–43.

Miner, A., Devaughn, M. and Rura, T. (2001). The magic beanstalk vision: commercializing university inventions and research. In C. Schoohoven and E. Romaneli (eds), *The Entrepreneurship Dynamic*. Stanford, CA: Stanford University Press, pp. 109–46.

Moore, J.F. (1993). Predators and prey: a new ecology of competition. *Harvard Business Review*, **71**(3), 75–86.

Moorman, C. and Miner, A.S. (1998). The convergence of planning and execution: improvisation in new product development. *Journal of Marketing*, **62**(3), 1–20.

Morse, J.M., Barrett, M., Mayan, M., Olsne, K. and Spiers, J. (2002). Verification strategies for establishing reliability and validity in qualitative research. *International Journal of Qualitative Methods*, **1**(2), 3–22.

Mosey, S. and Wright, M. (2007). From human capital to social capital: a longitudinal study of technology-based academic entrepreneurs. *Entrepreneurship Theory and Practice*, **31**(6), 909–35.

Mueller, S.L. and Thomas, A.S. (2001). Culture and entrepreneurial potential: a nine country study of locus of control and innovativeness. *Journal of Business Venturing*, **16**(1), 51–75.

Mustar, P. and Wright, M. (2010). Convergence or path dependency in policies to foster the creation of university spin-off firms? A comparison of France and the United Kingdom. *Journal of Technology Transfer*, **35**(1), 42–65.

Nijkamp, P. (2003). Entrepreneurship in a modern network economy. *Regional Studies*, **37**(4), 395–405.

O'Shea, R.P., Allen, T.J., O'Gorman, C. and Roche, F. (2004). University and technology transfer: a review of academic entrepreneurship literature. *Irish Journal of Management*, **25**(2), 11–29.

Podsakoff, P.M., MacKenzie, S.B., Lee, J.Y. and Podsakoff, N.P. (2003). Common method biases in behavioural research: a critical review of the literature and recommended remedies. *Journal of Applied Psychology*, **88**(5), 879–903.

Porter, M. (1998). Clusters and the new economics of competition. *Harvard Business Review*, **76**(6), November–December, 77–90.

Porter, M. (2000). Location, clusters and economic strategy. *Economic Development Quarterly*, **14**(1), 15–34.

Pries, F. and Guild, P. (2011). Commercializing inventions resulting from university research: analyzing the impact of technology characteristics on subsequent business models. *Technovation*, **31**, 151–60.

Qian, H. and Acs, Z.J. (2013). An absorptive capacity theory of knowledge spillover. *Small Business Economics*, **40**, 185–97.

Rasmussen, E., Mosey, S. and Wright, M. (2014). The influence of university departments on the evolution of entrepreneurial competencies in spin-off ventures. *Research Policy*, **43**, 92–106.

Saxenian, A. (1994). *Regional Advantage: Culture and Competition in Silicon Valley and Route 128*. Cambridge, MA: Harvard University Press.

Sosna, M., Trevinyo-Rodriguez, R.N. and Velamuri, S.R. (2010). Business model innovation through trial and error learning. The Naturehouse case. *Long Range Planning*, **43**, 383–407.

Spilling, O.R. (1996). The entrepreneurial system: on entrepreneurship in the context of a mega-event. *Journal of Business Research*, **36**(1), 91–103.

Strauss, A. and Corbin, J. (1990). *Basics of Qualitative Research: Grounded Theory Procedures and Techniques*. London: Sage Publications.

Swamidass, P.M. (2013). University startups as a commercialization alternative: lessons from three contrasting case studies. *Journal of Technology Transfer*, **38**, 788–808.

Teece, D.J., Pisano, G. and Sheun, A. (1997). Dynamic capabilities and strategic management. *Strategic Management Journal*, **18**(7), 509–33.

Thomas, L.D.W. and Autio, E. (2014). The process of ecosystem emergence. http:// smgworld.bu.edu/platformstrategy/files/2014/07/platform2014_submission_26. pdf (accessed 1 November 2014).

Venkataraman, S., MacMillan, I. and McGrath, R. (1992). Progress in research on corporate venturing. In D.L. Sexton and J. Kasarda (eds), *The State of the Art of Entrepreneurship*. Boston, MA: PWS-Kent, pp. 487–519.

Vohora, A., Wright, M. and Lockett, A. (2004). Critical junctures in the development of university high-tech spinout companies. *Research Policy*, **33**, 147–75.

Walsh, I.J. and Bartunek, J.M. (2011). Cheating the fates: organizational foundings in the wake of demise. *Academy of Management Journal*, **54**(5), 1017–44.

Walshok, M.L., Shapiro, J.D. and Owens, N. (2012). Transnational innovation networks aren't all created equal: towards a classification system. *Journal of Technology Transfer*, **39**(3), 345–57. doi: 10.1007/s10961-012-9293-4.

Wright, M. (2013). Academic entrepreneurship, technology transfer and society: where next? *Journal of Technology Transfer*, **39**(3), 322–34.

Wright, M., Clarysse, B. and Mosey, S. (2012a). Strategic entrepreneurship, resource orchestration and growing spin-offs from universities. *Technology Analysis and Strategic Management*, **24**(9), 911–27.

Wright, M., Mosey, S. and Noke, H. (2012b). Academic entrepreneurship and economic competitiveness: rethinking the role of the entrepreneur. *Economics of Innovation and New Technology*, **21**(5/6), 429–44.

Yli-Renko, H., Autio, E. and Sapienza, H.J. (2001). Social capital, knowledge acquisition and knowledge exploitation in young technology-based firms. *Strategic Management Journal*, **22**, 587–613.

Yosuf, M. and Jain, K.K. (2010). Categories of university-level entrepreneurship: a literature survey. *International Entrepreneurship Management Journal*, **6**, 81–96.

Zacharakis, A.L., Shepherd, D.A. and Coombs, J.E. (2003). The development of venture-capital-backed internet companies: an ecosystem perspective. *Journal of Business Venturing*, **18**, 217–31.

Zahra, S. and Wright, M. (2011). Entrepreneurship's next act. *Academy of Management Perspectives*, **25**, 67–83.

Zahra, S.A. and George, G. (2002). Absorptive capacity: a review, reconceptualization, and extension. *Academy of Management*, **27**, 185–203.

Zucker, L.G., Darby, M.R. and Armstrong, J. (1998). Geographically localized knowledge: spillovers or markets? *Economic Enquiry*, **36**(1), 65–86.

Conclusion: directions for future research

Phillip H. Phan

This volume presents research on questions of technology commercialization and entrepreneurship that has received less attention in the literature. It considers the institutional (regulatory, cultural and political) drivers and impediments of technology-driven economic development. The importance of the training and education roles of universities in economic and industry development are also examined. We focused on the problems attending the risky stage of technical translation, in which the concept or scientific discovery is converted to a workable prototype, including the identification of the fit between firm-level research and development (R&D) capabilities and stage of technology maturity, the problem of sustaining high risk investments and situations where international collaborations might pay off when going it alone domestically is risky. We also considered the relative value of general versus specific human capital development and the implications for entrepreneurship and wealth creation. In all these situations, the reader should note the counter-factual conclusions from the authors and in some cases, the counter-intuitive findings in the data. The aim is not to point out problems with the extant research, because this is a multifactorial and multidimensional phenomenon that simple theoretical frameworks cannot fully capture, but rather that future researchers should pay attention to the alternative explanations and 'tails of the distribution' in questions that they are trying to address.

The case study of a technology translation project, the Smart Kitchen, shows us how to describe the translation process. It demonstrates the importance of the learning goals in such endeavors, not only because this project takes places under the auspices of a training program, but also because the process of translation is itself a learning process. In order to do translation well, there is a non-avoidable improving-by-doing dynamic. The reason is that translation is not so much a hypothesis-driven discovery process but a trial-and-error learning process.

The chapter discussing how the lack of academic job opportunities can lead to more technology spin-offs is a study in surprises. The fact that technology startups, given their risks, represent a form of alternative employment is itself interesting. It tells us that future researchers should look for counter-factuals and consider the second order effects of a policy intervention. What is interesting from the authors' data is that technology spin-offs by individuals seeking alternative employment pathways or to exploit an identified economic opportunity are not different from each other. Although academics sometimes become entrepreneurs as a second-best solution, because of shortcomings in the market for knowledge, this is not necessarily a barrier to success. Hence, the provenance of a startup may be less important than the way it is managed, once launched. The third chapter also offers a surprising lesson for future researchers. The authors find that international R&D alliances can provide an alternative path to growing foreign markets, especially when such firms face difficulties in product development in more challenging domestic markets. This flies in the face of existing notions on internationalization pathways since international alliances add a level of complexity that remaining domestically does not. Future researchers should fully characterize the translation processes at the industry level of analysis, as these are unique to the technology and industrial context, before testing hypotheses about factors of success or failure. At minimum, such industry-specific factors should be included as control variables in the tested models.

The idea of a technology credit scoring model for biotechnology brings to the fore the importance of considering firm-technology interactions in explaining commercialization outcomes or 'bet-the-house'-type investment decisions. Combined with Phan et al.'s chapter examining governance and innovation and that by Paruchuri on the pace of organizational adaptation in fast-changing technological regimes, future researchers are advised to look beyond mere applications of extant theory when considering their research models in the life science industries. Received wisdom, whether in the management of technology (that places technology above that of firm capabilities) or governance of risky investments (that places the importance of the shareholder above the manager), may not provide a sufficiently rich theoretical foundation for investigating such volatile industries. Given the high rate of pervasive failure in this industry, researchers should focus their efforts on understanding the economic and technical nuances before applying theory. In short, theory in general is insufficient for testing specific phenomena when the latter are so volatile that the outcomes of strategic investments are difficult to predict.

Finally, the research presented in this volume, at the institutional level of analysis, suggest to future researchers that one should look at institutional impediments as much as enablers when trying to understand the interactions between cultural, regulatory and political regimes with technology and economic policy interventions. The extant research in this domain tends to employ a 'best practice' approach to understanding what and how policy interventions will work in regions seeking to develop technology-driven economic welfare. They seldom consider the negative effects of cultural and social norms that exclude the participation of large segments of the population (women, for example) or political regimes that slow the transmission of information and knowledge. Future researchers should focus on the negative interactions that impeding institutional artifacts can create. In the same vein, drawing the lessons from Guerrero et al. and Bock and Johnson, future researchers should be careful about applying normative theory to the value of university-centric economic development models. It turns out that universities may be most useful in their traditional roles of education and training to develop the general human capital that represents the feedstock to future entrepreneurial endeavors, rather than becoming engines of entrepreneurial activity themselves. They may be faced with cultural constraints and fundamental contradictions as public (and even privately funded) institutions trying to behave like private enterprises for wealth creation.

In summary, the combination of alternative theoretical interpretations of the empirical data is what distinguishes the contributions in this volume. I hope that they have provided technology entrepreneurship scholars with good reasons to continue their work and to look in new directions (or less well-trodden paths) for research questions. The theoretical insights from future research and the related policy implications for educators, practitioners and public officials may well have material impact on economic welfare and the health of the public purse.

Index

Abramovitz, M.A. 189, 193
academic spin-offs
  administrative inadequacy
    future research opportunity 59
    hypothesis posited 40–41, 43, 45
    impact on academic job positions
      43, 45, 48, 58
    results 54–8
    variables 49–50
  alternatives to 40
  heterogeneity in 43–6
  high teaching loads
    hypothesis posited 40, 42–3
    impact on academic job positions
      41, 43, 45, 48, 58
    results 53–7
    variables 49–50
  hypotheses development 41–3, 46
  Italian universities as study choice
    41
  lack of academic job positions
    future research opportunity 59
    hypothesis posited 40, 42, 45
    impact of administrative support
      43, 45, 48, 58
    impact of high teaching load 41,
      43
    moderating effects for 48
    ratio calculating 48
    results 52–8
    variables 49–50
  motivations 39–40, 45, 58–9
  organizational factors 40
  rate of establishment 39
  relevance of age 41–2
  research design
    models and variables 48–9
    sample 46–8
  results 49–58
  students willing to become faculty
    members 42

study conclusions 2–3, 58–9, 251–3
team ventures 41–2
Acs, Z.J. 7, 201, 222–3
activities of daily living (ADL) 16,
    18–20
Agarwal, R. 71, 222
agency theory
  assumption that shareholders are
    risk neutral 156
  attempting to align interests of agent
    and principal 189
  on boards
    and assessment of risk 174
    and custodians of shareholder
      value 163
    and decision control process 157
  calls for less negative view of 178
  effective employment of branches
    of 177
  on efficient innovation projects
    163–4
  on investors and firm-related risks
    162
  negative bias against CEO duality
    177
  normative view of 156–7
  positive 175
  recognition of different risk
    preferences 160
  on separation of decision control
    and monitoring 177
  and value appropriation 156, 162–3
Aggarwal, V.A. 67–8
aging
  analysis of 19–20
  commercialization recommendations
    for 24
  as receptive market for QoLT 20
  roadmap 25, 27
  similarity to Wounded Warrior
    pathway 28

Aidis, R. 187, 189, 195–7
Aldrich, H.E. 115, 157, 220, 237
Aldridge, T. 43, 187, 199
Allen, T.J. 121, 150
Almeida, P. 69, 121
Alvarez, S.A. 218, 237
Amburgey, T.L. 130, 148
American Chemistry Council 116–17
Anokhin, S. 7, 8, 27
Antonelli, C. 40, 43
Arora, A. 65, 68
aspirations
    competitive 76–7
    historical 76
    organizational vs. personal 87
    performance relative to 66–7, 69
        attainment discrepancy 75, 77, 87
        call for incorporation of 89
        hypotheses 71–2
        investment banks 72
        necessity of search influenced by
            70
        results 83, 86–7
assistive technologies
    kitchen as desirable site for 19
    previous studies 10
    purchase price influence 20
    suite of 16–18
    transfer of
        pathways for 27
        tensions existing within 9–10
Audretsch, D.B. 8, 40, 43, 185, 187–8,
    190–191, 193–4, 199–202, 206–10,
    221–3, 243
Autio, E. 66, 221, 234, 238, 241

Balkin, D.B. 166
Barnett, W.P. 116, 151
Barney, J.B. 218, 237
Bauer, S.M. 9–10, 20
Baughn, C. 188–9, 198
Baum, J.A.C. 67, 70, 72, 130
Baumol, W. 189, 193
Baysinger, B. 155, 160–162, 166–7, 174
Beach, S.R. 10, 20
Bessette, R.W. 206, 210, 212
biopharmaceutical industry *see*
    biotechnology industry;
    pharmaceutical industry
biotechnology industry

characteristics as evaluation
    elements 101–2
constituents 99–102
development largely based on SMEs
    93
as important part of world economy
    110
model for 103–5
reliance on research-intensive life
    sciences sector 94
support
    ability to access 100
    policies for 93
technology credit scoring model for
    data and variables 102–5
    introduction 93–4
    literature review 94–9
    overview 3
    results of logistics regression
        105–9
    study conclusion 110–111
ventures in
    data sample 72–4
    empirical analyses 74–80
    introduction 65–7
    overview 3
    results 80–85
    study discussion and conclusion
        86–9
    theory and hypotheses 67–72
    white, red and green 100–101
Bock, A.J. 218–19, 221, 223, 237
Boeker, W. 89, 160–161, 174
Bonacich measure 80, 129
Bonardo, D. 46, 59
Borisoff, J.F. 7, 10
Boyd, B.K. 163, 165, 178
Bramwell, A. 207, 209
Brandt, E.N. 117–18, 121, 123
Burt, R.S. 122, 129, 150
business licenses, obtaining 194–5

Cameron, A.C. 125–6
capabilities
    to evaluate, develop and transfer
        technologies 192
    lack of effective technical and social
        192
    social, to make institutional changes
        193

Carroll, G.R. 116, 151
Carver, C.S. 237, 241
Casper, S. 157, 159–60
CEO duality
  ability to erode board independence
    162–3
  as measure 165
  negative bias of agency theory 177
  positive correlation with ownership
    concentration 177
  positive implications for risky
    decisions 175
  positively related to R&D
    expenditure 4
  relation with innovation 163, 174
  results 170–173
Certificate Program in Leadership and
  Ethics (CPLE)
  Class of 2015 15, 21–2
  competency of civic/social
    engagement 14
  leadership course as integral part
    of 12
  raison d'être 15–16
  undergraduate team 12–13
Certo, S.T. 155, 160
change in R&D
  assimilation of new inventors
    analytical techniques and
      dependent variables 127
    control variable 130
    independent variable 128–9
    as process 122–3
    results 143–6, 148–9
  carriers of
    analytical techniques and
      dependent variables 126–7
    independent variable 128
    as process 120–121
    results 141–3, 148–9
  content of
    analytical techniques and
      dependent variables 125–6
    control variable 129
    independent variable 127–8
    leading, following or inertia
      118–20
    results 130–140, 147–8
  control variables 129–30
  vs. organizational inertia 117–18

performance implications 120
  analytical techniques and
    dependent variables 126
  control variable 129–30
  independent variable 128
  results 140–141, 148
Chrisman, J.J. 207, 210
Chung, K.H. 157, 159–60, 169
Clark, B.R. 207, 209
Clarysse, B. 42, 219, 222
Cobb-Douglas production function
  208
Cohen, G. 188, 192
Cohen, S. 121, 150
Cohen, W.M. 119, 130, 240
collaborative knowledge 233–4, 235–6,
  239–40, 243
Colombo, M.G. 39, 69, 209, 235
commercialization
  academic entrepreneurs usually
    lacking expertise in 222, 235
  of academic research
    administration affecting 54
    focus on technology 44
    teaching load affecting 58
  challenges to 10
  and decision to invest in R&D 174
  development requiring time and
    costs 110
  of intellectual property for profit 159
  modes for misfit technologies 27
  of new products 65, 67–8, 158–9,
    177–8
  novel paths for R&D alliances 66–9,
    71–2, 86, 88, 252
  at odds with traditional academic
    culture 232
  pathways to 10
    CSR/CSP concepts in 15
    as dependent on multiple factors
      29–30
    resources and staffing needs 23
    roadmaps for 23–7
    for technology transition of
      assistive technologies 27
  potential of technological 97, 101
  recommendations
    for Smart Kitchen technologies
      22
    for target populations 24

technology transfer implications
for 22
slow speed of product 106
translation phase of development
cycle 1, 6
of university technologies 8
coping strategies, entrepreneurial
237–41, 243
Cornell University 19–20
corporate governance
board independence 162–4
and innovation 4, 159–60
estimation 168–70
input decisions 156
linkage 155–6, 162, 164, 177–8
measures and variables 165–7
results 170–174
link with performance 155
ownership concentration 160–162
credit scoring models 95–6
see also technology credit scoring
model
Cueing Kitchen 17, 24, 27
Cyert, R.M. 70, 121

Daily, C.M. 155, 160, 163, 165–6,
174–5
Dalton, D.R. 155, 160, 163, 165, 174–5
D'Aveni, R.A. 163, 175
Decker, R. 12, 14
Decter, M. 222–3
Deeds, D.L. 65, 68, 79, 100
Degroof, J. 39, 59
developing and transitioning countries
(DTCs)
accessing accurate information 194
discrimination against women
197–8, 202
education and training systems
190–192, 198, 201–2
entrepreneurs facing risk and
uncertainty 191
as failing to create competitive
advantages 185
law enforcement 189–90, 196–7, 200
misuse of talent 193–4
need for functioning formal and
informal institutions 187
need to build social capabilities 193,
200

obtaining business licenses 194–5
policy recommendations for
200–202
social networks 195–6
technical and social capabilities
192–3
technology transfer
capability for 192
facing unique challenges in 200
missing links in developing 186
recognizing importance of 186
tribal/group identities 196
trust and cooperation 199
DiMaggio, P.J. 115, 120, 148, 189, 192,
195
DiMasi, J.A. 70, 101
Ding, D. 8, 16, 19
disabled people *see* aging; assistive
technologies; mass market users;
physically disabled; quality of life
technologies (QoLT); Wounded
Warrior/Traumatic Brain Injury
Dow Chemical
analytical techniques and dependent
variables 125–7
change in R&D 117–23
control variables 129–30
defining environment 124–5
independent variables 127–9
research design 123–4
results 130–147
study discussion 147–50
study limitations and conclusions
150–151
Dranove, D. 66, 69
DTCs *see* developing and transitioning
countries (DTCs)

economic development (technology-
driven), constraints *see*
institutional inertias
economic impact of public universities
methods
data and variables 210–212
estimations 212–13
overview 5
previous studies 206–7
results 212–14
study conclusions 214–15
theoretical background 207–9

ecosystem development in regenerative
  medicine
entrepreneurial ecosystems
    220–221
  characteristics 238–40
  coping strategies and institutional
    culture 237–8
  development paths 240–243
  differences across 232–4
  differences between informant
    roles across 236–7
  and informant role comparisons
    229, 232
  investigating 224–5
  knowledge spillover and creation
    222–3
  regenerative medicine 223–4
  university-centric 221–2
  findings 229–37
  introduction 218–19
  limitations and research directions
    243–4
  methods
    investigation 224–5
    long interview 225–7
    procedures 227–9
  overview 5–6
  study conclusion 244
  study discussion 237–43
education and training systems
  lack of effective 190–192
  opposing discrimination 198
  policy recommendations for 201–2
entrepreneurial ecosystems *see*
    ecosystem development in
    regenerative medicine
entrepreneurship capital
  as conduit 209
  explanations about level of 213–14
  representing capacity to engage in
    and generate entrepreneurial
    activity 206
  and role of universities 207
  universities associated with
    outcomes of 208–9
entrepreneurship, technology-driven,
    constraints *see* institutional
    inertias
Estrin, S. 187, 189, 195–7
Etzkowitz, H. 218, 221

Fama, E. 156, 160, 163
Feldman, M.P. 218, 221–3, 243
Fini, R. 40, 46–7
Finkelstein, S. 130, 163, 175
Fleming, L. 124, 130, 167
Folta, T.B. 67, 78–9, 84, 88
Freeman, C. 186, 188–9
Freeman, J. 115, 120, 147–8, 150
Fukuyama, F. 187, 196, 199
future research
  directions for 251–3
  suggestions for
    academic spin-offs 59
    change in R&D 150
    corporate governance model
      building 178
    economic impact of public
      universities 215
    ecosystem development 244
    mechanisms to effect changes in
      institutional inertias 202
    novelty in product development
      88

Gans, J.S. 65–6, 68
Genetics Institute 73–4
George, G. 218–19, 223, 237, 240
Goldberg, M.R. 10, 12
Greve, H.R. 66, 70, 75–7, 87, 89
Guerrero, M. 208–9, 213
Gugler, K. 157, 159–60

Hagedoorn, J. 69, 72
Hambrick, D.C. 130, 148
Hannan, M.T. 115–16, 120, 147–8, 150
Hansen, G.S. 156, 161–2
Haveman, H.A. 115–16, 147
Hayter, C.S. 39, 221
Helfat, C. 118, 129
Hensley, S. 168, 170
Hernandez, E. 79, 223
Hill, C.W.L. 155–7, 160–162, 166
Hoang, H. 71, 220
Hofstede, G. 195, 237
Holmquist, C. 67, 70, 78–9
Hsu, D.H. 67–8
human capital
  as driver to growth of start-ups 235
  education and training to develop
    253

enabling network ties and diverse
social networks 219–21
investment in 207
nature of 208
study supports attraction of 214–15
universities associated with
outcomes of 209, 213
Human Engineering Research
Laboratories (HERL) 8, 13–16,
20–23, 25–6, 28–9

iCorp program 1
industrial biotechnology
advances dependent on knowledge
100
also known as white biotechnology
100
association with technology and
marketability attributes 3, 102,
108, 110
domestic economy as factor 111
growth reliant on investment in
innovation projects 100
high R&D costs 100, 107, 110
nature of 100
reason for studying 94
requirements for firms 110–111
ROC curve applied to 109
role of market demand 100
sample 103
stepwise logistic regression model for
non-default 106
variables 105
inertia *see* institutional inertias;
organizational inertia
informants
coping strategies 234
differences in collaborative
knowledge 233–4
emphasis and preference for
outcomes 234, 237
motivations 232–3
role
differences between 234–6
differences between, across
ecosystems 236–7
and ecosystems comparisons 229,
232
types, in study 228–9
selection and interview 225–7

information, lack of accurate 194, 200
innovation
as catalyst for entrepreneurship
and economic development
strategies 186
and corporate governance 159–60
CEO duality 163, 173–4
influence of inside board members
174–5
institutional owners 161–2, 173
linkage with 155–6, 162, 164,
177–8
theoretical model 164
estimation 168–70, 175–6
external and internal 157
measures 166–7, 173
in pharmaceutical industry 157–9
risky investment in 156–7, 178
Innovation Institute 13
institutional culture 237–41, 243–4
institutional inertias
formal 189–90
capability to evaluate, develop and
transfer technologies 192
diminishing incentives and misuse
of talent 193–4
lack of accurate information 194
lack of effective education and
training systems 190–192
lack of effective technical and
social capabilities 192
obtaining business licenses at
minimum cost and time
194–5
social capability to make
institutional changes 193
informal 195
bypassing the law 196–7
discrimination against women
197–8
social networks 195–6
tribal cultural values and norms
196
trust and social capital 199
introduction 185–8
overview 4–5
policy recommendations 200–202
study conclusions 202
theory 188–99
Interactive Display 17–18, 24–5

international R&D alliances 84–5
  benefits of 66, 68–9
  biotechnology with highest density
    72
  boundary conditions for 87–8
  caution due to uncertainty and
    operational challenges 66
  choice to pursue 66
  empirical analyses
    attainment discrepancy 77
    control variables 78–80
    dependent variables 74–5
    estimation 80
    independent variables 75–7
  firms in study 72–3
    example case 73–4
    verification of national origin 74
  formation of 65–6
  vs. licensing out 65, 67–8, 86
  management perceptions of 69
  novel commercialization path 66–9,
    71–2, 86, 88, 252
  overlooking opportunities for 87
  partner choice 71–2
  performance relative to aspirations
    66–7, 69–72, 75–8, 83, 86–9
  and problemistic search 69–72, 78,
    86, 88
  results 80, 83
    descriptive statistics 81–2
    regression 84–5
  as strategy to access technological
    knowledge 69
  underperforming ventures' trouble
    forming 88–9
Italian universities
  possibility that results are specific
    to 59
  sample composed of spin-offs from
    46–8, 58
  statistics 49
  as study choice 41

Jennings, P.D. 224, 238
Jensen, M.C. 155–7, 159–60, 162–3,
  175, 177
Johnson, D. 237

Katila, R. 67, 101, 223
Keilbach, M. 207–10

KitchenBot 17, 24–6, 28
knowledge capital
  nature of 208
  as source of competitive advantage
    206
  universities associated with
    outcomes of 209
  universities contributing to 208–9
knowledge, collaborative 233–4, 235–6,
  239–40, 243
knowledge spillover and creation 222–3
Kochhar, R. 161, 178
Kohlbacher, F. 19–20
Kroll, M. 157, 159–60

Lane, J.P. 9–10
Lant, T.K. 76–7
Lavie, D. 72, 87
law, bypassing 196–7
Leahy, J.A. 10, 27
Ledford, H. 219, 223
Lehmann, E.E. 207, 222
Levin, R.C. 123, 150
Levinthal, D.A. 119, 130, 240
Liang, H. 189, 191
licensing agreements for international
  markets 24, 65, 67–8, 86
Link, A.N. 40, 43
loan defaults 94–6, 98–9, 102–3, 105–8,
  110–111
Lockett, A. 40, 54, 233
Lucas, R., Jr. 207–8
Lundvall, B.-K. 192, 195

Mahajan, H.P. 8, 16–17, 19
Mangematin, V. 11, 42, 93–4, 100–101
March, J.G. 70, 121–2, 195
Markman, G.D. 155, 158, 166, 186
Martinez, M.A. 220, 237
mass market users
  analysis of 20
  commercialization recommendations
    for 24
  roadmap 27
  suggested partnership opportunities
    28
Matraves, C. 157, 159–60
McCracken, G. 224, 227
McDougall, P.P. 68, 87, 209
Meckling, W. 157, 160, 162–3, 177

Meltzer, D. 66, 69
Meoli, M. 40
Miller, S.R. 72, 87
Miner, A. 218, 221, 241
misfit technologies 27
Mizruchi, M.S. 155–7
Moon, T.H. 96–9, 102, 107–8, 111
Mosey, S. 219–20
motivation
   to create academic spin-offs 39–40,
     45, 58–9
   diminishing, in DTCs 193–4
   of organizational inertia assumption
     147
   for technology transfer 222
   at UI boundary 223, 230, 232–3,
     236
Mueller, P. 206, 209–10, 212
Mustar, P. 44, 209, 222

Nath, V. 7, 21
Nelson, R.R. 115, 118–22, 148–9, 185,
   189
non-technology spin-offs
   abnormal spin-off activity 59
   administrative inadequacy 40–41,
     43, 45, 54–5, 58
   as common among academic spin-
     offs 44
   effect of teaching load 53–4
   explanatory case 45
   joint effect of moderating variables
     57
   lack of academic job positions 52–3
   organizational deficiencies 41
   in sample 47–8
   taxonomy and hypotheses 46
   technology transfer offices 55–6,
     58
North, D.C. 186–90, 193

organizational inertia
   assumption of
     differentiating various
       organizational theories 151
     motivated by 147
     and performance implications
       120
     rejection of 141
     vs. change in R&D 117–20

hypothesis of
   and performance implications
     124–5
   in sourcing 121, 126
   institutionalized goals and routine
     activities leading to 148
   inventors embedded in routine
     leading to 121
   notion of 115–16
   possibly dominant characteristic in
     organizational populations 150
O'Shea, R.P. 210, 222
Oviatt, B.M. 68, 87
Oxley, J.E. 69, 72

Paruchuri, S. 115
patents
   academic institutions
     preference for research and
       publications 223
     region comparison 226
     TTO and RM comparison 242
   chemicals industry filings 117
   disputes over 71
   Innovation Institute for 13, 23
   knowledge transfer 208–9, 233
   as measure
     in academic spin-offs study 49–57
     in change in R&D study 123–51
     in corporate governance study
       157–8, 164–9, 172–3, 176–8
     in international R&D alliances
       study 79, 82–3, 85–6
     in technology credit scoring model
       study 97–8, 100, 107, 110–111
   protection, for assistive technologies
     24
   and speed to market 70
   time and monetary cost of
     registering 194–5
Pearlman, J.L. 10, 12
performance relative to aspirations
   66–7, 69–72, 75–8, 83, 86–9
Pfeffer, J. 115, 119–20, 148
Phan, P.H. 8, 157
pharmaceutical industry
   corporate governance and
     innovation in
       introduction 155–6
       methods 164–70

results 170–174
study discussion and conclusions
4, 174–8
theory and hypotheses 156–64
innovation in 157–9
pharmaceutical development firms
domestic economy as factor 111
management factors and firm-
specific characteristics 3,
101–2, 110
nature of 100–101
reason for studying 94
requirements 102
ROC curve applied to 109
sample 103
stepwise logistic regression model
for non-default 106–8
research and development in 115–17
see also Dow Chemical
physically disabled
analysis of 19
commercialization recommendations
for 24
focus on KitchenBot technology 28
roadmap 25–6
Pirnay, F. 40, 44–5
Pisano, G.P. 70, 76, 79
Podolny, J.M. 122, 126, 129–30, 150,
199
Porter, M.E. 80, 115, 190, 218, 220, 240
Powell, W.W. 73, 115, 120, 123, 148,
189, 192, 195
problemistic search 69–72, 78, 86, 88
public universities in United Kingdom
see economic impact of public
universities

quality of life technologies (QoLT)
aging, as receptive market for 20
function and purpose 9
often not coverage by insurance 10
partnership's mission 13
widespread use of 29–30

R&D *see* research and development
(R&D)
Rajagopalan, N. 116, 151
regenerative medicine *see* ecosystem
development in regenerative
medicine

research and development (R&D)
biotechnology expenditures in
Canada 93
certification of venture companies
100
and commercialization 174, 178
as complex and costly process 158
continuous 110–111
costs for new products 100
expenditure
board involvement in 159–62, 164,
177–8
CEO accurately assessing risk/
returns 174
and corporate governance 156
discussion of appropriate levels
of 178
efficiency 157
estimation 168–70
as indicator of innovation 166–7
leading to patents 157
results of study 170–174
funding from external institutions
100
investment
increasing knowledge absorptive
capacity 158
innovation cycle beginning with
158
in pharmaceutical chemicals
industry 115–17
research-based innovation factors
100
SMEs, difficulty in affording 94, 107
see also change in R&D;
international R&D alliances
roadmaps
aging 25, 27
co-ordinated 24–5
mass market 27
physically disabled 25–6
technology 11–12, 21–2
Wounded Warrior/Traumatic Brain
Injury 25–6
Roberts, E.B. 39, 42, 44–5, 59
Roessner, D. 206, 209–10
Romer, P. 207–8
Rose, A. 93, 99
Rosenkopf, L. 72, 158
Rothaermel, F.T. 65, 68, 71, 79, 89

Sakhartov, A.V. 67, 78–9, 84, 88
Salancik, G.R. 115, 119–20, 148
Sampson, R.C. 69, 72
Saxenian, A.L. 121, 219
Schulz, R. 8–10
Scott, J.T. 40, 43
Scott, W.R. 159, 188–9, 192, 195
search behavior *see* problemistic search
Seelman, K.D. 7, 9–10, 20
service-learning project
    benefits of 29
    CPLE undergraduate team 12–13
    Human Engineering Research
        Laboratories 13
    Innovation Institute 13
    project participants 12
    purpose of 14–16
Shane, S. 39–40, 43, 67, 206
Siegel, D.S. 7–8, 40, 43, 186, 201, 206,
    210
Simha, O. 208, 212–14
Singh, J.V. 118, 130
Smart Kitchen technologies
    analyses 20–21
    deliverables 21–7
    introduction 2, 16–18
    methods 18–20
    service-learning project 12–16
    study
        approach to 8–12
        conclusions 29–30, 251
        discussion 27–8
    technology transfer
        of assistive technologies 9–10, 27
        university-industry 7–8
SMEs (small and medium-sized
        enterprises)
    biotechnology industry development
        based on research-intensive 93
    and competitiveness 106
    cooperation with high-tech firms
        110
    difficulties affording R&D 94, 107
    difficulties arising from capital
        problems 100
    economic indicators 99, 108
    funding problems 110
    influence of government financial
        systems on 95, 110
    and market potential 107, 110

profits generated from technology
    transfer 106–7
specific attributes 98, 106, 108
support necessary for 111
technology-based 102–3
technology factors 108, 110
Snell, S. 155–6, 160, 166
social capital and trust 199
social networks 195–6, 220–221
Sohn, S.Y. 94, 96–9, 102, 107–8, 111
Somaya, D. 65–6, 68, 71
Spreitzer, G.M. 116, 151
stepwise logistic regression model
    105–9
Stern, S. 65–6, 68
Stuart, T.E. 122, 126, 130
Swamidass, P.M. 8, 42, 221
SWOT analysis 22–3

talent, misuse of 193–4
TBI (Traumatic Brain Injury) *see*
        Wounded Warrior/Traumatic
        Brain Injury
technology commercialization *see*
        commercialization
technology credit scoring model
    for biotechnology industry 3, 94, 252
    data and variables 102–5
    economic attributes 98–9
    first developed 94, 96
    need for recent biotechnology data
        111
    ROC curves 109
    SME specific attributes 98
    stepwise variable selection scheme
        for 105–9
    technology-oriented attributes 96–7,
        110
technology-driven economic
        development, constraints *see*
        institutional inertias
technology roadmap 11–12, 21–2
Technology Roadmapping (TRM)
    10–11
technology spin-offs
    administrative inadequacy 54–5
    creation requirements 45
    distinguished from others 44
    effect of teaching load 41, 45, 53–4,
        58

explanatory case 44–5
joint effect of moderating variables
57
lack of academic job positions 52–3,
251–2
in sample 47–8
taxonomy and hypotheses 46
technology transfer offices 56
technology transfer
and administrative activity 54, 58
in areas of technological
sophistication and high levels of
uncertainty 237
in assistive technology industries
difficulties 20
impact on 9–10
and capability 192
as complex, non-linear process 185
drivers of motivation for 222
and DTCs
facing unique challenges in 200
missing links in developing 186
policy recommendations for
200–202
problems in capturing benefits of
efforts 190
recognizing importance of 186
women's level of involvement in
197–8
implications for commercialization
recommendations 22
objectives of 192–3
SMEs generating profit through
106–7
students learning about 15, 29
university-industry, benefits of 7–8
use of scoring models for effective
111
technology transfer offices (TTOs)
and academic spin-offs 42–3, 54–5,
58
activity in universities studied 226,
230, 233, 244
DTC opening, in engineering
schools 186
as important engines of economic
growth 221
in Smart Kitchen technologies study
23, 28
Teece, D.J. 115, 148, 240

Telson, J. 8, 16–17
'third mission' 40, 42, 45, 59
Thomas, L.D.W. 224, 241
translation project *see* Smart Kitchen
technologies
Traore, N. 93, 99
tribal cultural values and norms 196
Trivedi, P.K. 125–6
trust and social capital 199
Tsang, E. 12, 14
Tushman, M.L. 150, 158

United Kingdom *see* economic impact
of public universities
universities
as drivers of regional economic
outcomes 218
entrepreneurial 206–15, 240
Italian 41, 46–9, 58–9
role in knowledge creation 222
university-centric ecosystems 221–2
university-industry technology
transfer 7–8
university-industry (UI) boundary
ecosystems 218–44
see also economic impact of public
universities
University of Edinburgh 218–44
University of Wisconsin-Madison
218–44
Urbano, D. 208–9, 213

value appropriation
and agency theory 156, 162–3
and innovation expenditures 156
link with value creation 156, 174,
177
value creation
activities, less is more 159
and CEO duality 162–3
and corporate governance role 174,
178
indicator of potential 167
insiders for evaluation of strategies
175
linkage with value appropriation
156, 174, 177
outside ratio of board members 163
principal method of 157
and routine decision-making 177

Van de Ven, A.H. 155, 163
Van Vught, F. 208, 212
venture development
    associated with knowledge creation
        and collaboration 240
    clustered, benefits of 220
    comparison of factors across
        ecosystems 239
    coping strategies 234
    data structure 230
    de novo 243
    differences between informant roles
        234–6
    different emphasis on 237, 239
    disproportionately driven 239
    ecosystem and informant role
        comparisons 232
    funding linked to 235
    gaining knowledge through human
        capital and spillovers 219
    under irreducible uncertainty 223–4,
        240
    learning about 233
    motivation toward 232, 236
    regenerative medicine 222–4,
        242
    role of social networks 220–221
    TTO personnel influencing 233
    at university-industry boundary 218,
        222, 241, 243
Verheul, I. 200–202

Vuong, Q.H. 125–6
Vuong statistic 125–6, 131–40

Wang, J. 8, 16, 19
Welter, F. 188, 197–8
Wennberg, K. 67, 70, 78–9
White, H. 125, 127
Whitehead, D. 117–18
Whittington, K.B. 65, 87
Williamson, O.E. 148, 191
Winter, S.G. 115, 118–22, 148–9
Wolfe, D.A. 207, 209
women, discrimination against 197–8,
    202
Wounded Warrior/Traumatic Brain
    Injury
    analysis of 18–19
    commercialization recommendations
        for 24
    Cueing Kitchen for 17
    roadmap 25–6
    similarity to aging pathway 28
Wright, M. 41, 209, 218, 219–20,
    222–3, 233, 243
Wright, P. 157, 159–60

Yiin, W. 8, 16

Zahra, S.A. 86, 155, 160, 166, 170, 174,
    178, 218, 240
Zucker, L.G. 121, 189, 219